North, South, and the Environmental Crisis

Since the 1960s, awareness of the serious consequences of environmental neglect has been growing steadily. The composition of the atmosphere is changing, the ozone shield is being depleted, marine life is threatened by pollution and over-exploitation, and rapid population growth in certain areas has created an alarming imbalance between population and resources. As the wealthy industrialized nations grow richer, they spread their waste around the world. What will be the fate of the poorer nations and what will their relationship be to the wealthier nations if the gap between them continues to grow?

Rodney White's clearly written, accessible book describes the basic scientific changes taking place in the environment in ways that can be understood by non-scientists. It covers such key topics as global warming, acid rain, management of the oceans, water supply, urbanization, waste management, and use of land for food and energy. The book will be of interest to all who are concerned about environmental issues, those who set government policy, employees of development agencies, and teachers and students in the many courses that are growing up around this complex subject area.

RODNEY R. WHITE is Associate Professor of Geography, Institute for Environmental Studies, University of Toronto. A specialist in infrastructure planning in West Africa, he has acted as consultant to many international organizations including the World Bank, the Canadian International Development Agency, and the United Nations Development Programme.

North, South, and the Environmental Crisis

RODNEY R. WHITE

UNIVERSITY OF TORONTO PRESS
Toronto Buffalo London

© University of Toronto Press Incorporated 1993
Toronto Buffalo London
Printed in Canada

ISBN 0-8020-5952-X (cloth)
ISBN 0-8020-6885-5 (paper)

∞

Printed on acid-free paper

Canadian Cataloguing in Publication Data

White, Rodney.
North, South, and the environmental crisis

ISBN 0-8020-5952-X (bound). – ISBN 0-8020-6885-5 (pbk.)

1. Conservation of natural resources – International
cooperation.   2. Environmental policy – International
cooperation.   I. Title.

S944.5.I57W55 1993   333.7'2   C92-095048-5

This book has been published with assistance from the Canada Council and
the Ontario Arts Council under their block grant programs.

Contents

Tables and Figures

Preface

This book is an examination of the internationalization of environmental issues and the impacts this may have on the relationship between rich and poor countries – the North and the South. Over the past ten years it has become increasingly apparent that many environmental problems are operating on a global scale. The build-up of carbon dioxide in the atmosphere, the depletion of the stratospheric ozone shield, and the widespread acidification of the biosphere are just the most obvious examples at this time. Clearly, these global-scale problems require global-scale decisions if any remedial action is to be effective. Furthermore, environmental issues such as water supply, waste management, and land-use change, which used to be local concerns, must also be linked to the global *problématique*, as all are affected by the development path which was adopted by the first industrial nations, beginning in the late eighteenth century and continuing to this day. This path is based on the unsustainable consumption of fossil fuels and the depletion of Nature's stock of forests, clean air, clean water, and naturally productive soils. As industrialization cast a wider and wider net around the world in search of cheap raw materials those places that had been colonized by the early industrial states also sought 'development' based on fossil fuels. However, as these second-stage industrializers add their load of pollution to natural systems and as the early industrial countries consume ever-increasing amounts of Nature's capital and deposit more and more of their wastes, the natural systems have begun to change. This form of development also created an additional problem in that many of the countries that came late to development still have very poor populations, generally with high birth rates and falling death rates. Under such conditions their population expands rapidly. Unfortunately the earth may not be able to support *enough* of our wasteful development process to let these poorer countries reach a point where death rates and birth rates fall low enough to stabilize their population size. So these populations may continue to expand quickly, and the goal of development (based on an unsustainable rate of resource depletion and pollution) may recede before them. In the poorest countries population is still growing at approximately 3 per cent per year, while their economies grow more slowly, or even stagnate. In the marginal grasslands of Africa's Sahel, where I started work in 1970, the environmental implications of the pressure to produce more for a growing population were inescapable.

This is the big picture with which we have to come to terms. Once we recognize it I hope our international relations and global institutions will be transformed to allow them to deal with the issues. I do not expect that this transformation will result from the elevation of humanity to a higher moral plane; such altruism would make a pleasant change, but it is not very likely. However, what is distinctly possible is that more and more decision-makers (and the citizens who influence them) will come to see that we are all occupying a single, global lifeboat, and that it is directly in the interests of the richer citizens of the world to take an active part in the improvement of the human condition in general, including the poorest of the poor.

The origins of a new environmental consciousness lie in the outcome of the patient work of many people in every country of the world. Some of these people are striving to rectify local environmental problems; others work as scientists in the field and in the laboratory; others struggle within the political process. Many work on highly localized issues or particular scientific minutiae. Few may have seen much apparent linkage between such disparate issues as the ocean dumping of nuclear waste and the clear-cutting of forests in India and the Philippines or established a connection between these events and the accumulation of PCBs in the fatty tissue of penguins in the Antarctic. Yet all are linked to the development path charted by the first industrial nations in their search for greater material wealth. Many of these issues are quite technical, and their implications are constantly being disputed by the experts who are expected to be able to understand them. One of the purposes of this book is to make the technical issues more familiar to people other than scientists – people such as politicians, bureaucrats, journalists, schoolteachers, trade union leaders, employers, community leaders, and others who shape public opinion.

My own interest in trying to put the issues together has been forged by two associations in particular. One is the Institute for Environmental Studies (IES) of the University of Toronto, where I have been cross-appointed from the Department of Geography since 1981. The other is the International Federation of Institutes for Advanced Study (IFIAS), of which IES is a member. In 1980 IES received a grant from IFIAS to fund Project Ecoville, a study of the environmental implications of rapid urban growth, which itself was one part of a larger IFIAS study known as Analysing Biospheric Change (ABC). ABC included projects of agricultural change, coastal management, atmospheric change, and the development of environmental indicators. Project Ecoville was the brainchild of Ian Burton, then director of IES and, later, executive director of IFIAS. Through the ABC connection I came to know many interesting people, including the program leaders of the ABC projects – Ray Beverton, Blair Bower, John Firor, Rolando Garcia, Rob Koudstaal, and Frank Rijsberman. ABC was also encouraged by Ilya Prigogine and the interdisciplinary research group working on the analysis of complex systems at the Université Libre de Bruxelles. Some of us became very excited about the possibilities that complex systems analysis offered as an escape from lin-ar models into the more unpredictable environment into which the world seemed to be heading. To Peter Allen and Chico Perez-Trejo I am particularly grateful for opening my mind to this way of thinking.

It was Rolando Garcia who insisted that global change was not simply an environmental problem for natural scientists to study, but a political problem, in which we had to search for the 'metaprocesses' that had brought the world to the position it is in. This was the argument behind his ground-breaking study of the conjunction of climatic and political processes responsible for the 1972 drought in the Sahel – *Nature Pleads Not Guilty*. In 1986 Ian Burton and I offered a new course at IES, which in many ways was an outgrowth of our work with ABC; the course was called 'Environmental Issues in Developing Countries.' I suggested we offer the course following a fairly conventional sectoral plan, because that seemed to be the best way to bring in specialists to deal with particular topics like 'tropical deforestation,' or 'drinking-water in the Third World.' Ian was not happy with this and kept encouraging us to look for Rolando's metaprocesses. It was difficult enough to teach a course that was intelligible to engineers, biologists, geographers, and political scientists; but he persevered, and I accepted that he and Rolando, and others who shared this view, were correct. To the world's current problems there are no sectoral solutions.

A holistic solution was none too evident either, however. If all these physical environmental problems were to be dealt with as part of the political process, how were we even going to develop the vocabulary that would make the world of the physical scientist available to the everyday world of society, economics, politics, and law? It was fortunate that in Project Ecoville I had teamed up with Richard Stren, a political scientist, who, like me, worked mostly in Africa. With our African background in common we worked together very well as we asked different questions relating to the same problems. Richard convinced me that I should try to write about the environmental crisis for a wider audience, especially as the crisis seemed likely to prove to be an increasingly divisive issue for relations between countries of the North and the South, the rich and the poor. By now the ideas behind Project Ecoville and ABC are fairly tightly fused and it is difficult to distinguish who contributed what to the concepts we are trying to operationalize. But that is less important than the value of what is finally produced. To all who contributed I offer my thanks; any errors of interpretation are my responsibility.

Towards the end of the writing process I was lucky to meet Thomas Naff, who introduced me to the concept of the 'superordinate issue,' and Paul Demeny, who rescued me from my naïvety about the demographic transition. I am grateful too for a sabbatical from the University of Toronto which helped me conclude what, at times, looked like an endless task. I have been doubly fortunate to spend the sabbatical at the School of Geography of the University of Oxford, where I enjoyed the stimulus and welcome of Andrew Goudie and his colleagues, both at the school and at the Environmental Change Unit.

At the University of Toronto Press I owe many thanks to the patience and encouragement of Ron Schoeffel and Ian Montagnes, and to the perceptive comments of their 'Outside Reader' who helped me to re-examine the structure of the manuscript. To Anita, Julia, Philip, and Robin I owe a special 'thank you' for the loan of 'Windy Ridge' in Pangbourne where I wrote the penultimate version of what I hoped would eventually turn into a book. Above all, I am indebted to my family, whose faith and patience never ran out.

RODNEY WHITE
Oxford, June 1992

Acronyms

AIDS	Acquired immune deficiency syndrome
ENDA	Environment and Development in the Third World
GATT	General Agreement on Tariffs and Trade
GEMS	Global Environmental Monitoring Systems (part of UNEP)
ICSU	International Confederation of Scientific Unions
IFDA	International Foundation for Development Alternatives
IFIAS	International Federation of Institutes for Advanced Study
IIED	International Institute for Environment and Development
IMF	International Monetary Fund
IPCC	Intergovernmental Panel on Climate Change
NGO	Non-governmental organization
NIMBY	Not-in-my-backyard syndrome
OECD	Organisation for Economic Cooperation and Development
OPEC	Organisation of Petroleum-Exporting Countries
SCOPE	Scientific Committee on Problems of the Environment (part of ICSU)
TNC	Transnational corporation
UNCED	United Nations Conference on Environment and Development
UNCHS	United Nations Centre for Human Settlements (HABITAT)
UNCTAD	United Nations Commission on Trade and Development
UNDP	United Nations Development Programme
UNEP	United Nations Environment Programme
USSR	the former Union of Soviet Socialist Republics (most of which is now the Commonwealth of Independent States)
WCED	World Commission on Environment and Development
WHO	World Health Organisation
WMO	World Meteorological Organisation
WRI	World Resources Institute

North, South,
and the Environmental Crisis

1

Snapshot of a Changing Earth

The [Rio conference] will be held against a background of sharp controversy about how development can take place in ways that support and sustain the environment. In particular, developed and developing countries differ profoundly, sometimes bitterly, about issues and priorities – about trade-offs between present and future generations. (World Bank, *United Nations Conference on Environment and Development: Network News*, 1991, 1: 1)

The context and purpose of this book

In its pursuit of material prosperity the human species has proliferated so quickly that it may well destroy the only home it has. People are not equal in their struggle for access to resources. Some are rich, and live in green and pleasant suburbs or modern cities; others are trapped halfway along the path to material wealth, in polluted villages and towns; while many scratch a meagre living on tiny farms threatened by drought and soil erosion. The gap between rich countries and poor countries is growing, and the global environmental crisis may force them even further apart.

The distinction between rich and poor countries was symbolized by a line drawn across the globe between the 'North' and the 'South' by the Brandt Commission in 1980. The 'North' consisted of North America, Europe, the Soviet Union, Japan, Australia, and New Zealand. All the rest belonged to the 'South.' The commission's concern was focused on inequalities in economic development, but the general distinction serves quite well for the increasingly divisive impacts of the global environmental crisis. Indeed the Brandt Commission mentioned the linkages between environment and development (1980: 113–16).

Environmental issues that already affect international relations include global warming, regional acidification, depletion of ozone in the upper atmosphere, marine pollution, nuclear safety, and the disposal of toxic wastes. These are issues that have come to public attention quite recently, and most governments remain ambivalent about how much should be done to control them. There is much scope for disagreement especially when the actions of one country affect the quality of life, even the livelihood, of its neighbours. Clean technology costs money to develop, to install, and to maintain. The benefits are difficult to quantify, and, as will be shown in this book, there are now limits to the extent to which an individual country can clean up its own environment and enjoy the benefits of its own investments and regulations without the active cooperation of its neighbours.

The great achievement of the World Commission on Environment and Development, or Brundtland Commission, authors of *Our Common Future* (1987), was to make explicit the linkages between global environmental deterioration, poverty, and rapid population growth. It described how both industrialization and overpopulation contribute to the degradation of environmental support systems. Thus, any solution to the current global crisis should also be linked through these issues – industrial activities must be cleaned up, poverty eradicated, and the size of the global population stabilized. How may this be done? That is the question to which this book is addressed. The starting-point is with the physical processes themselves. How is the global environment changing? What are the driving forces? What are the likely consequences? What remedial steps can we take?

Human response to biospheric change

More and more people are becoming aware that human use of the global environment has begun to affect the major natural cycles on which people depend for existence – the cycling of air and water around the globe and the cycling of essential nutrients for the plants and animals that provide the human diet. The climate is changing, and soil productivity is declining in many regions. These impacts are becoming so intense that what used to be localized problems now affect large regions of the earth, the atmosphere, and the oceans. Physically, the earth must now be studied as a single interlinked system.

In addition to the physical uncertainty, we face major institutional unknowns. The historical responsibility for changing the natural cycles lies with the rich countries that have gone through the modern agricultural and industrial revolutions. The poor countries are caught in a situation of rapidly growing populations and very few resources available to maintain economic growth and social services. For the poor countries, global environmental change is a long way down their list of priorities. Yet, without their active cooperation, reform on the required global scale is not possible. It is also clear that the current distribution of the world's riches is not sustainable. This impasse obliges all decision-makers to try to identify new forms of cooperation. To what extent will the countries that have grown rich from despoiling the environment be prepared to transfer capital and technology to the poor countries? For some politicians, the answer to this question is a curt 'very little.'

The major threats to earth as a home for human beings are the continued rapid growth of the human population and the proliferation of unwanted 'residuals' (or pollution) from our economic activities – agriculture, mining, manufacturing, transportation, and so on. Although one can distinguish between these two processes, they are closely related. It was the improvement in the efficiency of these economic activities that reduced human mortality rates and spurred the modern rise of population from 1800 onwards. In the early industrializing countries of North America and Western Europe the fall in the death rates was followed (about eighty years later) by a fall in birth rates and a stabilization in the size of the population. Before this transition to stability took place, the population of Europe more than doubled in size. This demographic transition is beginning now in the South. There is nothing inevitable about it. It could take place much faster than it did in Europe and North America, or it may not happen at all. If the transition is not completed, then the human population could find itself in some dreadful oscillation, with high death rates, high birth rates, and a population that grows, then collapses, and grows again. Many factors could delay the demographic transition in the South. A key factor is the persistence of grinding poverty. Conditions have improved in some countries, but others remain as wretched as they were fifty years ago and they show little potential for 'progress.' What has happened to the process known as economic development?

The impact of the international development effort

The pre-eminent agency in terms of international economic development is the World Bank, for which the early successes came from the reconstruction of war-damaged economies, where it helped to replace damaged infrastructure and put already skilled workers back on the job. The type of projects in which the World Bank specialized involved physical infrastructure – roads, railways, dams, and ports. The supplying of improved infrastructure became the classic prescription for development. This prescription was really the distillation of the American frontier experience, where lands were developed rapidly with the application of new technology and capital. As the World

Bank is a bank as well as a development agency it focused on short-term loans of five years. If the projects were well designed there was no reason for a longer-term commitment except in cases such as railway projects, irrigation projects, and other large-scale infrastructure projects, which were built in a series of five-year stages. Banking prudence required this caution.

When it became clear in the 1960s that the development of the poorest countries was not following the same path as that of the American frontier or the reconstruction of Europe, the Bank took the lead in broadening the concept of what this phase of global development entailed and what kind of projects would be required. It moved into social infrastructure (health, education, housing, family planning), 'directly productive activities' (industry, agriculture), and 'institution building' (management training). When projects faltered, the remedy was to be found in 'appropriate technology,' as opposed to the straight transfer of the technology of the North. The Bank worked with the governments of the client countries; the governments created bureaucracies to manage aid-funded projects in utilities, marketing, forestry, and almost every other aspect of the national economy. Eventually it was accepted at the Bank that the partners and clients – the governments of the Third World – were part of the problem. This led to efforts since the late 1970s to get governments out of agriculture and to privatize services. The staff of the Bank moved away from Keynesian interventionism to rediscover the market-place as the key to development, and they adopted the belief that if you could 'get the prices right' then producers would respond by producing more goods. Where local demand was weak, emphasis should be on 'export-led growth.'

The need for environmentally sustainable development has now been added to the list of requirements for well-designed projects. However, the environment is not just another add-on element; it goes to the heart of the development issue. The essential difference between the development of the South and the development of North America and the reconstruction of Europe is that the South is experiencing very rapid population growth, with its economy still based, in most low-income countries, on traditional peasant agriculture. This places an immense and growing burden on the environment. It is not at all clear that a development option exists in these circumstances. If it does exist, then it will require that two very difficult conditions be met. One is a much greater mobility of labour, so that peasants with unviable farms can move to the cities, to less crowded lands in the South, or to the rich countries of the North. The second condition is the 'empowerment' of the remaining farmers, to give them freedom to make the best of their very difficult lot; they need freedom to choose the crops they grow and the markets for which they produce. As has often been noted, with the proper incentives peasant farmers can increase their productivity (Dumont and Mottin 1982).

Economic development, especially of the sustainable variety, requires a social revolution. Through painful experience, some of the classical development strategists have recognized this fact (Hirschman 1984). However, it is difficult for the Bank, the other development agencies, and their client governments to face this reality. The Bank, by its statutes, is supposed to provide capital and technology – not ideology, as Stanley Please explains in his aptly titled book *The Hobbled Giant: Essays on the World Bank* (1984). For the governments this attempt means nothing less than organizing a peaceful revolution to remove themselves from power. Obviously, this change of viewpoint will be difficult to achieve. The development agencies will have to travel much further along the path from five-year projects to permanent programs. Structural adjustment programs are a step on this journey, but they are still narrowly conceived in terms of traditional macro-economics – and they pay scant attention to the environment.

The Bank now recognizes, however, that, 'for developing countries, curbing poverty, improving the quality of life, and safeguarding the environment must be mutually supportive objectives' (World Bank 1989: 7). As noted in the same report: 'This marks a major redirection of World Bank activity. Although the Bank did not ignore environmental issues altogether in the past, it did not give them sufficient attention. The dangers of understating environmental concerns, however, have become progressively clear. Governments and their publics have begun to see better environmental management as a priority. The Bank, along with other development institutions, has had to change' (p. 9).

Until 1987 environmental assessment was simply another step in project design, and it was left to a handful of Bank staff. Now the aim is to have '4,000 environmentally sensitive staff at the Bank' (World Bank 1989: 9). In addition to embedding environmental considerations within the whole process of project design, the Bank is also producing papers on environmental issues and is working with thirty countries to produce environmental action plans. The Bank's papers include highly country-specific issues such as deforestation in Brazil's Amazon, global issues such as the 'greenhouse effect,' and broader intellectual concerns, such as the evolution of paradigms for environmental management (Mahar 1989; Arrhenius and Waltz 1990; Colby 1990). In 1990 the Bank produced its first annual report on *The World Bank and the Environment* (World Bank 1990), and in 1992 it devoted its entire annual *World Development Report* to 'Development and the Environment' (World Bank 1992).

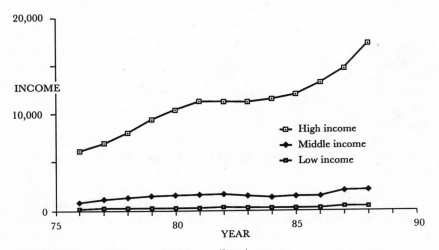

Figure 1.1. Changes in per capita income ($U.S.)

Within the Bank it is now apparently accepted that the environmental outlook is highly uncertain and that the situation requires urgent attention. Unfortunately, during the years that elapsed while this evolution was taking place, the condition of many of the countries of the South deteriorated alarmingly.

The evolution of the South

In broad economic and social terms, it is sobering to see that four 'decades of development' (1950–90) have hardly made a dent in the world's intertwined problems of poverty and environmental degradation. Figure 1.1 shows per capita gross national product in the World Bank's threefold division of high-income countries, middle-income countries, and low-income countries (World Bank 1978–92). All three groups have seen per capita GNP increase between 1976 and 1988, although this does not allow for inflation, which would probably wipe out any gains in terms of real income. Even so, just taking the incomes without allowing for inflation, it is a sobering picture. For the low-income group the 'increase' took the average from $150 per year to $320; for the middle-income group the change was from $750 per year to $1,930; for the high-income countries, from $6,200 to $17,080. Trends in life expectancy (Figure 1.2) and adult literacy (Figure 1.3) show a period in the latter half of the 1970s when low-income countries did appear to be making substantial gains, but this trend flattened out after 1980. Infant mortality (birth to one year of age) – the key indicator of the quality of life – illustrates the same situation (Figure 1.4). There appeared to be an encouraging improvement in the late 1970s, but little change in the early 1980s.

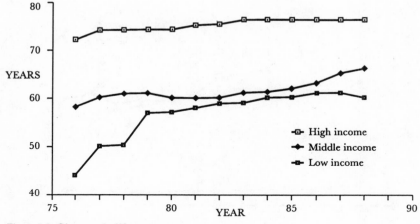

Figure 1.2. Changes in life expectancy

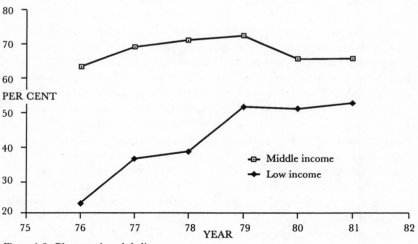

Figure 1.3. Changes in adult literacy

Since 1984, both life expectancy and infant mortality show an alarming divergence between middle-income and low-income countries. Adult literacy, life expectancy, and infant mortality were the indicators used by Morris D. Morris in his 'physical quality of life index,' the precursor for the Human Development Index first published by the United Nations Development Programme in 1990 (Morris 1979; UNDP 1990: 11–16).

It is true that most of the national economies of the poor countries have grown throughout this period (despite the 1980–3 recession), but only a small

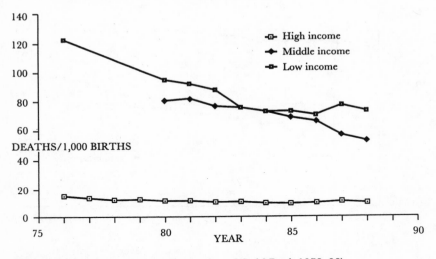

Figure 1.4. Changes in infant mortality (from World Bank 1978–90)

handful have kept ahead of population growth. The handful for which the economy grew faster than the population comprises the 'little dragons' of Hong Kong, Taiwan, South Korea, and Singapore. The per capita GNPs of Hong Kong and Singapore now exceed those of some European countries, and therefore the distinction between North and South economies has become quite blurred (Table 1.1). The population of Singapore has stabilized and the government is now encouraging immigration from Hong Kong.

Despite the evident shortcomings of the statistics used in such a comparison, it would seem, according to the GNP per capita, that at least three of these former 'developing' countries have evolved into modern economies, without the aid of oil export revenues. (The World Bank has not reported figures for Taiwan since 1979.) For most of the rest, immense political and financial difficulties remain. Some are large enough to weather the vicissitudes of the international commodity price swings, while others still remain precariously dependent on the price of one or two crops or minerals. Some have managed to maintain a productive agricultural sector, while others have seen theirs dwindle and thereby contribute to a growing 'food gap' between production and consumption. Their cases are diverse, but all (except the 'little dragons') have a long way to go before they will have the capital resources and the freedom of action to develop their own clean technology, sustainable agriculture, and renewable sources of energy.

To some extent the North has been able to ignore the failure of four decades of development in the South. Business has continued and some modest

TABLE 1.1
GNP per capita for selected countries, 1988 ($U.S.)

Countries formerly classified as South		Countries formerly classified as North	
Korea, Republic of	3,600	Portugal	3,650
Hong Kong	9,220	Greece	4,800
Singapore	9,070	Spain	7,740
		Ireland	7,750

Source: World Bank, *World Development Report, 1990*: 179

gains, on a country-by-country basis, have been posted in education, life expectancy, declining birth rates, and economic growth. On average, though, the picture is not good. Some of those countries that have made economic and social progress are now threatened by unpayable foreign debts, uncontrolled growth of cities, life-threatening pollution, desertification, and soil erosion. For almost all of them the growing pressure of rapid population growth will be the reality for at least another thirty years, on the present trajectory.

What needs to be done now, to make the best of a very bad situation, is painfully clear. The development effort to reduce global poverty must be stepped up to a completely new level of commitment, and the demographic transition must be completed in the South as quickly as possible. However, goods must now be produced using a clean technology that does not destroy the habitability of the planet. As a global society we might approach international aid in the same sense of self-interest that led the nineteenth-century middle-class ancestors of the inhabitants of today's rich North to build city drains, set up rudimentary health services, and offer (indeed enforce) free elementary education for rich and poor alike. Because global systems – both physical and economic – are now highly interconnected, we are now virtually obliged to extend this nineteenth-century attitude on a global scale, for much the same reasons that those ancestors did. A mass of poor, uneducated people cannot be absorbed into an intricately linked, complex, materially wealthy, modern society. This is particularly true at a time when that wealthy segment of the global society has discovered that its road to materialism has entrained heavy (still unknown) costs to the planet it inhabits. It needs a new organizational basis for maintaining its wealth, and that basis must include the replacement of mass poverty with a tolerable standard of living for all.

None of this will be easy; but the longer we delay, the more difficult it will be. There will be more malnourished people to cope with, and there will be fewer usable ecosystems available to humans in their struggle for survival.

Those countries of the South that did not begin to build a strong national economy in the immediate post-colonial period, and now have little or no chance of doing so, will be pushed to the brink of survival as national units. Those that have enormous natural resources left untapped because of war (Sudan) or misgovernment (Zaire) will find themselves under international pressure to put their resources at the disposal of the world community. Those countries for which the resource base is too weak to support their growing population (like the countries of the Sahel and the Horn of Africa) will come under similar pressure to seek a regional, internationally supervised solution.

Why might these things happen? Why will the human species not just muddle through in its usual way? The reason is that this environmental crisis is unlike other problems that afflict the human race, like war and the threat of war, the narcotics trade, and the everyday violence of human society. Such problems are self-inflicted, and we might imagine a day when society may be free of them. Similarly, natural disasters like hurricanes, droughts, and earthquakes which wreak terrible damage may be regarded as acts of God. The environmental crisis is unlike these problems. Much of the impact of environmental change is invisible to the naked eye. And, while many of the cruelest blows will fall on the poor, in the not-too-distant future the general deterioration will affect the rich as well. This crisis has been a long time coming. Why have most of us become aware of it only recently?

The emergence of public concern over the environment

The environmentally oriented concerns that emerged in the postwar period did not reflect the global nature of the crisis. In the rich countries of the North, in this century, three concerns were pursued more or less independently. They can be grouped, loosely, as conservation, potentially toxic chemicals, and resource depletion. Of these three, the modern conservation movement has the longest history, being rooted in a concern for the preservation of remaining 'natural' landscapes, the last reserve for wildlife. The world's first national park, Yellowstone, was established in the United States in 1872; other rich countries followed suit. In some poor countries, colonial governments established parks, most notably in eastern Africa. The emphasis here was firmly on the preservation of endangered species of birds and animals for hunters and nature lovers; plants were usually a secondary concern.

Public concern about potentially toxic chemicals became widespread in the United States, probably because it was the first country to turn to chemicals on a large scale to increase agricultural output, by applying fertilizers, pesticides, and herbicides. (Related uses included the application of pesticides, like DDT, to the eradication of mosquitoes, and the use of herbicides to clear vegetation from roadsides and power corridors.) It was Rachel Carson's *Silent Spring* (1962) which did most to focus early attention on the impact of some of these chemicals on wildlife. Later it was realized that it was not only wildlife that would be affected but humans also, and not only in rural areas, but, even more likely, in urban areas, close to toxic-waste dumps which, until then, received little supervision. The *cause célèbre* for the toxic-waste scandal was the Love Canal dump, near Buffalo, New York, of which the health impact became public knowledge in 1977.

Both conservation and the impact of improperly handled chemicals were the concerns, by the 1960s, of either small or specialized interest groups. In the United States some of the conservation groups were national societies with large memberships, like the Sierra Club (founded 1892) or the Audubon Society (founded 1885). They had influence, but not on the scale of manufacturing companies like Dupont, Dow, or General Motors. The people who were worried about improperly handled toxic chemicals were localized community groups, who believed that the health of their families was threatened.

Another environmental problem directly affected the real powers in the Western economies – the big companies. Their concern was resource depletion, especially the threatened scarcity of key fuels and minerals. It was the fear of industrial society running out of accessible raw materials that lay behind the foundation of Resources for the Future, for example, in Washington, DC, in 1952. This fear became reality in the 1970s when OPEC raised oil prices from $2 to $30 per barrel over the decade (International Monetary Fund 1989: 12).

Limits to economic growth

It was the spectre of resource depletion that accounted for the impact of *Limits to Growth* when it was published in 1972 (Meadows et al.). A group of systems analysts, with backgrounds principally in engineering and economics, developed a computer model that put together globally aggregated projections for population growth, agricultural and industrial output, 'resources,' and 'pollution.' ('Resources' stood for land, minerals, and water; 'pollution' was unspecified in the general model.) The level of aggregation was crude, but the conclusion was very clear: you cannot have infinite economic growth in a world of finite resources. An important finding of the research was that collapse could happen suddenly.

Limits to Growth was translated into twenty-nine languages and sold over nine million copies – a remarkable reception for a book full of graphs based on a computer simulation. The backlash was also strong. On technical grounds it was easy to criticize the oversimplifications of the model. For example, everything was aggregated to a global total, and there were no real data for the dose/response assumptions for human vulnerability to pollution. 'Anyway,' critics said, 'how could you propose to limit economic growth when over half the world's population suffered from malnutrition?' Even as the book sold, the criticism mounted. Yet, despite the critics, the book's publication (in the same year as the United Nations' Stockholm Conference on the Human Environment) contributed enormously to the growing concern that the environmental niche of human beings was threatened on a global scale, not just in a few polluted localities. The book linked projections of population, resources, and economic growth at a time when the overriding goal of economic growth was virtually unquestioned.

It is true that *Limits to Growth* was based on a rather simple projection of the diverse elements of the global system – although it was more complex than anything that had been attempted at the time. It is also true that it assumed that society would continue to pursue a fairly limited range of policy options to combat the twin threats of resource depletion (including land) and pollution. Yet, again, the range of options it considered was far wider than any under serious discussion at that time – or even today, nearly twenty years later. Another feature that attracted criticism was the apparent omission of the price mechanism. In fact, the authors of *Limits to Growth* had folded the price/technology/exploration relationship into their model by assuming that there would be discoveries of additional resources and better technologies as consumption rose, but that such responses were, ultimately, finite. However, this implicit treatment of the price mechanism was not enough for some critics, because, in the field of resource economics, it was a fundamental assumption that, as the price for a natural resource increased, either new supplies would be found or more efficient means of processing materials would be discovered. This belief appeared to be confirmed by the market's response to the OPEC price shock, which led to new sources of petroleum being brought in from the North Sea, Mexico, the North Slope of Alaska, and the Canadian Arctic. The price shock also spawned grandiose plans for recovering tar and oil shale from western Canada and Venezuela and for the development of the Hibernia oilfield off the coast of Newfoundland. By 1986, the price of oil, in real terms, had fallen below the 1974 price. Oil was the key to twentieth-century industry, and market forces appeared to have proved that they were capable of resisting and finally breaking an oil-producers' cartel. The collapse of the oil price convinced politicians, almost worldwide, that the market was truly the only road to prosperity. This tide of opinion banished the 1960s and 1970s spectre of resource depletion and removed notions like 'limits to growth' from the policy agenda.

Global environmental change

Yet, if the market had disproved the notion of 'limits to growth,' why was *The Global 2000 Report to the President* somewhat pessimistic about the evolution of humankind (Council on Environmental Quality and the Department of State 1977)? Why was the World Commission on Environment and Development (Brundtland Commission) set up in 1985, and why was its report, *Our Common Future*, sold out within days of its publication in 1987? Why did these reports attract worldwide interest, while the equally important report of Willy Brandt's international commission, *North–South: A Programme for Survival* (published in 1980), received only brief attention in the press and in the corridors of power (Head 1991: 9)?

The answer is that one of the assumptions of the *Limits to Growth* model was more right than anyone suspected at the time. No one knew how right it was because the measurements had not been made when the model was developed. Even though we still do not have much dose/response data (outside the laboratory) on human susceptibility to 'pollution,' we now know that the pollution side-effect of industrialization is having widespread impacts on the major bio-geochemical cycles on which the habitability of the earth (for humans) depends. These measurements were becoming available at the time President Carter's *Global 2000 Report* was being written. The data showed a build-up of carbon dioxide in the atmosphere, widespread acidification of the ground adjacent to industrial regions, and depletion of the stratospheric ozone layer which screens out cancer-causing ultraviolet radiation.

These global changes can be linked to more-localized impacts of industrialization such as marine pollution and the accumulation of toxic wastes on land. A poor quality of life, due to a deteriorating physical environment, can be linked to the persistence of high death rates in the poorest countries. Furthermore, as these very countries struggle for economic growth along the Western industrialization path, they will contribute more and more to the carbon dioxide build-up, ozone depletion, and acidification problems. Since the late 1970s it has become increasingly evident that we are all in the same trap. Because the negative side-effects of industrialization cross national boundaries, there is no privileged escape route for the wealthy. Japan cannot clean up its 'own' environment without China doing the same; the United States cannot escape without Mexico, nor can France without Algeria. Scientists call this phenomenon system closure. It was the underlying theme behind Barry Commoner's effective book, *The Closing Circle*. The mental compartments that we used to separate one place from another are no longer useful in a world undergoing widespread environmental transformation. In such circumstances the old notions of a country's 'exclusive economic zone' of the ocean and sovereign airspace are inadequate for the formulation of environmental policies. Similarly, we can no longer assume that the side-effects of one region's economic activity and population growth can be disposed of 'elsewhere,' with emigrants leaving crowded nineteenth-century Europe or toxic wastes being exported around the globe in the twentieth century. There are no more 'elsewheres' to absorb surplus people and wastes.

Instinctively we can see that small islands are fairly closed systems, at least from the perspective of terrestrial plants and animals. Their environmental niche is clearly delineated. Now, since the first photographs from space, people can see that the earth itself is an island in the solar system. From this perspective the atmosphere no longer appears as the limitless sky, but as a thin mantle of life-giving gases.

Some implications of system closure on a global scale

What is novel about the present situation is that humanity is facing system closure on a global scale. The problems no longer fade away. There is no unpopulated shore or forest for the boat people to colonize; there is no isolated refuge where a community can protect itself from AIDS. (AIDS spread from the forests of central Africa to the High Arctic in less than three years.) With its five billion people rapidly on their way to doubling to ten billion in the lifetimes of those alive today, humanity has to confront *itself* − not the limitless frontier. Like the Sorcerer's Apprentice we have unleashed a system of resource exploitation that has run out of control. The global climate is changing, and we can only guess what we have done to the ocean. Meanwhile, the world's poorest people die of starvation.

System closure for the world's physical environment has some interesting political implications. It implies that *only* a cooperative strategy will solve the major elements of the environmental crisis. Unfortunately, we are no closer to a fruitful cooperation between rich and poor countries now than we were in 1980 when the Brandt Commission observed (in a different economic context): 'the self-interest of nations can now only be effectively pursued through taking account of mutual interests' (Brandt Commission 1980: 269). Despite the fact that cooperation is a necessary condition for an effective response to the environmental crisis, this has not yet accelerated the emergence of such cooperation.

Nevertheless, there is a growing understanding that our current environmental crisis is a by-product of the North's industrial development, while the most vulnerable victims will be the poorest countries; although, so far, these uncomfortable truths have not softened the North's unwillingness to restructure its relationships with the poorest countries. This unwillingness was epitomized by Margaret Thatcher at the Commonwealth Conference in Kuala Lumpur, in October 1989, when she made clear her view that 'in a free market economy the poor nations should pay for their own development in an environmentally responsible manner' (quoted in the Toronto *Globe and Mail*, 21 October 1989).

It is quite possible that one of the earliest casualties of the crisis is likely to be whatever goodwill remains in North–South relations. Just as a heavy wind will blow down a damaged house, so the pressure of the crisis will expose the weaknesses, the papered-over ambiguities, and contradictions that form the basis of relations between rich and poor countries. If the damage from the process of environmental change is to be minimized it will require a radical change in attitude to the growing gap between rich and poor.

This change may well mean the end of the nation-state – the political system that reshaped Europe in the sixteenth century and drove the Europeans to establish their worldwide empires, and eventually to transform India, China, and all the non-Western societies. In the 1950s and 1960s some of these nation-states responded to part of the pollution legacy of their industrialization by passing Clean Air acts which served to improve air quality in their cities. What was not realized at the time was that the problem was not simply one for local and national governments, but one of international concern. In the 1980s a new consensus began to emerge, and, by 1988, a conference in Toronto produced the following remarkable statement:

> Humanity is conducting an unintended, uncontrolled, globally pervasive experiment whose ultimate consequences could be second only to a global nuclear war. The Earth's atmosphere is being changed at an unprecedented rate by pollutants resulting from human activities, inefficient and wasteful fossil fuel use and the effects of rapid population growth in many regions. These changes represent a major threat to international security and are already having harmful effects over many parts of the globe.
>
> Far-reaching impacts will be caused by global warming and sea-level rise, which are becoming increasingly evident as a result of the continued growth in atmospheric concentrations of carbon dioxide and other greenhouse gases. Other major impacts are occurring from ozone-layer depletion resulting in increased damage from ultra-violet radiation. *The best predictions available indicate potentially severe economic and social dislocation for present and future generations, which will worsen international tensions and increase risk of conflicts between and within nations.* It is imperative to act now. (Environment Canada 1988: 1; my emphasis)

This is not an isolated opinion. Later the same year, the following statement appeared in a newsletter prepared jointly by the University Corporation for Atmospheric Research and the American Meteorological Society:

> The world is increasingly aware that the global climate is changing as a
> result of human activities that are altering concentrations of trace gases in
> the atmosphere and characteristics of the earth's surface. *In the next few
> decades, we can expect a significant global warming, an increase in sea-level, and marked
> changes in regional and local climate.* These can dramatically change agricultural
> productivity and human habitability in many parts of the world. The release
> of chlorofluorocarbons has reduced the amount of ozone in the stratosphere,
> with potentially disastrous effects on life on the planet, if left unchecked.
> Even with the vigorous effort that we must make to slow the emissions of
> heat-trapping gases, *major climate changes are already unavoidable.* (*UCAR Newsletter*,
> November–December 1988: 2; my emphasis)

One factor which makes it difficult to comprehend the many implications
of the environmental debate is that the *net effects* of a particular process are
often difficult to calculate. Global warming may bring advantages to some
places. (From the perspective of a Canadian winter this sounds like a distinct
possibility.) Some soils will benefit from acid rain. While no one will benefit
from stratospheric ozone depletion, many people do benefit from the products responsible for this depletion (such as refrigerators), and many more had
hoped to do so. Some people might be prepared to trade off the increased
risk of skin cancer against the improved nutrition made available from re-
frigerated food. Increased carbon dioxide will tend to increase plant yields,
but increased tropospheric ozone will inhibit growth – how will these effects
net out for a particular plant species in a particular location?

Furthermore, the solution to one kind of problem may intensify another.
For example, the replacement of coal by natural gas will reduce carbon dioxide emissions, so reducing global warming, but it will put more sulphur
dioxide in the air, thereby intensifying acid rain. There are very few obvious
options. Instead we must analyse a long list of complex, poorly understood,
trade-offs. These problems are complex not only in natural science terms,
but also in human terms. The sum of individuals' preferences, as now struc-
tured, will not lead to a general improvement. Companies seek profits, governments seek power (sometimes by intermediate goals such as high
employment rates), and individuals seek their own financial and medical security. There is a distinct lack of potential 'biosphere managers.' Yet few, if
any, of the problems can be solved piecemeal; we must have cooperation at
all levels to clean the seas, the air, and the ground. This suggests that massive
resources will have to be transferred from the rich countries to the poor in a
way that does not undermine the integrity of the poorer societies with a new
wave of imperialism cloaked in 'conditionality.'

The communication challenge

The shift toward a multidisciplinary, cooperative view of the global environment will be made difficult by many limitations in the human communication process. Not only are there barriers between different kinds of scientists; there are even more impenetrable barriers between scientists and journalists, and between the public and decision-makers. Efficient exchange of information does not come easily. Scientists have difficulty communicating with the public and with politicians. Politicians probably find the numbers used by scientists very confusing. The 'parts per million' of the greenhouse gases seem too small to cause concern; yet the quantity of forest lost per year, consolidated into an area the size of Belgium, seems impossibly large.

All these barriers exist within a single country, using one language (or two at the most) for communication. The problems multiply once the language is translated. Yet, ideas might still, painfully, be transferred within a fairly homogeneous class of Western-style scientists or consumers. Of these well-fed people only a tiny number have the slightest conception of the way much of the world still lives – sleeping on the street in a Third World city or raising a meagre harvest to feed a family suffering a lifetime of malnutrition.

Why has it suddenly become important to try to bridge all these communication gaps on a subject for which the complexity can baffle even the scientists who spend an entire lifetime studying a small part of it? The reason is simple. The changes we are already witnessing will affect everyone – rich and poor – down into the very details of their daily life. In the past even the most dreadful wars affected only a small percentage of the world's population on a daily basis. Yet this environmental crisis will affect us all, for the rest of our lives and our descendants' lives. Already, in many cities of the rich North, people are recycling some of their garbage – a small beginning, but the practice will grow. Some politicians have understood that this period of environmental concern is not just a fad; it affects the way people vote. In North America, the cars on the street are smaller than they used to be, and even the most reluctant industrial countries are changing over to lead-free gasoline. Environmental issues are in the elementary school curriculum, and they are becoming the concern of a growing number of parents, community leaders, union leaders, and bureaucrats.

The scope of this book and some reasons for optimism

The current environmental crisis is difficult to comprehend, given the complex interplay of the forces that are responsible for changes in the earth's chemistry and physiology. From reading magazines and books on the subject it might be easy to go from a state of disbelief to a state of despair, with no intervening stage of constructive involvement. This book takes a more 'academic' view of what is happening. It describes in non-technical language how the major bio-geochemical cycles are changing; it identifies some of the causal links and proposes some remedial policy alternatives. This book stresses the physical processes involved in global environmental change. For example, it explains why ozone is essential to human life in the stratosphere and inimical to the same in the troposphere; it describes which gases contribute to global warming and which contribute to acid precipitation; it identifies the various sources of these gases. The economic changes that engendered these environmental changes, such as the industrial revolution, are analysed, to show how human beings became dependent on fossil-fuel-based development. The circumstances under which this dependence might be broken are reviewed. No attempt is made to deal with the myriad other social problems we have created for ourselves, such as the pursuit and constant threat of war, use of addictive drugs, AIDS, mindless consumerism, and the weakening of family life in industrial countries. These processes could be included in a work of this kind, but they are beyond the present scope.

No easy solutions are identified because one of the fundamental difficulties in resolving the environmental crisis is the gap that has opened up between rich and poor countries. The rich are largely responsible for such phenomena as global warming, ozone depletion, and marine pollution; yet they appear reluctant to rehabilitate the ecosystems they have degraded and to make available to poor countries, at no cost, the best low-waste technology. How can such environmental conservation and rehabilitation be paid for? Is there any way the rich countries can have their materialist 'cake' and eat it too? Maybe. Large sums of money are at present being spent on unproductive activities such as war, and preparation for war, advertising and packaging of useless, even harmful, things, and wasting energy and water because there is no incentive to do otherwise.

War-related activities may have been considered untouchable if it were not for two recent developments. First, the United States and the former Soviet Union are seriously overextended and seem to be pursuing detente. In the 1980s this led to the closing down of some of their 'proxy' wars in countries like Afghanistan and Angola. Second, environmental problems may soon appear to pose a greater threat to the national security of the superpowers than fear of foreign invasion. For example, if things do not improve all round, the former Soviet Republics and the United States may suffer the desiccation of their central grain-producing areas, and the United States may be flooded by economic and environmental refugees from Latin America and the Caribbean.

So this may be a time when we can contemplate major changes in global society with the expectation that many groups will see that they have a common interest in changing the status quo, which is nothing other than the destructive development of the earth's resources for the short-term benefit of a minority of its inhabitants. It is hoped, therefore, that this book will end not with a vague list of wishes for a better world but with a realistic agenda that might be considered practical in the near future.

The next chapter sets up a framework for analysis. It traces those concepts that are fundamental to a general understanding of environmental change at the end of the twentieth century. The next eight chapters look at a set of related problems. The first four are best viewed on the scale of the whole globe (three are concerned with the atmosphere, one with the ocean). These problems are dealt with first because it is the changes to the atmosphere that have produced the most widespread concern in the North and have reopened the environmental debate at the international level. Next are two chapters that may be viewed within the context of very large regions (land-use change and water supply). Chapters 9 and 10 cover problems that traditionally have been the concern of local government, although both are now growing to be matters of regional, if not global, scale (urbanization and waste management). References will be made throughout the book to the impact of various aspects of the environmental crisis on the relations between rich and poor countries, between North and South. Chapter 11 shows how these relations have been affected, already, by the crisis. The last chapter offers some suggestions for further analysis of the crisis and makes proposals for its mitigation. The book is written in the belief that all is not yet lost.

2

A Framework for Analysis: Systems, Cycles, and Transitions

Report on the meeting of the leading western industrial nations (the G7) in London, July, 1991: Leaders had only 10 minutes to debate the environment ... [yet] ... despite the lack of discussion ... summiteers managed to fill up a quarter of the declaration with the subject. Mr. John Major, the British prime minister, again stressed that the UN environment and development conference in Rio next June would be 'immensely important.' (*Financial Times*, London, 18 July 1991: 4)

How can we begin to even think about the complex interconnections between human beings and their global home? The natural world was already a highly complex system even before people made it more complicated by changing the composition of the atmosphere, diverting rivers, and extinguishing species. In this chapter we will begin to assess the evolving human impact as people change their diet, consume more energy, extend their life expectancy, and increase their number. The scope is vast even if we limit our concerns to that part of the global environment known as the biosphere, which is 'that portion of the earth in which organisms and people can live, that is the biologically inhabitable soil, air and water' (E.P. Odum 1989: 28). Perhaps the only language broad enough to encompass the breadth of subject-matter is general systems theory (GST), which is flexible enough to be applied to the world of economics and to the world of natural science. Notions of structure and feedback also point the way to the evolutionary paradigm of Ilya Prigogine.

This chapter brings together a number of concepts that originate in very different fields of enquiry. The result is not neat, but it does go some way towards the provision of an integrated approach to the analysis of human and natural systems – an analysis which is required by the current environmental crisis. Terms such as 'environmental pathways' and 'bio-accumulation along the food chain' may not be familiar to every reader. No attempt is made to present an exhaustive introduction to such terms in this chapter; rather, they are introduced very briefly and then used with examples in subsequent chapters. (Technical terms are briefly described in the Glossary, as are some key environmental incidents like Bhopal and Love Canal.)

Systems theory, economics, ecology, and energy

Since general systems theory emerged in the early postwar period it has steadily grown in its range of applications, embracing both natural and human systems (von Bertalanffy 1968; Wilson 1981, for example). The term 'natural systems' is used here to refer to systems that can function and evolve without input from people. Although that is not to suggest that many, if any, terrestrial systems now operate outside human influence.

The heart of GST is the notion of boundaries and feedbacks. The boundaries distinguish between what is inside and what is outside the system; inflows are called inputs, outflows are called outputs. Processes that encourage the system to grow are called positive feedbacks; processes that restrain or reduce the size or complexity of the system are negative feedbacks. Materials that no longer serve to enhance the system are residuals. The places in which residuals are discarded are sinks.

A key concept in systems analysis is the degree of openness or closure of a system. We saw in the previous chapter that the world itself should now be treated by the human species as a single closed system. When humans were less numerous they used smaller parts of the world as open systems, moving their villages to practise hunting, herding, and shifting cultivation. Now many of our environmental niches are dangerously closed, so much so that we are sometimes unable to dispose of our wastes. For example, some cities find their atmospheric wastes trapped under a temperature inversion for days, and the particulate matter, extruded from their factories and vehicles, rests suspended in the air. Other cities dump their wastes into coastal bays, little touched by tidal scouring. Generally, the more open environmental systems are said to have a higher absorptive capacity for the admission of wastes because the quantity of other inputs and outputs (circulating water and air) dilutes the concentration of wastes.

The variables that change the status of the system are known as the driving (or forcing) variables. For example, the driving variable behind the world's weather is the amount of solar radiation that strikes various locations on the surface of the earth. The driving variables that stress the planet's ecosystems are the growth of the human population and that population's growing per capita consumption of resources.

Systems operate on a variety of spatial and temporal scales, and systems interact with one another. In human affairs some of the large-scale systems have a controlling influence over small parts of the system. One of the purposes of this book is to identify those large-scale processes Rolando Garcia calls metaprocesses. For example, we need a better understanding of the way in which decisions taken in corporate boardrooms and government offices affect the peasant trying to keep a family alive on a one-hectare farm.

In the twentieth century economists have approached such interlocking influences from the standpoint of equilibrium theory. This theory is based on the assumption that the efficient allocation of resources is assured by a market which produces prices to balance demand and supply. Admittedly this equation is constantly shifting as a result of a multitude of factors, such as the impact of the weather on crops, the changing tastes of consumers, new technology, and resource depletion. But the price mechanism works constantly to bring demand and supply back towards equilibrium. Market systems undergo many oscillations, but there remains a theoretical equilibrium price to dampen the oscillations. As indicated in Chapter 1 there was a renewal of faith in this equilibrating role of the price mechanism during the 1980s after the rules of demand and supply humbled the powerful OPEC cartel. Economists recognize that this equilibrium exists only in a general sense, and that in the real world there are many factors that may lead to 'market failure.'

Despite such irregularities, economists have been able to use concepts such as the interplay of demand and supply to analyse the way in which people transform raw materials into goods. Sometimes the transformation is improved to maximize the output of goods from a given resource base; sometimes the objective is to minimize the cost of provision of an essential service. The search for optimization can adjust to the physical realities of natural systems. For example, when fish stocks were seen to be stressed by people trying to maximize their individual catch, fisheries biologists developed the concept of maximum sustainable yield for the fishery as a whole. A similar concept has also been applied to forestry.

Physical scientists, also, have accepted the need to simplify their objects of study in order to further their knowledge. Much of the methodology of natural science is based on experimentation, which allows scientists to reduce systems to their elemental composition, to control many of the variables in the process, so that they can see how variable A affects variable B. Recently, scientific attention has shifted to larger complex systems, such as the interaction of human beings with the environment (Allen 1980; Allen and Sanglier 1981). Scientists recognize that they cannot predict and control very much of what they are studying on such a scale. They accept that these systems are complex, and inherently unpredictable. In place of human control, human adaptability is now emphasized. Holling (1978) called this new approach 'the science of surprise.' From this perspective scientists are less concerned with the maximum productivity of a system than they are with its resilience under stress (Burton 1983; Munn 1986: 333).

Since Ilya Prigogine published his Nobel prize–winning work on irreversible changes in physical chemistry, the systems approach to scientific understanding has been greatly extended (Nicolis and Prigogine 1977; Prigogine 1980; Prigogine and Stengers 1984). What Prigogine discovered was that, under certain conditions, a system, at the molecular scale, would cease to oscillate between one condition and another, and instead would be pushed 'far from equilibrium,' and, as a result, would change its structure irreversibly (Prigogine and Stengers 1984: 146–70). It is this irreversible change that is responsible for the evolution of systems, both natural and human (Lovelock 1988: 215). It is worth noting that these changes of structure may occur suddenly, as a function of the combination of a multitude of non-linear interrelationships. The application of this evolutionary paradigm to the study of human systems and natural system interaction produced some interesting results (Allen 1980; Allen and Sanglier 1981). As world population grows and humans place more and more stress on the planet it would appear that such notions as optimization and maximum sustainable yield are not broad enough to provide a basis for policy and that the evolutionary paradigm may be more appropriate. In terms of human population growth and its impact on the global environment, we are clearly moving through a situation which is far from equilibrium, and we are making irreversible changes to the environment through the extinction of species, the clearance of tropical forests, and the salinization of vast tracts of land.

Ecologists have applied systems theory to the study of botanical and zoological ecosystems. A habitat is shared by many living organisms on a cooperative and competitive basis. Within a habitat each organism has its niche, defined by a set of inputs and outputs. This approach to systems ecology is exemplified by the work of Eugene Odum (1989) and Howard Odum (1983). A typical producer-consumer system is illustrated in Figure 2.1, which shows the inputs of solar radiation, nutrients, and gases necessary for photosynthesis. All systems produce wastes, or residuals, which continue to cycle through the system. As matter is neither created nor destroyed, but only transformed, it might be difficult to see why any change in such a system should be irreversible.

Central to an understanding of this problem of irreversibility is the role played by energy – in this example, solar radiation. The system – in this example, photosynthetic plants – uses this energy to break down available

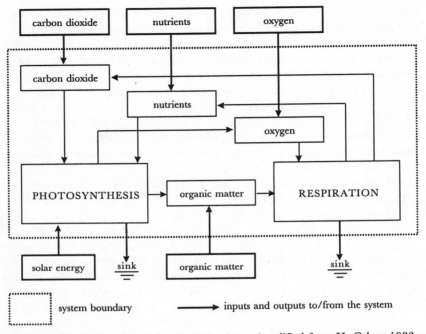

Figure 2.1. Typical producer-consumer ecosystem (modified from H. Odum 1983: 20). Arrows linking photosynthesis (of terrestrial plants, for example) and respiration (of bacteria, for example) constitute a 'feedback.' Unusable 'residuals' from these processes (photosynthesis and respiration) are deposited in 'sinks' outside the system, as defined by the boundaries.

organic and inorganic nutrients needed for plant growth. As long as the biological system functions it can make use of this 'available' energy. Once the system is disturbed (by the draining of a wetland, for example), the original plant community may no longer be able to use the energy. It is easy to see how, in such intricately interwoven ecosystems, the mode of functioning may change irreversibly. That is not to say that it will necessarily change for the worse. For example, a natural ecosystem, like a wetland, may be drained and then replaced by intensive agriculture. Agriculture will continue to make use of solar radiation, to provide food energy (known as somatic energy) for human beings. Nevertheless, the new habitat no longer provides a niche for many of the former occupants, such as migratory birds.

Howard Odum extended his energy/ecology analysis to human systems, showing how various human production processes may be evaluated in terms of the energy they use and the energy they produce. By taking the commercial cost of energy production for human use he put a dollar value on all energy-transforming systems, so that we can begin to measure efficiency in biological terms and financial terms simultaneously (Odum 1983: 476–570). However, as René Passet observed, this transformation is somewhat arbitrary, as the value placed on the biological production of energy is thereby made dependent on the cost and efficiency of the commercial energy system with which it is being compared (1979: 197–8).

Another concept from systems ecology, which can be used at all scales, from that of a small wetland area to that of the global circulation of the atmosphere and the ocean, is that of the environmental pathway. This is, literally, a description of the route taken by a substance through the environmental circulatory system (Mackay 1991). For example, when a substance like DDT is sprayed on a tropical wetland to control the breeding of mosquitoes, some DDT attacks the target organism, but most of it is vaporized into the atmosphere or falls on the soil or is washed away by surface water. Then it is ingested by micro-organisms, which are subsequently consumed by larger organisms, and so up through a chain of consumers, perhaps eventually including people. (In the days when large carnivores ate human beings those carnivores enjoyed the dubious honour of being at the 'head' of the 'food chain.') At each higher stage of the chain, it is possible that more and more of a harmful substance stays within the body of the organism and in this way the dose accumulates (Figure 2.2). This process – the sum of all substances travelling down their myriad pathways – adds up to a process of bio-accumulation or bio-magnification. As they pass along the food chain, certain residuals which are harmful to human health, like DDT, may accumulate, especially if they are insoluble in water.

The accumulation of harmful residuals in the food chain is only one example of the way in which the interaction of human beings and natural systems may malfunction. Another example is provided by the human use of the energy available to them. People spend a lot of time and resources on improving the quality of the energy they use, for example by damming rivers and drilling for oil. Yet, so far, they have spent little time looking at the energy they have wasted, or the renewable energy sources (like forests) which are being demolished to produce a short-lived fragment of 'usable energy' such as charcoal. In material terms, this energy wastage becomes 'residuals' which are lost into sinks. However, if we can take an approach such as 'residuals and environmental quality management' (Bower 1977), we can develop a more holistic view. Similarly, in economics, impacts outside the system under study, such as wastes from production, are categorized as externalities and are ignored in the calculation of costs and benefits. Now, under the pressure of new environmental regulations, there is a tendency to

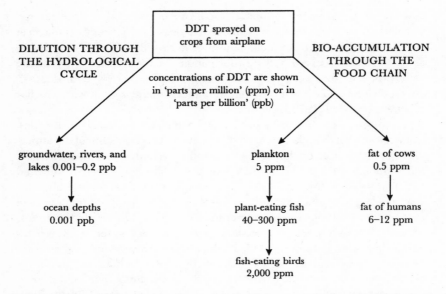

Figure 2.2. Typical branches within a food chain to illustrate bio-accumulation of DDT (dichlorodiphenyltrichloroethane). The figures are typical of the United States in 1970, before the use of DDT was banned. (Adapted from Turk and Turk 1988: 553)

'internalize' more and more of these former externalities, as an integral part of the calculation.

Our measurement of the status of any system depends on the identification of key indicators. For example, for the composition of the atmosphere, scientists are not so interested in the quantity of its major components, oxygen and nitrogen; what they measure is the parts per million of water vapour and trace gases like carbon dioxide, nitrogen oxide, ozone, methane, and artificial gases like chlorofluorocarbons. It is the increase in these trace gases that is responsible for current concerns about human-induced (or anthropogenic) climate change. For aquatic systems a key indicator is biological oxygen demand (BOD), which measures the amount of oxygen used by organic substances (alive or decaying) in the water. The dumping of wastes, like sewage and run-off fertilizer into water, increases BOD, thereby reducing the amount of dissolved oxygen (DO) available to other organisms, like fish and aquatic plants.

The key global indicators for the evolution of the human race are the total human population, its birth and death rates, its life expectancy, and its income level. These indicators determine the probable level of resource use, and hence the impact on natural systems. Other human system indicators, such as the gross national product (the value of all goods and services produced in a country each year), give a rough indication of the quantity of fossil fuels, fertilizers, and other resources that a country's human population consumes, although economies vary greatly in the amount of resources they consume to produce a given unit of GNP.

All the concepts mentioned above, such as equilibrium analysis, irreversibility, environmental pathways, driving variables, and indicators, are elements of a language that we may use to describe the symptoms of the environmental crisis and to identify some of the causes. Within this broad field various intellectual disciplines used to concentrate on relatively small subsystems. Natural scientists worked with controlled laboratory experiments on problems such as metal uptake in plants or fish, economists with models of the price mechanism, and fisheries biologists with models of the abundance of a particular species of fish. What has happened as people have steadily become more numerous, in absolute terms and relative to the planet's resources, is that many subsystems that we used to analyse in isolation now daily impinge on one another. For example, the 'market' for a species of fish disappears if the fish is exploited to extinction. Similarly, the contamination of the fish through bio-accumulation while alive, or through improper handling after being caught, may force governments to ban its sale. In order to gain an overview of this multitude of interlocking processes we need to analyse the largest of earth's systems – the natural elements that circulate around the globe.

Environmental pathways and global cycles

The concept of an environmental pathway can be applied readily to movements on a global scale. Some movements are relatively slow, like continental drift; others are more turbulent, like the movement of the atmosphere. Others are somewhere between the two, like the movement of water over the surface of the earth in lakes and rivers, through the ground, or in deep, salty currents in the ocean. The fluidity or turbulence of all these moving systems determines the rate of passage of particles – solid, liquid, and gaseous – through their various pathways. For example, we will see that some gases (such as sulphur dioxide) remain in the atmosphere for only a few days, while others (like carbon dioxide and chlorofluorocarbons) may remain aloft for a hundred years or more. We measure the mean passage time of a typical particle along the many segments of its environmental pathway, and we can then estimate the probable concentration of particular substances in various locations.

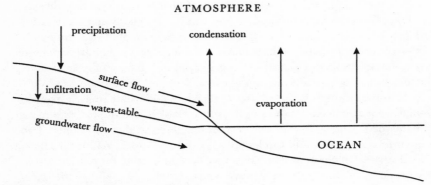

Figure 2.3. The hydrological cycle

In this way we can estimate, for example, the rate at which heavy metals, like mercury, cadmium, lead, and other by-products of industrial processes, may become absorbed by plants and animals or lodged in lake sediments. For example, as a result of metal uptake studies we should be able to estimate how much mercury will be found in the tree stumps left behind, to be flooded, in a new reservoir. As the stumps rot under water, the concentrated mercury is released in the lake; it is then absorbed by fish, some of which are eaten by people. As a result of a number of such accidental poisonings in Canada and Japan we know roughly what the dose/response relationship is between mercury and human health, and new policies can be developed to regulate the preparation of valleys to be flooded by reservoirs and the discharge of chemicals by industries into sheltered bays and estuaries. Landmark cases for mercury poisoning are Minamata, Japan, and Grassy Meadows, Canada.

Scientists study the movement of water through the global ecosystems by an examination of the hydrological cycle which describes the flow of water over land to the ocean, evaporation to the atmosphere, and deposition as precipitation (Figure 2.3). This is the cycle that carries the residuals from fossil-fuel combustion through the atmosphere, acidifying the water vapour before precipitating on the ocean and the land. (See Chapter 5 on acid rain.) Just as we can study the passage of water over land to the oceans and the atmosphere, we can also study the movement of other materials through the air and the ocean on a global scale.

Another approach to studying global cycles is to take each of the key plant nutrients in turn. In this way we can isolate the flow of carbon, oxygen, nitrogen, potassium, and phosphorus. The flows of such elements through air, sea, and over land are sometimes known as bio-geochemical cycles. Because of the universality of the global cycle models they were adopted as the framework for the study of global change by the Scientific Committee for the Protection of the Environment, set up by the International Committee of Scientific Unions (Munn 1986: 331). These cycles are introduced in more detail in the next four chapters. There are important gaps in our knowledge, especially in the movements in the deep ocean and in the interaction between air and ocean. As we shall see, these knowledge gaps must be filled so that we may gain a more accurate understanding of the impacts of human activities on the major natural cycles.

The human species in transition

Individuals' reactions to the modern growth of the human population are quite varied. Some, quite confidently, will sketch in a rapid levelling off, with a total population of less than ten billion. Some believe that technology can keep up with population growth indefinitely. Some feel hopeless and depressed, while others just refuse to think about it.

What will actually happen is far from clear. Compared with the rest of the animal kingdom, human beings have demonstrated an unprecedented capacity for learning and adaptation. A third of the current human population (living in the North) has already passed through the demographic transition to lower death rates and lower birth rates to produce a stable population; however, most countries of the South appear to be at the early stages of the process (World Bank 1984: 51–79; Meade, Florin, and Gesler 1988: 104–13). Population growth rates associated with the various stages of the transition are illustrated in Figure 2.4. The demographic transition is part of the key to economic development and high levels of material prosperity. On a global scale it is the key to the survival of the human species. As explained in the previous chapter, if this transition is not completed, worldwide, in the next thirty or forty years, human beings could go into some frightful oscillation of rapid growth and collapse in a cyclical fashion, like rabbits or fruit flies. We might interpret the AIDS epidemic as a warning that members of the human population are so closely interconnected now that any new contagious disease will diffuse very rapidly through the world system of settlements. Only recently we have witnessed the rapid resurgence of cholera through western parts of Latin America and southern Africa.

The key to reducing the diffusion of such diseases is the improvement of health and education, worldwide. Yet, in some countries, progress in these areas has come to a halt and, in others, even gone into reverse, as population growth has outstripped the meagre resources made available for health and education (World Bank 1984: 71). In low-income countries half of the deaths

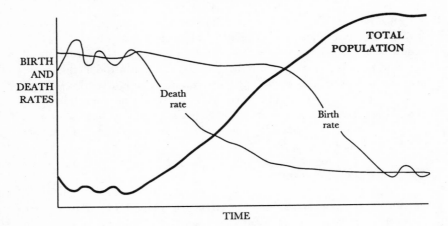

Figure 2.4. The demographic transition model

occur among those under five years of age, where the main identifiable causes of death are infectious and parasitic diseases. As countries pass through the mortality transition the threat to children is reduced. In the later stages of the transition, mortality is positively correlated with age, with cancer and heart disease becoming the principal causes of death.

The diet transition is a shift in human food preferences that has affected all cultures as they have moved from a traditional form of society to a modern, internationalized (i.e., Western-style) society. The major features are shown in Figure 2.5, shifting from left to right. Part of this shift represents a shift by human beings up the food chain from cereals to meat. In energy terms this is very inefficient: as domestic animals eat cultivated grains and grain products like meal and oil, as well as pasture, the protein afforded to humans from this meat is much less than the protein in the grains that the chickens, pigs, and cattle consume. Despite this, more and more land is planted to cereals and other oil-bearing plants for livestock to eat. It may be that what is required here is not to try to encourage poorer people through this transition as quickly as possible (as in the case of the demographic and mortality transitions), but to persuade richer consumers to step back and eat lower down the food chain, as recommended by Frances Moore Lappé in her admirable book *Diet for a Small Planet*.

The diet transition is just one aspect, albeit a crucial one, of the general consumption transition that people pass through as they become wealthier. As people become richer their individual impact on the environment steadily increases as they consume more resources and produce more waste (Uusitalo 1986: passim). This trend is accompanied by increasing levels of

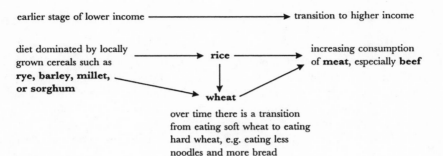

earlier stage of lower income ————————————▶ transition to higher income

diet dominated by locally
grown cereals such as ——————▶ **rice** ——————▶ increasing consumption
rye, barley, millet, ⟍   of **meat**, especially **beef**
or sorghum   ⟍—————————▶ **wheat** ⟋

over time there is a transition
from eating soft wheat to eating
hard wheat, e.g. eating less
noodles and more bread

Figure 2.5. The diet transition

urbanization, so that not only do people produce more waste per capita, but also the wastes become more concentrated spatially, thus increasing the load on the absorptive capacity of the local environment.

The last great transition considered here is the energy transition, in which the North has passed from fuel wood through fossil fuels, and will soon (we hope) go on to renewable energy, such as tidal, wind, and solar power. It is possible that countries in the South could go through an accelerated energy transition and pass directly to the use of renewable resources, without adding their own massive consumption of fossil fuels with its attendant impact on the environment. There is also a hybrid stage that could be encouraged in the South based on the renewable use of biomass fuel such as methane digesters and the planting of renewable wood lots. However, it might be difficult to make the land-use changes necessary to support the larger settlements in this way.

In summary, it appears initially that the following adjustments to these transitions, as experienced by the North, should be considered:

- *Demographic and mortality transitions*: Pass to 'replacement only' stage as quickly as possible with the North's support for health and education services in the South; this would be helped by better access to Northern markets and freer migration from South to North (see below).
- *Diet transition*: The North to reduce its meat consumption so as to free up land now devoted to animal feedstuffs and grazing, in order to grow crops for human consumption; thus the North should eat lower down the food chain, while the South should not be encouraged to adopt unnecessary elements of the current Western diet.
- *Energy transition*: The North to move to renewable sources as quickly as possible and to make this technology available to the South, hoping the South can minimize the fossil-fuel dependence stage in which the North now finds itself; perhaps the South could use biomass fuels on a strictly

renewable basis until other renewable sources, such as wind and solar, are commercially viable on a large scale.

As yet, none of the above proposed adjustments are under serious consideration. Instead the human population is passing through these transitions without visible modification, and, even though some transitions will improve the lot of individuals, they will, at the same time, impose heavier burdens on the environment. The human population is still growing rapidly, and is expected to increase from 5.3 billion in 1990 to 8.5 billion in 2025 (World Resources Institute 1990: 50). People in some of the wealthier countries are now at, or even below, replacement level; however, they are the heaviest consumers of fossil-fuel energy and of somatic energy (biological energy derived from food and water). There is widespread scepticism about the sustainability of these trends even if the global economic system were rearranged to permit the poorer countries to increase their energy intake while reducing their rate of population growth. Before concluding this chapter some mention should be made of the options for any such rearrangement of global political and economic relationships.

Economic growth, conflict, and sustainable development

The current phase of rapid population growth has its origin in the agricultural and industrial revolutions that began in Western Europe in the eighteenth century. It is no coincidence that the emergence of these revolutionary forms of production and consumption took place at the same time that the nation-states of Western Europe were extending their political and commercial control around the globe. The intensification of the rate at which these early industrial nations extracted resources was commonly assumed to require access to the raw materials of their colonies. The economic hinterlands of the biggest industrial cities spread to every part of the world (White and Whitney 1992). By the end of the colonial era economic development, when viewed on a global scale, was highly uneven, as the early industrialized countries continued to extract more and more resources for their material benefit. While some maintained that economic growth and development would eventually diffuse from the industrial heartland to the rural periphery, dependency theorists argued that this unevenness (which is today the division between North and South) was an essential element of capitalism, which required a cheap pool of labour and raw materials.

Within the capitalist countries there were profound differences of opinion as to how best to expand a particular country's trading niche in the world economy. Mercantilism was an early form of protectionism, with each country trying to secure its own zone of influence through control of colonial trade.

As British interests became global in the late nineteenth century its governments usually championed free trade, with markets open to the most efficient trader.

Early in the post-colonial (post–Second World War) period it appeared that the running battle between free-traders and protectionists in the industrial countries was turning in favour of the former. The United States, like Britain in the previous century, saw great promise in free trade as it occupied a heavily dominant position in the world economy. Japan and Europe preferred to protect their domestic markets, especially in agriculture and in older labour-intensive industries like steel and textiles. However, although the industrial nations see one another as 'the competition,' it is the low-income, former colonial providers of raw materials and labour that now suffer the heaviest penalty from protection, as markets are restricted for many of their raw material exports (such as vegetable oils, sugar, and fruit) and their labour-intensive manufactured goods.

Now, as the population of the low-income countries continues its rapid rise, the conflict is sharpened between these different visions of economic and political evolution. During the Cold War between the United States and the former Soviet Union, with its constant threat of nuclear war, this difference in vision within the industrial nations was less evident. Now that Eastern Europe and the former Soviet Republics are abandoning communism in favour of integration with the Western economies, the 'free trade versus protection' argument once again assumes a central role. On a theoretical basis, the argument in favour of free trade is overwhelming, and it appears to offer the best hope of eventual escape from the morass of poverty. In the arena of domestic politics, however, the theory proves hard to embrace, as is demonstrated by the collective insanity of the European Community's Common Agricultural Policy, to mention only the most prominent example of the protectionist viewpoint (*Economist*, 29 June 1991: 10–11). This is a policy that is designed to protect the incomes of some of the world's richest farmers at a financial cost to European taxpayers of $80 billion per year and that requires the application of environmentally damaging chemicals, the use of scarce water resources, the storage of the output for which there is insufficient demand, and the denial of markets to those countries most desperately in need of trade.

Of the many reasons for which protectionism is not sustainable the most serious are those that have been introduced in this chapter: rapid population growth and the persistence of poverty. 'According to one model used by the European Commission, the Arab countries of the Mediterranean seaboard will have 100 million more mouths than they can easily feed by the year 2000 (*Economist*, 1 June 1991: 45). This disequilibrium suggests that large numbers of people can be expected to move, whether legally permitted to do so or not (Grenon and Batisse 1989: 51). Under these circumstances the rich industrial countries face a number of choices: they may struggle to maintain current policies against ever-increasing pressures (financial, environmental, and demographic); they can increase their aid, loans, and commercial investments in low-income countries; they can open their domestic markets to the world; and they can permit a substantial number of immigrants from poorer countries, on a scale comparable to their own out-migration during their own period of demographic explosion.

As long as the present protectionist and exclusionary policies are pursued by the richer countries the danger of violent conflict will increase. Thomas Homer-Dixon has suggested that environmentally related conflicts can be expected on several scales – those of the individual, the group, and the state. The first level would be fuelled by an individual's sense of relative deprivation, the second by forces such as ethnicity and religion, exacerbated by forced migration in search of resources, and the last by the structure of social and material constraints within and between states (Homer-Dixon 1990: 16–22). 'In the simplest terms, [these theories] assert that people will rebel when they believe the distribution of economic goods is grossly unfair and when there seems to be little prospect of improving the situation through peaceful means' (ibid.: 18).

In order to reduce the probability that such conflicts might occur, there is clearly a need for a more sustainable form of economic and social development. The form of development that benefited today's wealthy nations is not replicable worldwide, nor is it sustainable even at its present extent. The compartmentalized thinking which lies behind the classical scientific method (which supported the economic growth of the agricultural and industrial revolutions) must be replaced with a more holistic vision. Systems ecology puts people back into the physical environment on which we all ultimately depend. An appreciation of the global bio-geochemical cycles gives us some idea of the extent to which people have begun to change major ecosystems with consequences that we cannot compute. A study of the historical transition of the human species as a reproducer of itself and as a consumer of energy makes it very clear that our development path is not sustainable. What are the chances of our putting these insights to good use?

Decision-making

Citizens in the richer countries who enjoy the right to vote for their politicians will be faced with an ever-growing array of difficult choices, choices that relate to places they will never visit and to time-frames beyond their own lifetime. Local and national considerations will be forced to make room for these global, long-term issues. This mental transition will be difficult because until very recently our reactions to the degradation of the environment were guided by the visibility (or, sometimes, the stench) of the problem. The Clean Air acts of the 1950s and 1960s in Europe and North America were a reaction to the observation that people often could not see very far in cities; nor did they breathe very well on foggy days. Acid rain surfaced as a problem because people saw no fish in their Swedish and Canadian lakes, and because the German forests appeared to be dying.

For a time, traditional resource economists could fit these visible 'market failure' problems into their old framework. Polluters should internalize their externalities and pay for the clean-up; or they should buy 'pollution rights' and consumers should pay the full 'replacement cost' of restoring 'environmental goods' like clean air and water. All these good intentions are steps in the right direction, but they are not enough. They are examples of small changes in the old way of doing business; they are not an adequate response to the new reality.

The new reality requires major changes in the way that we inhabit the globe and measure the impacts of our activities on the ecosystems on which we depend for our existence. Among the concepts we need is that of an environmental currency, something that reflects the health of the critical ecosystems. Finding such a measurement – one as simple to understand as the dollar cost of a clean-up – will not be easy (Hamel et al. 1986). We can estimate the entropy in the energy system; we can measure the biomass of vegetal systems; we can measure the human-support potential of systems. But all of these either operate only over a partial range of the human-planetary interface, or else are multidimensional measures that are much more complex than the simple dollar. However, the conviction that we must re-evaluate our traditional concepts of wealth is now becoming widespread (Ekins 1992; UNDP 1991: 162–3, 191).

While we are waiting for someone to devise a simple environmental currency there are a number of concepts we can put to work. Certainly, the idea of residuals management is a necessity. Not only must waste be reduced, but all wastes must be identified as the responsibility of some group of individuals, companies, and institutions within the producer/consumer/regulator matrix. This is the new meaning of 'product life-cycle engineering.'

As we shall see in subsequent chapters, there is much we do not know. Many of the current predictions as described in this book may have changed by the time you read this. Given the rate of change of human knowledge of environmental matters at this time, that is almost inevitable. However, the overall process is more important than the details. What is certain is that the human impact on the global environment is currently outside anybody's control; the changes that will occur are unknown, and some of those impacts are very likely to be life-threatening. Sea-level rise and stratospheric ozone depletion alone could account for the deaths of millions within our lifetime.

We do not know exactly what needs to be done, but the need to act on certain problems, now, is none the less very clear. As was noted in the *Economist* (16 December 1989:15), on the global warming controversy: 'even if the earth is not likely to warm up, there are good environmental and economic reasons to adopt policies whose by-product will be a curb on greenhouse gases. Even a small chance of global warming means that governments should see a small extra argument for such policies ... Wise governments will take the cheapest, most cost-effective steps first ... Just as apocalyptic visions of science are usually followed by a skeptical backlash, so the backlash is followed by calmer calculation.'

What we do know is that the heart of the matter is the reduction of our species' rate of growth, its energy demands, and the management of its residuals from production and consumption. In systems terms, we have destabilized the ecosystem which is our only home. The ecosystem – the earth – is now evolving very rapidly, under human impact, and, on this trajectory, it is almost certain to become increasingly unpredictable and uncomfortable as a home for all of us. And nowhere in the scientific debate is there more uncertainty mixed with the prospects of widespread discomfort than on the topic of global warming. This is the subject of the next chapter.

3

Global Warming

There is virtually no doubt among atmospheric scientists that increasing the concentration of carbon dioxide and other trace gases will increase the heat trapping and warm the climate ...

The developed world might have to invest hundreds of billions of dollars every year for many decades, both at home and in financial and technical assistance to developing nations, to achieve a stabilized and sustainable world. (Stephen Schneider 1989: 70, 78)

The topic of global warming has become extremely contentious. Although the weight of scientific opinion inclines firmly towards the belief that human activities will result in the steady warming of the atmosphere, there is what the *Economist* described as a backlash against this opinion (see the conclusion of the preceding chapter). That such a backlash should occur is not at all surprising given that the database is still small, given the uncertainty of the implications of such a warming, and given the tremendous changes in behaviour that the acceptance of a belief in global warming would imply.

Before the issues are examined in this chapter it should be noted that the sceptics raise one or both of the following objections. First, while none deny that the carbon dioxide build-up is taking place, some doubt that the build-up will have a warming effect at all. (Of course, there is also much disagreement among those who do expect a warming effect as to how big that effect will be.) Second, some of the sceptics concede a warming effect but object to the predictions relating to its implications, notably sea-level rise and widespread climatic change.

In order to put the arguments in perspective we need to understand how the earth's climate changed before human, or anthropogenic, effects became noticeable.

Climate change before human interference

The greenhouse effect is a major factor in making the earth habitable in the first place. Without it the average temperature of the earth's surface would be 32° Celsius less than what it is, something like the surface of Mars. However, the temperature at which humans have flourished has been no higher, and mostly somewhat lower, than it is now. The last ice advance reached its maximum 18,000 years ago, when average temperatures on the earth's surface were only 4° or 5° Celsius lower than they are today. Since then the average temperature has slowly increased, albeit irregularly, and the ice cover has retreated. We know now that there have been many oscillations in that short period, but all have been well within the 2° range. Temperature changes are accompanied by changes in humidity. From excavations of ancient lake beds in northern Mali, Nicole Petit-Maire and her colleagues have reconstructed a much more variable climatic history than was previously assumed, and this greater variability obviously has implications for predicting current climatic changes (Petit-Maire and Riser 1983; Petit-Maire 1984). However, there has been a long-term trend towards warming since the last ice age, and it was this warming tendency that allowed people to expand from their East African and Middle Eastern heartlands across Europe, through Asia, and over the Bering land-bridge to the Americas. Others moved through southeast Asia, across the islands, and on to Australasia.

The reasons for the climatic oscillations that produced the glacial and interglacial periods are incompletely understood; however, it is worth a brief description of the various climate-change hypotheses to put the modern age of global warming in the geophysical context (Goudie 1983: 207–22). The hypotheses may be grouped as: (1) variations in solar radiation, (2) astronomical periodicities, (3) volcanic dust, (4) changing distribution of land and sea, and (5) auto-variation.

Extensive research has been carried out on the connection between variations in the level of solar radiation and climatic change. Correlations have been identified between them and also with changes in the earth's magnetic field. However, the causal association is not fully understood. The second hypothesis is based on known fluctuations in the stretch of the earth's elliptical path around the sun, variations in the time of the equinox (the time when the earth is nearest the sun), and changes in the obliquity of the elliptic (the tilt of the axis on which the earth rotates). Together these are referred to as the Croll-Milankovich hypothesis. The third possibility is that volcanic dust is sometimes emitted in such quantities that it could reduce the amount of incoming solar radiation, perhaps enough to lower the temperature of the surface of the earth long enough to induce an ice age. Impressive quantities of such dust have been found in ice sheets and in geological strata. The fourth hypothesis also has some fairly evident implications. As the earth's major tectonic plates shift, the distribution of land and sea changes. That distribution, with the associated changes in relief, is a major factor in determining climatic regions. However, it is doubtful that such long-term movements could account for comparatively rapid climatic changes like the ice ages.

Lastly, and these more closely fit the time scale of the ice ages, are various auto-variation hypotheses in which small, random oscillations flip the system into a new, relatively stable, state. These are oscillations within the 'normal' short-term variability of the climatic system. Examples are the build-up and sheering of ice on the West Antarctica ridge, natural oscillations in the production of carbon dioxide (CO_2), the interplay between higher sea levels in the interglacial periods and the amount of precipitation, and the impact of volcanic dust on the albedo effect of snow-covered ground. Broecker and Denton propose that the alternation between glacial and interglacial periods is linked to changes in the behaviour of the 'Atlantic conveyor,' a deep salty current, which, in turn, responds to variations in the amount of CO_2 at the atmosphere-ocean interface (1990: 53–6). Such a hypothesis accords very well with the implications of Prigogine's evolutionary paradigm which demonstrates how new system states may be produced by relatively small, random variations within the process itself.

This is not the place to evaluate the relative merits of these hypotheses; as one hypothesis does not exclude another, there is a very complex set of interrelations. However, the background of natural change must be borne in mind when we try to estimate the importance of human impact on the climate. For example, it is quite possible that the observed anthropogenic tendency toward global warming is running against a natural tendency toward cooling. However, the human impact could also accentuate a natural warming of the climate.

The impact of human activities on the atmosphere

As noted in Chapter 2, humanity's survival on earth depends on several biogeochemical cycles, of which the most important for human beings are water, carbon, oxygen, nitrogen, phosphorus, potassium, and sulphur. Despite dramatic changes in climate and the distribution of land and sea through geological time the cycling of these elements has not changed much in the past two million years. For example, the amount of carbon in the atmosphere is estimated to have changed by not more than 40 per cent over the past several million years (Flavin 1989: 10). It can be seen from Figure 3.1 that carbon cycles through almost every part of the earth's ecosystems on which

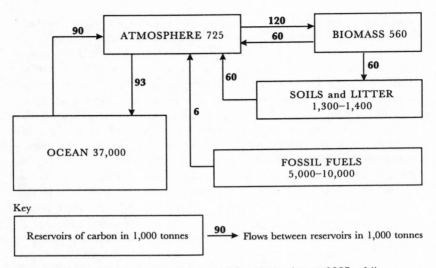

Figure 3.1. The global carbon cycle (adapted from UNEP/GEMS 1987a: 14)

humans depend for respiration and on which plants depend for photosynthesis. Carbon dioxide in the air also plays an essential role in radiating back to earth the heat radiated from the earth's surface (Figure 3.2).

Once human beings passed into their fossil-fuel-based industrial revolution they began to seriously disturb the natural carbon cycle. Stephen Schneider describes the impact thus: 'As humanity burns the organic matter from past geologic periods (or the forests of today) to power the engines and economies of modern society, we are injecting our fossil carbon legacy into the atmosphere at an incredibly accelerated rate. CO_2 is dumped into the atmosphere at a much faster rate than it can be withdrawn or absorbed by the oceans or living things in the biosphere' (1990: 20–1).

Nearly one hundred years ago Svante Arrhenius (in 1896) proposed that human activities such as the burning of fossil fuels (then principally wood and coal) could alter the balance of the carbon cycle. Since his time the consumption of fossil fuels (now including petroleum and natural gas) has grown by nearly ten times. Concern about this activity, which was associated with the worldwide intensification of industrial activities and transportation, resurfaced in 1957 when a report from the Scripps Institute of Oceanography suggested that half of the carbon released by the combustion of fossil fuels remained in the atmosphere (Flavin 1989: 11). The Scripps report predicted that this carbon dioxide in the atmosphere would radiate an increasing amount of the earth's short-wave radiation back to earth, producing a steady

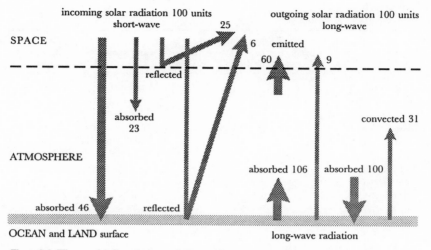

SPACE

incoming solar radiation 100 units
short-wave   25

outgoing solar radiation 100 units
long-wave

6   emitted

60   9

reflected

absorbed
23

convected 31

ATMOSPHERE

absorbed 106   absorbed 100

absorbed 46   reflected

OCEAN and LAND surface   long-wave radiation

Figure 3.2. The earth's heat balance (adapted from UNEP/GEMS 1987a: 9)

warming of the earth's surface and of the lower layers of the atmosphere.
(The sceptics on global warming estimate that more solar radiation will then
be reflected away by clouds, the density of which will increase as part of the
initial warming and humidifying effect.)

The year following the Scripps report Charles Keeling began to monitor
atmospheric carbon from a site high up on Mauna Loa, Hawaii, as far away
as possible from industrial activities. Even at this remote site he found that
indeed the concentration of CO_2 in the atmosphere was steadily increasing
(Keeling 1987). His results were soon corroborated from several sites, including Sweden, Alaska, Samoa, and the South Pole (Kellogg and Schware
1981: 36).

Carbon dioxide is estimated to account for only half of the increased heat-
trapping capacity of the atmosphere. Other contributing gases include methane (CH_4), nitrous oxide (N_2O), and chlorofluorocarbons (CFCs). These are
all by-products of industrialization. However, methane also occurs naturally,
and some is produced by agricultural activities such as the growing of paddy
rice and the raising of livestock. Collectively carbon dioxide, nitrous oxide,
methane, and the CFCs are referred to as the greenhouse gases. Other important by-products of industrialization include sulphur dioxide (SO_2), nitric
oxide and nitrogen dioxide (NO and NO_2, usually grouped as NO_x), carbon
monoxide (CO), and ozone (O_3). The effects of some of these other emissions are discussed in the following two chapters. Their sources and impacts
are summarized in Table 3.1.

TABLE 3.1
Impact and characteristics of trace gases

	Greenhouse effect	Stratospheric ozone depletion	Acid deposition	Anthropogenic sources	Residence time in atmosphere
Carbon dioxide (CO_2)	+	±		Fossil-fuel combustion, deforestation	100 years
Methane (CH_4)	+	±		Rice fields, cattle, landfills, fossil fuel production	10 years
NO_x: Nitric oxide (NO) and nitrogen dioxide (NO_2)		±	+	Fossil-fuel combustion, biomass burning	Days
Nitrous oxide (N_2O)	+	±		Nitrogenous fertilizers, deforestation, biomass burning	170 years
Sulphur dioxide (SO_2)	−		+	Fossil-fuel combustion, ore smelting	Days to weeks
Chlorofluoro-carbons	+	+		Aerosol sprays, foams, refrigerants	60–100 years

Note: ± indicates that the impact of the gas depends on its altitude.
Source: Adapted from Graedel and Crutzen, *Scientific American*, September 1989: 41

Deforestation, which accelerates the trend toward global warming, is a multifaceted process, some of the ramifications of which will be discussed in Chapter 7, Land for Food and Energy. At this point we are concerned more narrowly with the impact of deforestation on the process of global warming. Trees and other vegetal matter take carbon dioxide from the air and fix the carbon within their tissues. Deforestation reduces the quantity of woody materials available to fix new carbon, while the burning of trees releases previously locked-up carbon back to the atmosphere. The disturbance of the litter cover on the forest floor further exposes woody matter to disintegration and releases locked-up carbon.

Thus, deforestation contributes to the warming process, both by release of carbon to the atmosphere and by reduction of the possibility of converting carbon dioxide back to carbon in the form of biomass. It is estimated that it would take a newly wooded area the size of France to absorb the current annual increment of carbon in the atmosphere (UNEP/GEMS 1987a: 36–7). It is this two-pronged attack on the stability of earth's carbon cycle that makes the process difficult to predict and potentially so disastrous. It is estimated that over 80 per cent of anthropogenic (human-produced) carbon dioxide is

TABLE 3.2
Estimated carbon emissions from deforestation and fossil-fuel
consumption from selected countries in the South, 1980 (million tons)

Country	Carbon from deforestation (1980)	Carbon from fossil fuels (1987)
Brazil	336	53
Indonesia	192	14
Nigeria	60	9

Source: Based on Flavin 1989: 29

the result of burning fossil fuels (principally coal, oil, and natural gas), while
most of the rest comes from burning timber. This equation is not constant
across the world; nor is it constant over time. For some countries their carbon dioxide contribution is almost wholly from fossil-fuel combustion; for
others, deforestation is more important (Table 3.2). However, the rate of
forest loss combined with the industrialization of some of these countries may
soon reverse this position.

   Figures 3.3, 3.4, and 3.5 illustrate some of the complexities of regulating
carbon emissions. Output per country is a function of population size, wealth
per capita, and efficiency of fuel use. (Asterisks on the figures indicate the G7
group of countries, the world's seven largest market economies.) Thus,
relatively efficient but wealthy countries, such as Canada and the United

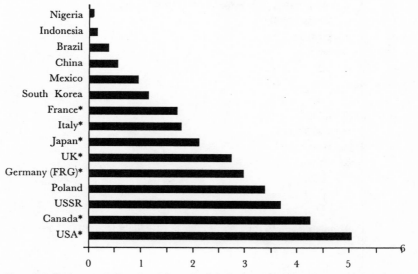

Figure 3.3. Carbon emissions (tons) from fossil fuels per capita (data from IIED/WRI 1987)

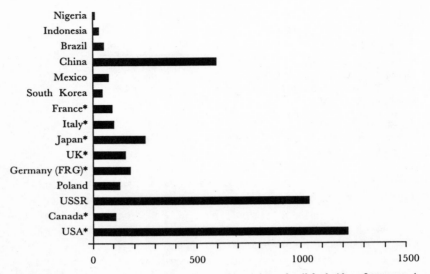

Figure 3.4. Total carbon emissions (millions of tons) from fossil fuels (data from IIED/WRI 1987)

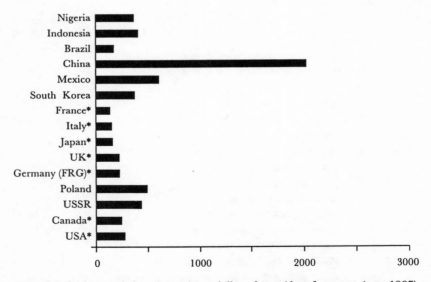

Figure 3.5. Carbon emissions (grams) per dollar of GNP (data from IIED/WRI 1987)

TABLE 3.3
Carbon emissions by type of fuel
(grams of carbon per kilowatt-hour of energy)

Conventional coal	304
Pre-gasified coal	270
Steam-injected gas	118
Solar thermal with gas	47
Nuclear	43
Geothermal	2.5
Photovoltaics, wind	0

Source: Based on Flavin 1989: 45

States, produce slightly more carbon per capita than poorer but less efficient countries, like Poland and the former Soviet Union (Figure 3.3). The highest absolute levels of carbon emissions come from the populous (China), the large (USSR), and the wealthy (USA) economies (Figure 3.4). If we want to identify the economies that produce a lot of carbon in relation to GNP then China is the most obvious culprit among the group of countries shown in Figure 3.5. The data are subject to all the problems inherent in world estimates of GNP and population (lack of monetary values for auto-consumption and barter, lack of census data, etc.) plus the difficulty of measuring carbon emissions based on the application of very rough constants applied to very approximate figures of the tonnages of various fuels that are consumed. The figures applied to the fuel sources are clearly not constant across countries. The values in Table 3.3 are commonly quoted for carbon emissions.

Most countries of the North claim that they are reducing their consumption of fossil fuels, and that they are using fossil fuels more efficiently. However, the issue is much deeper than this 'gross domestic product approach' to carbon dioxide emissions. Some of the products of the South's deforested lands, such as timber and beef, go to meet the demands of the rich North. So who is producing the carbon dioxide in such a case? The current situation is important because we need to know what physical measures are required to improve the situation. However, the cumulative historical record should be used to assign responsibility for the clean-up, preferably going back to the beginning of the industrial revolution. Whether one makes the argument that most countries of the South simply cannot afford corrective measures, or one argues that countries of the North are responsible based on their past (and present) contribution to the problem, the conclusion is the same: most of the resources for clean-up will have to come from those countries which have already become rich by degrading the environment.

Implications of anthropogenic climate change

Prospects are beginning to look slightly better for international action on controlling the emissions of greenhouse gases and controlling the rate of deforestation. However, enormous inertial forces stand in the way of a quick resolution of the problem. Inertia resides in the physical systems (for example, the ocean acts as a sink for carbon dioxide) and in institutions. Much resistance to action remains, especially among major polluters like Britain, the United States, the former Soviet Union, and Japan. The resisters are worried that a reduction in energy use will curtail economic growth. There is also an unwillingness to concede the scale of transfers that will need to be made from the North to the South. The political possibilities range from the extreme of continuing along the present path to the other extreme of rapidly enacting an internationally binding Law of the Atmosphere to regulate all emissions. For the moment it will suffice to look at the probable evolution of the atmosphere based on the assumption of some improvement in national policies, but with strong undercurrents of resistance to an adequate response. A middle-of-the-road hypothesis could well produce a doubling of carbon dioxide in the atmosphere over the next thirty years. The estimated impact of that kind of evolution points to a warming of the average surface temperature of between 2° and 5° Celsius, with a sea-level rise of between 30 and 100 cm according to the report of the Intergovernmental Panel on Climate Change to the Second World Climate Conference in Geneva, in November 1990 (Houghton, Jenkins, and Ephrauns 1990). Changes of this order have been confirmed by subsequent meetings (Jäger and Ferguson 1991).

To the layperson, familiar with daily and seasonal swings much greater than 5°, this might not seem very much, but in the words of Jeremy Rifkin, this 'would exceed the entire rise in global temperature since the end of the last ice age. If the scientific projections are correct, the human species will experience the unfolding of an entire geological epoch in less than one lifetime' (1989: 9).

Furthermore, this temperature change would not be uniform. The incoming solar radiation and the re-reflected radiation warm dry land faster than the surface of the ocean. Because so many implications of the changing factors are unknown there is wide disagreement as to what the changes will bring to each region. Most projections show the temperate vegetation belts moving polewards. The tropics may have even more rain than they do now, while predictions for the savannah lands are mixed. Drier conditions are also expected for the continental heartlands of North America and Eurasia. This will push the wheat belts northwards, in most cases onto poorer soils, so yields may fall.

The effect on crop yields is very difficult to predict because the increase in carbon dioxide could increase the growth rate of many plants, including sorghum, wheat, and barley. Whether these potentially higher yields can be supported will depend on, among other things, the availability of nitrogen and moisture in the soil. It is likely that increased yields will require more synthetic fertilizer. Another unknown factor is the effect of carbon dioxide on weeds. It is always possible that the growth of weeds will outstrip the growth of food and fibre crops. The case of rice – the world's most important food crop – is critically important. Whereas an increase in carbon dioxide would tend to increase growth, higher temperatures in the tropics, where almost all the crop is produced, would reduce productivity. The warming trend itself would, however, improve productivity in the cooler rice-growing regions of China, Korea, and Japan. The overall interplay between rice and global warming is further complicated by the fact that flooded rice fields are a major source (25 to 30 per cent) of methane, itself a greenhouse gas. With so many feedbacks the net effect is difficult to predict. As explained by Keith Ingram of the International Rice Research Institute, 'We know quite a bit about how temperature and carbon dioxide affect rice, but not much about how they work in combination' (IRRI 1990: 2).

The effect of global warming on energy demands will vary greatly from region to region. Cities like Washington and New York will require more air-conditioning in summer, but New York might require less heating in winter. The higher temperatures will, however, probably increase the demand for water, which will require pumping (hence energy) over longer distances. A greater disparity in production between regions would require more transportation of food from surplus areas to deficit areas. What is sure is that the level of climatic uncertainty will increase. What actually happens depends not only on the ultimate CO_2 levels at stabilization, but also on the rate and type of change. The ocean will continue to act as a buffer, but with a lag time in the change of its surface temperature of perhaps twenty years relative to that of the land; in the transition period conditions could be more severe than after a new equilibrium has been reached.

The impact of global warming on sea level is one of the most hotly disputed topics. There are arguments for and against a reduction in the extent of the ice caps. Some projections show the disappearance of the shallow Arctic Ocean ice cover; others predict that it will remain intact. Some predict an increase in snowfall over the Antarctic, bringing a gradual extension of its ice cap. More studies predict a diminution of both ice caps; some go so far as to predict that huge portions of the Western Antarctica ice ridges will sheer off into the sea. It is also possible that the edges of Antarctica might melt, while higher precipitation would lead to further ice accumulation in the interior (Peltier 1990). If the whole of the Antarctic and Arctic ice were to melt, sea level would rise by 80 metres! However, no one is yet predicting that that would happen.

Most scientists estimate that, whatever happens to the ice caps, sea level will rise anyway because of the thermal expansion of the oceans, since the volume of water will expand as it is heated. As nearly one-third of the earth's people live within 60 km of the sea (UNEP/GEMS 1987a: 32) even a relatively low predicted rise of 30 cm above the present sea level would have dramatic effects, especially in highly populated areas of the Ganges, the Mekong, and the other rice-growing coastal lowlands of southeast Asia. The prospects for the Nile Delta are likewise very poor. Those coastal areas that would not disappear under a new high water mark would still expect to suffer much more from spring tides, storms, and the salinization of coastal aquifers. Preparations are already being made in parts of Atlantic Canada to re-enforce storm-water barriers. Areas in hurricane paths will become more vulnerable with even a slightly higher sea level. The key to surviving such environmental changes will be forewarning and the capacity to develop remedial action, such as changing over to crops with different tolerances, strengthening sea defences, and relocating people from threatened areas. In virtually all these respects the poorer countries, almost by definition, will be less capable of responding.

All countries will suffer from disruption of food supplies because of climatic change and general uncertainty. The North, with nearly stable populations, huge food surpluses, elaborate storage systems, and the ability to buy food anywhere in the world, may not be severely disturbed. With their scientific knowledge the rich countries may also be able to devise alternative cropping strategies. The South, with a still rapidly growing population and a weak food technology situation, will soon find itself in dire straits. Particular regions will find themselves with additional difficulties.

As indicated above, sea-level rise will hit hardest those agricultural societies living on coastal plains, which, in most low-latitude countries, are the country's main source of grains. With the advent of serious flooding – first on an occasional basis, then regularly – production bases might be destroyed long before conditions stabilize in a way that might allow replacement productive systems to be developed inland of the present areas of production. That is, the sea-level effect may strike its blow before the climatic effect has time to establish more beneficial production conditions further inland.

As far as North and South are concerned the summary is this: the North is largely responsible for the conditions that established global warming, but it seems highly probable that it is the South that will suffer the worst impacts.

Policy options

The options available to decision-makers vary with the nature of the economy, the climate, and the capital and technology available to them. Choices also vary with different levels of government: national, regional, and metropolitan. However, before these distinctions are made a brief description is given of the options in general.

First, the systems approach prepares us for the interlocking nature of both the roots of the problem and the elements of a solution, although some of the interconnections are poorly understood, especially when it comes to estimating the net effect of several conflicting trends. Timing is also very difficult to predict, and often the rate of change is critical to the choice of the best response. For example, in the long run, it is possible, once people are no longer producing extra carbon dioxide by burning fossil fuels and trees, that the oceans will absorb all the extra carbon dioxide that has been put into the atmosphere. 'But meanwhile [the ocean] has more than it can handle, and there is a temporary pile-up of the gas in the atmosphere' (Colinvaud 1982: 107). But what Colinvaud regards as 'temporary' will bring little comfort to today's decision-makers, as he prefaced this prediction with another: 'The concentrations [of carbon-dioxide] in the air when the fuels are spent and our civilization is no more will be nicely adjusted back to 0.03 per cent by volume' (ibid.: 106). Thus, although the build-up of carbon dioxide in the atmosphere may be only a temporary problem for the earth, it may imply something rather more terminal for our civilization.

Second, the concept of bio-geochemical cycles helps us to identify the broad options. We know there is a great deal of inertia in the carbon cycle as the mean passage time of carbon dioxide in the atmosphere is about one hundred years. We know that the ocean as a sink also works very slowly, with the difficult consequences described by Colinvaud. It takes even longer for the carbon in the ocean to become fixed in the mud to become a potential fossil fuel. But the notion of the cycle points us in the direction of the possible solutions: we can reduce our carbon output and we can change our patterns of land use to absorb more carbon inputs. Similarly for the other greenhouse gases.

Third, the transitions through which the human population is moving – in demography and consumption, especially fuel use – mean that the nature of our greenhouse gas problem is changing all the time, whether we adopt any remedial policies or not. As the population increases more trees are cut down, and more fossil fuel is burned. Even if the rapidly growing populations begin to stabilize they will most likely do so because they are becoming wealthier, living longer, and consuming more resources, thus increasing their personal contribution to greenhouse gases.

What then are the options? Broadly, they are: reduce emissions of carbon dioxide; reduce emissions of the other greenhouse gases (methane, CFCs, nitrous oxide); reforest, to absorb more carbon dioxide; prepare to adapt to the impacts of a changing atmosphere (build sea walls, prepare to relocate people, etc.). The mix of options selected by a particular group of decision-makers will vary according to the factors mentioned at the beginning of this section. Also the means of pursuing these goals will vary.

Reduce emissions of carbon dioxide. There are three main elements of emission reduction: use cleaner technologies that put less carbon dioxide into the air, switch from high-carbon fuels like coal to lower-carbon fuels like oil and gas, and reduce the amount of energy consumed. Obviously there are a great variety of ways of achieving these things depending on the activity under analysis, be it industrial production, household management, or transportation. Energy use is the key. There are more efficient ways of burning coal, giving more heat and producing less carbon. Some forms of energy are very wasteful. For example, heating a house electrically is far more energy intensive than burning natural gas. Insulation of the house will reduce energy demand whatever form of input is used. Some cars do many more kilometres per litre of gasoline than others. Large carbon savings can be achieved by changing vehicles over from gasoline to natural gas. Public transport is far more energy efficient than private cars, which in North America and Western Europe at least, spend much of their time transporting a single person, not to mention sitting idly in congested traffic.

Cleaner technologies exist, but how can their use be encouraged? The two main options are by regulation and by the price incentive. Much of what we need to do can be achieved by the price mechanism, by simply taxing more highly those activities that produce more carbon. A carbon tax is now being implemented in several European countries (*Financial Times*, 19 November 1990: 6). Additional revenue from such a tax can be used to promote cleaner technology by providing subsidies for research and subsidies for the cost of conversion to the cleaner technology. There is some interest in charging industrial polluters for their output of pollutants and allowing them to trade these rights to other operators.

Reduce emissions of the other greenhouse gases. The strategy for each of the gases varies according to its source, the use to which it is put, and its behaviour when released into the atmosphere. One of the principal sources of methane is the manufacture of gas as a by-product of coal, and as leakages during the transportation of natural gas. Much natural gas is still flared off from oilfields because its world price does not always justify the heavy capital outlay for its liquefaction and transportation to the market. For example, all the natural gas has been flared off from the Nigerian oilfields since they were first developed in the late 1960s. Methane is allowed to leak from landfill sites. Burning it off would reduce its impact; better still would be to use the energy, thereby cutting down on some other fuel which might produce carbon. The other main source of methane is rice paddies (as mentioned above). The reduction, or use, of this source is more problematical, as it is more diffused and is more likely to be distant from potential industrial or urban users. Additional methane would be released, too, if global warming melts the now frozen tundra lands of northern latitudes in America and Eurasia (Government of Canada 1990: 19). Nitrous oxide is produced mainly from chemical fertilizer; it could be reduced by changing over to organic farming, which uses natural fertilizer.

Reforest, to absorb more carbon dioxide. There are several advantages to increasing the forest cover, worldwide, but one of the most compelling is that trees are our most flexible means of absorbing additional quantities of carbon. As the additional load of carbon dioxide is well mixed in the atmosphere, more trees will help the work of carbon dioxide uptake. Different growing conditions (age, climate) and different species have different rates of uptake, but the main principle is to halt deforestation (again, for many reasons other than the CO_2 problem) and to replant. Tree planting produces additional benefits, especially in the cities of the North, in that trees reduce ambient temperatures in the summer (thus reducing the need for energy for cooling), and they act as windbreaks in the winter, raising ambient temperatures (thus reducing the need for energy for heating).

Prepare to adapt to the impacts of a changing atmosphere. Given the amount of inertia in the system – in both the time taken by human institutions to adjust and the time carbon dioxide particles stay in the atmosphere – whatever we do now we will have to be prepared to adjust to the impacts of increased carbon dioxide in the atmosphere. Some of the countries that can afford it are already strengthening their coastal defences, but no one yet is preparing for massive relocation of populations or for major changes in the food production capacity of the earth. The sooner these preparations are made and costed the better. Once these reactive strategies are costed then decision-makers will be in a better position to move ahead on preventive activities, which almost certainly will be found to be more cost-effective.

*

Every country will need to make its own 'battle plan,' because circumstances vary widely. There will be particularly wide differences between the countries of the North and the South. (These differences will reappear in each aspect of the environmental crisis covered in this book.) The overwhelming problems of most countries of the South are rapid population growth, environmental deterioration, and a crippling financial indebtedness to the North – all of which make it very difficult to embrace new policies, environmental or otherwise. True, many useful policy changes could be made immediately in the South, but probably not on a scale to assist in the control of the most probable global warming scenario. Under these conditions how can the decision-makers develop useful strategies to reduce the risks of global warming?

The reduction of emissions of gases of industrial origin requires a combination of new technology and new regulations, including taxes that reflect environmental impact. Right now the main responsibility to develop and disseminate improved industrial technology rests with the North. If this technology were made available to countries in the South they would have to ensure that such technology were adopted. The other major contribution of the South would be to complete the demographic transition as soon as possible. Both policies will require financial and technical resources from the North.

So far this discussion has been at the level of national governments. But in many countries (like Canada, the United States, and Mexico) there are important intermediary levels of government between the central authority and the city. The European Community will exemplify this tripartite division of territorial power, as the former nations become 'provinces' of Europe. As of now there are no clear guidelines as to how the different levels of government will integrate their jurisdictions to deal with problems like global warming. In Canada, for example, policy documents have been produced by all three levels of government – federal, provincial, and municipal (Government of Canada 1990; Ontario Ministry of Energy 1990; Metropolitan Toronto Government 1991; City of Toronto 1991). So far it is urban governments that are most specific about policy, perhaps because their responsibility lies with visible, community-scale actions. This urban level of activity is the focus of Chapter 9, Urban Management.

This chapter has focused on the incipient problem of global warming, but environmental decisions must take into account all the major processes currently under way in the transformation of the planet and humanity's increasingly tenuous place in it. By now it is widely believed that global warming represents a potentially terminal threat to human occupancy of the planet. According to the current evidence we must start to curtail it right away. At the same time the world's poorest people must pass through the demographic transition.

If these issues cannot be dealt with simultaneously, then the world may slide into a hopeless trajectory. The North might set itself up to reduce carbon dioxide emissions, while leaving the mostly agrarian countries of the South to 'pay for their own development in an environmentally responsible manner' (to quote Margaret Thatcher; see Chapter 1). This the South cannot afford to do; nor does it have any overriding incentive to do so, as it has more urgent problems, like feeding and housing its people, educating its children, and paying the interest on its debt. Left unaided to face the environmental problems generated by the North, the governments of the South will probably collapse, with terrible consequences for the rest of the human habitat.

Global warming and sea-level rise are only a part of what may happen to the biosphere as a result of population growth and industrialization based on the combustion of fossil fuels. The complete picture includes the interplay of the changes associated with stratospheric ozone depletion, acidification, and increasing marine pollution (especially from hydrocarbons and agricultural and human waste), deforestation, desertification, and increasing scarcity of accessible fresh water. These problems are discussed in subsequent chapters, beginning with the thinning of the ozone shield which protects us from cancer-causing ultraviolet radiation.

4

Ozone and CFCs

Some 25 kilometres above the Earth's surface lies a delicate veil that protects
the inhabitants of this planet from the direct gaze of the Sun. This veil,
thinner than gauze itself and just as delicate, is the ozone layer.

Life on Earth depends as much on the presence of this ozone as it does on
the presence air and water. Without it, lethal levels of ultraviolet radiation
would reach the Earth's surface, extinguishing life on the green planet just as
surely as if the atmosphere were removed altogether. (Mostafa Tolba,
Executive Director, United Nations Environment Programme, Foreword to
The Ozone Layer, UNEP/GEMS, 1987b: 3)

The role of ozone in the atmosphere

Ozone (O_3) is a pungent, trace gas of which the molecule consists of three
atoms of oxygen, rather than the two atoms found in the oxygen molecule,
on which humans and other animals depend for respiration. The ozone problem is a more difficult topic to grasp than global warming (or acid rain perhaps) because it is really two problems, not one. The duality of the problem
lies in the fact that ozone, from the human perspective, plays both a beneficial role in the upper atmosphere and a harmful role near the ground. At the
higher levels, as described by Mostafa Tolba in the introductory quotation,
it protects us, while, near the earth's surface, it is a threat to animal and plant
health. An additional difficulty in understanding the ozone problem is the
lack of a homely analogy, such as the one provided by the greenhouse effect
to describe the impact of CO_2 build-up.

About 90 per cent of the earth's ozone is found in the stratosphere, that
band of the atmosphere between 10 and 45 km above the earth's surface
(Figure 4.1). In that location it interacts catalytically with the most potentially damaging wavelengths of ultraviolet radiation (UV) coming from the
sun. The UV breaks down the ozone into an oxygen molecule and an oxygen
atom, and then breaks the molecule into free atoms, which recombine into

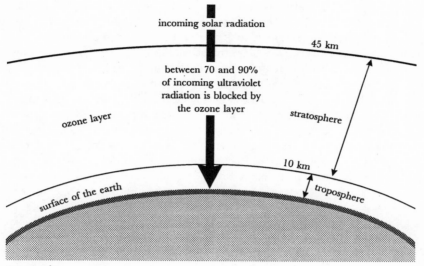

Figure 4.1. Ozone in the stratosphere

ozone. (This process is described in more detail below.) Meanwhile the UV has been transformed into harmless infrared radiation. The quantity of ozone remains unchanged. Without this catalytic operation, life on earth would be very different from what it is today. As UV is cancerous, affecting the skin, the eyes, and the immune system, it is unlikely that the human species, and a large number of our plant and animal neighbours, would have evolved at all. Phytoplankton, the basis of the ocean's food chain, is very sensitive to ultraviolet radiation.

In the troposphere (the lowest ten kilometres of the atmosphere) ozone used to exist in low concentrations (low compared with the stratospheric ozone which absorbs the UV), usually about ten parts per billion. This, again, is very fortunate for plant and animal life, as ozone is poisonous. It irritates the eyes and lungs, it inhibits plant growth, and, at higher concentrations, it will kill plant tissue. Furthermore, in the troposphere ozone also acts as a greenhouse gas. (For a useful discussion of the interplay between global warming, ozone depletion, and acidification see James C. White, *Global Climate Change Linkages*, 1989.) Plants are more visibly susceptible to ozone than are people. It has been estimated by the U.S. National Crop Loss Assessment Network that ozone damage to crops in the United States already amounts to something between one and five billion dollars per year (IIED/

WRI 1987: 155). Field measurements of the impact of high ozone levels have shown a 30 per cent reduction of yields for wheat seeds, 25 per cent weight reduction in potatoes, and 20 to 55 per cent reduction in the mature height of trees like poplars, maple, pine, and ash (ibid.: 154). Ozone is now thought to be responsible for much of the tree decline once attributed to acid rain.

Industrialization, motor vehicles, and the burning of bush vegetation (to create farmlands) have produced a steady increase in this low-altitude, harmful ozone. Much of the increase in ozone near the ground can be attributed to the catalytic effect of nitrogen oxides (released by the combustion of fossil fuels) which combine molecular and atomic oxygen to produce ozone (O_2 + $O = O_3$). Tropospheric ozone levels are now generally two to four times what they were in pre-industrial times. In regions with heavy industrialization and/ or high sunshine levels, readings of ten times the old norm are commonly recorded (Graedel and Crutzen 1989: 60). This is the case in parts of California, the northeastern United Sates, Western Europe, and Australia. Visible evidence of ozone build-up can be seen in the photochemical smogs of Los Angeles, for example. In 1988 the concentration of ozone above Los Angeles exceeded the safety level set by the World Health Organisation on 130 days. However, in Mexico City the count was 312 days, at much higher levels of concentration (*Economist*, 18 February 1989: 43). Because the evidence of this ozone build-up near the ground is so visible, and because the harmful effects are felt daily in our cities, there is some movement towards curtailing ozone production in the worst-affected places, particularly by the application of converters to motor vehicles. By comparison, the threat to the beneficial ozone shield in the stratosphere is less visible, though the problem is even more insidious there and more difficult to treat.

The impact of CFCs on stratospheric ozone

Some of the resistance to the thesis that the burning of fossil fuels was responsible for carbon dioxide increases in the atmosphere was due to the fact that carbon dioxide occurs naturally in the earth's ecosystems. So the source, as well as the magnitude, of the increment was very difficult to measure. The depletion of stratospheric ozone was even more difficult to measure than the build-up of CO_2 as it occurs not in parts per hundred (like CO_2) but in parts per million (Shea 1988: 5). However, the agents responsible for the depletion were easier to identify, as they were artificial substances for which the history of production is recent, and relatively easy to measure. The main culprits are chlorofluorocarbons (CFCs), especially CFC 11 and CFC 12 (CCl_3F and CCl_2F_2). CFCs have been widely used since the 1930s, beginning in the United States, for refrigeration, and subsequently becoming even more widespread with the adoption of air-conditioners and the growing use of foam packaging and aerosol products. Other compounds which contribute to ozone depletion are CFC 113, CFC 22, methyl chloroform, carbon tetrachloride, and halons. The last (used in fire extinguishers) are even more destructive of ozone than CFCs. As early as 1974 Mario Molina and F. Sherwood Rowland proposed that CFCs would seriously damage the stratospheric ozone shield (Molina and Rowland 1974; Roan 1989). For further measure, CFCs are currently estimated to account for 15 to 20 per cent of the greenhouse effect.

CFCs are extremely long-lived. They take several years to travel to the stratosphere, where they are slowly broken down under sunlight, specifically ultraviolet radiation. Their residence time in the stratosphere is estimated at around one hundred years. When CFCs break down under sunlight the chlorine atoms become detached from the carbon and then break down the ozone molecules (Worrest, Smythe, and Tait 1989: 68). This is a catalytic process. The chlorine leaves the oxygen molecule it has helped to create and is then free to break down more ozone molecules. Thus, taking CFC 12 as an example, the CFC is broken down by the ultraviolet radiation, so releasing the chlorine atom, known as a chlorine radical:

$$UV + Cl-\underset{\underset{F}{|}}{\overset{\overset{F}{|}}{C}}-Cl = Cl-\underset{\underset{F}{|}}{\overset{\overset{F}{|}}{C}} + Cl$$

The chlorine radical breaks an ozone molecule into oxygen and chlorine oxide:

$$Cl + O_3 = ClO + O_2$$

The chlorine oxide then detaches an oxygen atom (from another ozone molecule) to form more oxygen. The chlorine radical is then released to break down more ozone:

$$ClO + O = Cl + O_2$$

Net effect: $O_3 + O = 2O_2$

In the above equations, UV is ultraviolet radiation, C is carbon, Cl is chlorine, F is fluorine, O_3 is ozone, and O_2 is oxygen.

Diminution of upper-atmospheric ozone was first reported from research stations in the Antarctic in the 1970s (UNEP/GEMS 1987b: 23). Predictably, the causal association of these reports with the production of CFCs was disputed by the $2.2 billion CFC industry, which, at that time, had no alternative products to offer (Roan 1989: passim). Despite the resistance, frivolous uses (such as aerosol cans for deodorants) were banned in the United States (the leading producer) in 1978. Bans followed in Canada and Scandinavia. These bans reduced production of CFCs by about 20 per cent, but in the 1980s production increased again as more countries became involved in their manufacture (IIED/WRI 1987: 335). Through the late 1970s and early 1980s more data came in which suggested that there had been a general stratospheric ozone reduction of 4 per cent since measurements had first been made. Yet, public interest appeared to have waned until the publication of data by Joseph Farman and his colleagues (1985) which demonstrated the opening up of a huge 'hole' in the ozone layer over the Antarctic. This information, and the satellite maps which supported it, reawakened public concern. The maps, which were widely reproduced in newspapers, probably gave the public a vivid sense that the 'sky was falling,' especially as it was widely understood that increased ultraviolet radiation was linked to skin cancer. The impact would be greatest in the higher latitudes, which in the northern hemisphere meant the home of sun-loving, but generally sun-deprived, citizens of the wealthy industrial nations of northern Europe and North America.

Data collected at Antarctic research stations through the early 1980s showed the rapid enlargement and increasing duration of the area of ozone depletion, which persisted into springtime in southern Chile, Argentina, New Zealand, and Australia. In September 1987 a NASA airborne collection program confirmed the role of CFCs in the ozone breakdown process, and early in 1988 the Russians reported the existence of a similar hole over the Baltic Sea (*Globe and Mail*, 6 March 1989: 1, 5). This time, more than aerosols would have to go.

Implications of the depletion of stratospheric ozone

On an annual basis, UV radiation is greatest at the equator, although equally high rates are found at higher latitudes on clear days in the summer. People who normally live in higher latitudes seem to be more susceptible to the effects of the incoming UV radiation, as evidenced by skin cancer (including melanoma, which can be fatal), ageing, wrinkling, infections of the skin, sunburn, retinal damage, and cataracts. Among white-skinned people there is already a strong correlation between latitude and the incidence of skin cancer. For example, people in Texas have nearly three times the incidence of people in Iowa, and Australians have the highest rate among white-skinned people (UNEP/GEMS 1987b: 28). In general, increased radiation weakens the body's immune system, and thus there is the potential for accelerating the spread of AIDS (*Independent*, 9 February 1992).

Experiments have been carried out on many plant species to estimate their response to increased UV radiation. Response is varied, but generally yields are reduced through damage to plant hormones and chlorophyll. In some cases yields drop consistently, per cent by per cent, with increased UV radiation. Trees would be affected along with more vulnerable crops like soybeans and cotton. Plants would therefore be subjected to an ozone effect on two fronts. Ozone depletion in the stratosphere leads to an increase in harmful UV radiation, while build-up of ozone near the earth's surface contributes to the reduction in plant yields, as mentioned at the beginning of this chapter. Working against the negative effects of this redistribution of ozone would be the build-up of carbon dioxide, which is generally thought to be beneficial to plant growth. It is the multiple nature of the impacts which makes it difficult to estimate the net effect of global warming and stratospheric ozone depletion.

More vulnerable even than terrestrial plants are aquatic algae, the basis of the marine food chain. Their demise would reduce fish stocks worldwide. Further decreases of fish stocks would be expected as a result of the direct damage from UV radiation to fish larvae. For example, it has been shown that anchovy larvae, down to a depth of 10 metres, are killed by fifteen days' exposure to UV radiation at a level of only 20 per cent higher than normal (UNEP/GEMS 1987b: 29).

The role of CFCs in manufacturing

The property of CFCs that made them so attractive to their discoverers was that they are insoluble and unreactive, at least in the lower atmosphere. Thus, in the 1930s they were first used as a coolant in refrigerators (8 per cent of CFCs used in 1985). Later, they were used as solvents (19 per cent) and in aerosols (25 per cent), for deodorants, hair sprays, and furniture polish. Production grew steadily with the growing demand for insulation (19 per cent) food packaging, carpet padding, foam cushions (7 per cent), and car seats. They are an ingredient in ski waxes too (*Economist*, 23 December 1989). An important recent application has been as a cleaner for circuit boards and microchips. Another boost came from the ever-growing demand for air-conditioning (12 per cent) for buildings and cars. The highest per capita use is in the United States, closely followed by Europe and Japan. In 1986, these three and the other OECD countries accounted for 70 per cent of world consumption, with 14 per cent in the Soviet Union and Eastern Europe, 2 per cent in

China and India, and the remainder (14 per cent) in other countries of the South.

Until recently CFCs were known to consumers by their patented names, like Du Pont's Freon for refrigeration and Dow's Styrofoam for cups and insulation. Production grew steadily from 545 tons in 1931, to 20,000 tons in 1945, to 40,000 tons in 1950, and to over a million tons in 1987. The banning of the use of CFCs in aerosols in North America and Scandinavia brought about a temporary reduction in production but this was soon followed by a renewed increase, as other uses were discovered and as newly industrializing countries adopted them as well.

Many of these uses are reserved for the wealthiest sectors of global society – 80 per cent of the cars sold in America are air-conditioned (Shea 1988: 19). Some uses, such as ski waxes and deodorant aerosols, may be dismissed as frivolous. At the same time it was the wealthy (conscious of their suntan) who felt most at risk. This is one reason why the aerosol ban was a relatively easy decision to make, like boycotting consumer goods from one source when similar goods can easily be bought from another source. The solvent and refrigeration uses are more difficult to deal with. Although CFC-free substitutes are being developed, their efficiency (so far) is lower than that of CFCs. More significantly, the companies that are developing them want assurances from governments that new rules will not be introduced to make the substitutes unacceptable at a later date; specifically, they want governments to guarantee long-term markets for the substitutes they are developing (*Globe and Mail*, 6 March 1989).

The CFC issue has split the old industrialized countries from those that are newly industrializing. The latter, being all in the lower latitudes, are probably less at risk to skin cancer and eye infections. Also they do not have the industrial infrastructure to manufacture substitutes for a product for which they are developing an increasing appetite – at least for solvents and refrigeration. They are reluctant to sign an agreement to ban those useful CFCs unless the rich countries will provide them with an adequate substitute at no additional cost. These differences in attitude were very apparent at the March 1989 London Conference on Saving the Ozone Layer (*Globe and Mail*, 6 March 1989: 1, 5).

Some aspects of the ozone crisis make the problem more manageable than that of global warming. First, CFCs are only one segment of modern industrial society, whereas the problems of global warming and fossil-fuel consumption involve every energy-using activity and even the most rudimentary forms of land use. Second, there is widespread scientific agreement on the causal link between CFC use and stratospheric ozone depletion, although this agreement was a long time coming (Roan 1989). There is also broad agreement on the implications of increased ultraviolet radiation as it is potentially very destructive of plant life and directly threatens human health, particularly the health of the rich. Lastly, as CFCs are a human artefact they can be replaced, albeit perhaps by more expensive or less efficient alternatives. However, in another important respect the CFC problem is similar to the CO_2 problem in that the molecules have a long lifetime in the atmosphere – approximately one hundred years. This not only means that the impacts of atmospheric change will endure long after remedial action has been taken, it also means that the gases are so well mixed in the global circulation that the inputs of each nation form only one indissoluble part of the problem. This aspect of system closure, whereby the global environment must be treated as a single entity, means that cooperation among nations is an essential element of success.

On this issue opinion is split widely between North and South. The North can develop CFC-free substitute technology, once it is required to do so by government regulation, and it has many incentives to do so – from the macroeconomic, to the personal, to the fear of the unknown (aptly played upon by Tolba's pronouncement, quoted at the opening of the chapter). The South, however, has far more urgent matters to attend to, some of which are explored in later chapters. Furthermore, the South has so far contributed much less than the North to the emergence of the ozone-depletion problem. There is justifiable fear in the South that the banning of CFCs will render their industries obsolete, making the South more dependent than before on Northern technology and on Northern terms of technology transfer. Some even fear that a CFC ban will become a formidable non-tariff barrier to international trade, further distancing the poorer countries from the global economic mainstream.

Physical system closure again implies the need for new forms of international relations, forms which look for cooperation rather than competition at any cost. Despite all these difficulties substantial progress has already been made on the ozone issue, under the aegis of the United Nations.

Steps toward the elimination of CFCs

Among those United Nations agencies, like UNEP, which work towards international agreements, the sequence of steps usually follows from a convention (which is a statement of concerns and priorities) to a protocol (which sets targets for action) to a treaty (which is legally binding). Thus, once the ozone-depletion process was confirmed, continued concern led to the Vienna Convention in March 1985, which was signed by twenty-seven countries. The convention was simply a statement of principles, a call for further research, and a pledge to work out a protocol for the implementation of a freeze on production at present annual levels. The protocol, which called for a reduction in annual production by 20 per cent of the 1986 level of production by 1994, and 50 per cent by 1999, was signed by twenty-four countries in September 1987 in Montreal, where a supervisory agency was established (*Globe and Mail*, 17 September 1987; Government of Canada 1990: 117). However, there were many loopholes in the agreement concerning trade in CFC products, and there were lengthy delays before complete phase-out, particularly to accommodate developing countries and the Eastern Bloc. There were hold-outs, too, among the industrialized nations – interest groups who wished for a more thorough analysis of the problem and of the options. Neither methyl chloroform nor carbon tetrachloride, which account for 16 per cent of the ozone-depletion effect, were covered by the Montreal Protocol; nor were halons.

By 1988, however, the data suggested strongly that the general rate of ozone depletion around the globe was faster than had been expected, and a new sense of urgency pervaded the discussions. Even the sceptics appeared to be converted. A total phase-out of CFCs by the year 2000 ('if possible') was agreed to by eighty-one countries and the EC at Helsinki in May 1989 (UNEP 1989: 1). In March 1990 a conference was held in Geneva to add methyl chloroform to the convention (*Globe and Mail*, 9 May 1990). By June 1990 the number of signatories of the Montreal Convention had risen to fifty-six.

Both 1990 and 1991 produced record depletions of the ozone layer. Many countries have now promised to phase out CFC production completely by the year 2000. Canada is committed to complete phase-out by 1997, and several European countries are aiming for 1995 (*Globe and Mail*, 12 October and 21 November 1990; *Independent*, 10 February and 2 March 1992). The northern 'ozone hole' is now expected to affect Canada and Britain every spring, and people have been warned to wear sunglasses and sun cream to protect them from getting cataracts and cancer. In Chile, which has been affected by the southern ozone hole since the 1970s, there are alarming reports of blind fish, rabbits, and sheep, deformed tree buds, and an upsurge of 'patients with allergies, eye irritations and skin complaints' (*Financial Times*, 6 November 1991). Apart from the risk to human health, there are fears that increased ultraviolet radiation will have major effects on Chile's economy because of the impacts on fish, fruit, and wood products.

Despite the new sense of urgency there are still at least two major points of concern. First, even if all further production is banned, if all uses are banned, and if all existing CFCs (i.e., those now in use, approximately two million tons) are destroyed, ozone depletion will continue for the one hundred years or so of the remaining lifetime of the CFCs already in the atmosphere, unless some means can be found for recovering them (Shea 1988: 22). Second, it is unlikely that the poorer producing countries (especially the emerging industrial giants like China, India, and Brazil) will cease production unless a substitute technology is available for their use. Industrial companies in the richer countries are highly unlikely to make a gift of the substitutes they are now developing. The question then comes back to the governments and taxpayers of the richer countries: how are they going to finance the transition to a less-threatening evolution of the atmosphere? One calculation that may move private-sector opinion in the industrial world is the cost of delay. In addition to the damage to plant life and marine life there are several economic activities which will be immediately and heavily affected by the threat to human health. The obvious examples are sun-based tourism, sun-based retirement communities, life insurance, and the increased cost of health care.

Although the observed rate of ozone depletion continues to exceed predictions, there are positive changes appearing from the technical side, with substitutes soon to be available for those uses considered essential. For cleaning printed circuit boards the substitute was both more effective and cheaper – warm, soapy water was the answer (*Globe and Mail*, 16 April 1990; *International Herald Tribune*, 16 May 1990)! Technology has been developed to recycle CFCs rather than release them to the atmosphere (*Globe and Mail*, 12 September 1987). Many improvements could be made in the handling of CFC products to prevent their wasteful release. The World Resources Institute estimated that a combination of recycling, elimination of aerosols, and the use of already available substitute chemicals could quickly reduce ozone depletion by one-third (IIED/WRI 1987: 159).

Such improvements may be expected as long as citizens and non-governmental environmental organizations keep the pressure on their governments and as long as those governments regulate manufacturers and consumers. The unresolved problems, on a global-management scale, are how to transfer the improved technology from the rich countries to the poor, and how to monitor and control the atmospheric changes in order to minimize the side-effects. The Helsinki Declaration did promise to 'facilitate the access of developing countries to relevant scientific information, research results and training, and to seek to develop appropriate funding for the transfer of technology and to replace equipment at minimum cost' (UNEP 1989: 1). However, a budget is required to make this 'facilitation' a reality. An impasse exists because some industrial countries (especially the United States) do not share the sense of urgency over the problem, as expressed by the four continental Scandinavian countries, for example. The hold-outs have so far refused to transfer technology or funding to poorer countries. Among the latter, those who are industrializing on a large scale, like Brazil, China, and India, do not consider ozone depletion as a priority, certainly not as important as domestic poverty and (for Brazil) the overriding problems of inflation and the size of national debt owed to foreigners. Right now, the industrializing countries of the South are waiting to see if the rich countries will demonstrate their concern by transferring the technology that might enable low-income countries to do their part.

5

Acid Rain –
The Global Implications

It is now generally accepted that acid deposition impairs sensitive aquatic ecosystems and corrodes materials ... The potential effects on human health, crops and forests, soils and groundwater are still controversial and under continuing study ... Increased acidification exhausts the buffering capacity of the ecosystem and thus increases nutrient and water stresses which in turn decrease tree vitality. Also, as a result of increased leaching of toxic heavy metals, human heavy metal intake via drinking water and through the bio-accumulation process in the aquatic food chain may have become higher. (OECD, 1985a: 32)

Acid precipitation

Acid rain was the subject of the first atmospheric 'transboundary dispute' to force its way into the popular imagination and onto the political agenda. In everyday life, the term 'acid' suggests corrosion; clearly, it is something that, in large quantities, would be unhealthy. Coming down with the rain it sounds distinctly threatening.

The scientific term 'acid precipitation' includes acidic deposition from snow, fog, dew, and cloud moisture, as well as the more familiar acid rain. It is the product of the reaction, in the atmosphere, of water with sulphur dioxide (SO_2) and nitric oxide and nitrogen dioxide (NO, NO_2, symbolized collectively as NO_x) to form sulphuric acid and nitric acid. The rapid increase of sulphur dioxide and NO_x in the atmosphere is largely due to the use of fossil fuels for electricity, transportation, and various industrial processes. The smelting of sulphate ores (to obtain nickel, zinc, and copper, for example) is also a contributor to sulphur dioxide in the atmosphere. In mining countries, like Canada and Norway, smelting is a bigger source of SO_2 than the combustion of fossil fuels.

This increase in the acidity of the atmosphere is passed on to terrestrial and aquatic ecosystems through wet and dry deposition via the hydrological cycle. On plants it has a growth-inhibiting effect; although much of the forest die-back once ascribed to acid rain is now thought to be largely due to ozone, as mentioned in Chapter 4. It was in lakes that the connection between industrialization and ecosystem damage was first noticed in the 1950s and 1960s. Continued acidification successively attacks fish larvae, molluscs, aquatic plants, fish, and thence throughout the food chain. If continued, the acidification process will render some lakes almost lifeless. To counteract this effect, the Swedish government has poured over 700,000 tons of crushed limestone into the worst-affected lakes since the mid-1970s (OECD 1985a: 31). However, the lifeless lakes may be the less- dangerous part of the acidification threat.

Acidification of water and soil accelerates the release of heavy metals and aluminum, which may then enter the human food chain through the process of bio-accumulation, described in Chapter 2. The threat to human life through soil, water, and the food chain is still disputed and certainly is less visible than the absence of biota in lakes. Probably it is for this reason that acidification appears to be less immediately threatening to humans than stratospheric ozone depletion or global warming. However, from another perspective, it is amazing that there has not been more public concern and international action on the acid-rain issue. In the previous two chapters we have seen how the long lifetime of CO_2 and CFC emissions in the atmosphere means that there is a global mixing of the troublesome gases. Thus, although we can estimate roughly which country put which percentage of the compounds into the atmosphere, we cannot trace which country damaged another. However, SO_2 and NO_x, the agents of acid rain, stay in the atmosphere only for a few days or, at most, a few weeks; after that they either settle in dry form or are brought down with precipitation. It is estimated very roughly that one-third of the load falls within 200 km of the point of emission, one-third between 200 and 500 km, and the rest beyond that. In this situation, one *can* roughly estimate how much one country deposits on another. Despite this potentially interesting situation the culprits have been reluctant to make amends, and the victims appear to have been reluctant to press for compensation. Cooperative agreements have been very slow to emerge, and in the case of some of the major culprits (such as America, Britain, and France) hardly anything has yet been done. Perhaps one reason for this inaction is that many of the victims are culprits too, and, in trying to get their guilty neighbours to pay their environmental bills, they might be forced to pay what they themselves owe to others.

The problem of acid deposition has grown in spatial extent as industrial systems have become more extensive, and as local pressure for clean air obliged emitters to construct higher smokestacks. True, the local air quality might thereby be improved, but the same quantity of emissions would eventually be deposited further away. In this way a local environmental problem became a regional problem, and eventually the regional problem has become a transboundary or international problem.

Human acidification of the environment becomes an international issue in three different ways. First, among the old industrialized countries of the North there are clearly established patterns of emission and deposition related to prevailing winds and the intensity of rainfall. Thus, eastern Canada lies downwind of the old American industrial heartland from New Jersey to Illinois. Scandinavia is downwind of the industries of Britain, France, and Germany. Second, the newly industrializing countries of the South are becoming large enough to pass on SO_2 and NO_x to downstream neighbours in the North. Thus the growing economy of Mexico will affect the southwestern United States, North Africa will affect southern Europe, and China and the Koreas will affect Japan. Already studies have shown that, in the winter, of the sulphur found in Canadian Arctic smog, 25 per cent comes from Western Europe, 25 per cent from Eastern Europe, and 50 per cent from the former Soviet Union. One of the scientists who made these measurements said that 'air pollution is not a regional problem but a global one when affecting the Arctic' (*Globe and Mail*, 11 January 1991). There is even evidence of high-level transport of SO_2 and NO_x across the Atlantic and across the Pacific. Soon, acidification will become recognized as a problem of global atmospheric circulation, too, even though only a fraction of the total load will travel across the oceans. Acidification will also affect marine life, perhaps with international implications. Finally, acidification will become a more and more widespread problem as fossil-fuel combustion continues to increase, and the general North–South issues of clean technology transfer, already encountered in Chapters 2 and 3, will emerge.

What happens to an acidified environment and how does the process relate to other aspects of the global environmental crisis?

Acidification of the environment

For some readers the chemistry involved in the acid-rain controversy may appear to be even more complicated than that of the CFC-ozone problem. Also the eventual implications of acidification for plants, animals, and people themselves are, at this stage, less clear than is the ozone-depletion situation. An appreciation of what is happening requires an understanding of three topics: the measurement of acidification in the environment; the natural cycles of sulphur and nitrogen in the environment; and the changes in levels of acidification due to the increasing presence of nitrogen and sulphur emitted by industrial activities.

The measurement of acidification is based on the presence of atoms that carry a net electrical charge, known as 'ions.' For example, free hydrogen atoms are positively charged (H^+), while free oxygen ions are negatively charged (O^-). Some compounds, like ammonia, are net positive; others, like hydrogen carbonate, are negative. When a water molecule breaks up, it splits into free hydrogen atoms (H^+) and hydroxyl ions (OH^-). The higher the concentration of free hydrogen ions, the more acid the water. Acidity is measured on the pH scale (pH for positive hydrogen ions), with zero being the most acid condition and 14 the most alkaline; 7 is neutral. Normal precipitation is slightly acidic (about 5.6) because of the interaction of water with carbon dioxide to form a weak carbonic acid. (It is this weak acid that erodes limestone, which then precipitates to form stalactites and stalagmites in limestone caves.)

It is important to understand the natural cycles of sulphur and nitrogen because they are important plant nutrients. Nitrogen is essential for the building of protein, amino acids, nucleic acids, and vitamins, while sulphur is required for the production of proteins and vitamins. Although nitrogen exists in abundance in the atmosphere (accounting for 78 per cent), it is not directly accessible to plants, which must absorb it in the form of some compound. Atmospheric nitrogen is transformed biologically by micro-organisms and then joins the food chain. Nitrogen is released back to the atmosphere by organic decay, microbial action, and combustion. Whereas nitrogen is based in the atmosphere, most of the sulphur is found in the ground as elemental sulphur, sulphides, sulphates, and sulphur dioxide. Microbes, interacting with plants, release sulphur to the atmosphere, from which it is redeposited on the ground. Volcanoes release sulphur, and sulphur is found with coal.

People have changed these natural cycles in a number of ways. First, one of the main components of the fertilizers that people apply to soils is nitrogen, because many crops take out more nitrogen than they put back. In this situation, in sulphur- and/or nitrogen-deficient soils acid deposition could be beneficial. (Like global warming, a little acidification might be good for some places.) Second, unintentionally, the burning of fossil fuels has greatly increased the quantity of acidic materials in many parts of the earth's surface and atmosphere. This human augmentation of acidification is out of all proportion to the localized agricultural deficits in nitrogen or sulphur. Once again, the environmental change engendered by people is uncontrolled; the odd beneficial side-effect is overwhelmed by the negative implications. How has this unintended effect happened?

Human emissions of SO_2 and NO_x into the atmosphere interact with water to produce sulphuric acid and nitric acid. When these acids are deposited on vegetation and soils they interfere with the complex process of cation exchange whereby plants assure their access to soil nutrients like calcium, sodium, and phosphate. The impact is greatest in environments that are already slightly acidic, particularly rocks with a high silica content such as granite and sandstone; here the breakdown of clay particles in soils is accelerated by acid deposition. Clay particles play a key role in holding nutrients in the soil, keeping them accessible to plant roots. The net effect of acidification is to break down the clay, thereby making it easier for moisture percolating through the soil to wash away plant nutrients and, at the same time, release aluminum and heavy metals such as cadmium, zinc, and copper. The nutrient loss inhibits plant growth, and the heavy metals are free to accumulate in the food chain. This is most readily observable in fish in lakes, particularly lakes in granitic areas such as the Canadian Shield, Highland Scotland, and the Fenno-Scandinavian Shield.

The effect of acidification on these fragile lake systems is now well known. However, the impact on soils and terrestrial plant life is more difficult to measure because it must be separated from similar damage attributable to the build-up of ozone and other pollutants. If the soil and water environment in an acid deposition zone is initially alkaline (e.g., in limestone areas) the effects may be buffered. This means that the deposition of acid precipitation does not appear to interfere with the stability of the nutrient cycle or the distribution of heavy metals.

The effect of atmospheric pollution on buildings was noticed long before the acidification of Scandinavian and Canadian lakes came to public attention. The effect was particularly dramatic in the unhappily weathered faces on statues set around famous buildings made of vulnerable limestone and sandstone. What is less visible is the general corrosive effect of acid rain on all buildings and structures such as highways and bridges. Again, it is difficult to separate out the impact of SO_2 and NO_x from that of other pollutants. However, the sheer quantity of these compounds released by human activities must mean that they play a major role. It is estimated that Britain emits six million tons of SO_2 yearly, while New York alone emits two million tons (Briggs and Smithson 1985: 522). The impact on human health may be fairly direct from digestion of toxic materials in food and water and from inhalation of acidified air. The former effect is now well researched, but the latter has not yet received much attention.

The regional impact of acidification

Since people lit their first fires the balance of the sulphur and nitrogen cycles has been in jeopardy. The use of fire for clearing bush in the tropics is still a major contributor to acidification. However, it was not until the beginning of the coal-burning age (and the sulphide-metal-smelting age) that the impact became noticeable. This contribution has exploded since the Second World War.

Acidity can be measured in the rainfall and in lake water and the soil. Trends in rainfall acidity are now very clear after thirty years of measurement. The effect can be seen in the spreading and deepening of the acid-rain 'shadow' over northeastern North America and northern Europe. The spatial specifics of acid deposition are much clearer than the estimated regional impacts of global warming or ozone depletion because we can easily identify the sources of the industrial activities responsible for SO_2 and NO_x emissions (Figure 5.1). The impact of these emissions can be measured either from the pH of the lake water or by changes in the levels of the metals that are released by the acid-deposition process. Data from Lake Ommern in Sweden illustrate the latter relationship quite dramatically (Figure 5.2). Estimates can be made of the percentage of each country's deposition that comes from outside its own boundaries. For Britain, the figure is a low 20 per cent, for Sweden it is 82 per cent, and for Norway 92 per cent (much of Norway's load coming from Britain). However, although it may appear that laying the blame would be as simple as pointing to the source of the prevailing winds, the pattern of deposition is more complicated than that. For example, France dumps 167,000 tons of SO_2 on Germany; but Germany, in its turn, drops 124,000 tons on France. Thus, the settling of accounts (such as paying some monetary compensation), even if aggregated at the national level, would be complicated.

Other complications come from lack of agreement about the problem we are trying to solve. These complications are a very awkward mixture of the technical and the moral. They are illustrated by Figures 5.3 to 5.6 based on OECD data, which are used because that organization was the first international body to collect a broad range of environmental statistics that established the basis for relating national economic output to environmental impact (OECD 1985a, 1985b, 1991a, 1991b). Twelve countries are selected to show the performance of three groups of market economies:

- the G7 or the seven biggest market economies (United Kingdom, Italy, Germany, France, Japan, United States, and Canada)
- four relatively 'green' countries, or at least countries in which environmen-

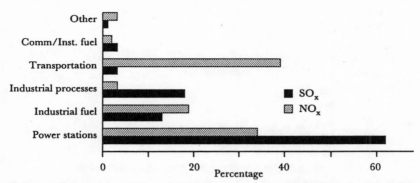

Figure 5.1. Percentage of SO_x and NO_x emissions by source (from Bubenick 1984)

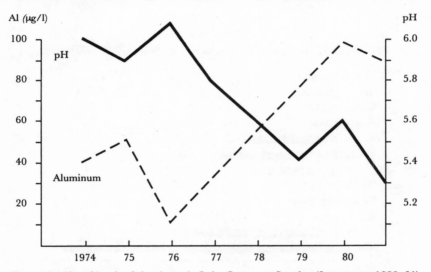

Figure 5.2. pH and levels of aluminum in Lake Ommern, Sweden (from OECD 1985: 31)

tal issues have been prominent in political debate for the past twenty years (Denmark, Sweden, Norway, and the Netherlands)
• one relatively poor OECD country, which illustrates the difficulty in expecting poorer countries (whether from the North or the South) to remain economically competitive while meeting environmental standards (Portugal)

One approach to the reduction of global warming is to define the problem in terms of national economies and the quantity of emissions they each produce. Quantities vary according to the type of emission, but let us take

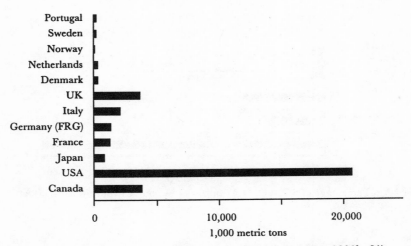

Figure 5.3. Total sulphur oxide emissions, late 1980s (from OECD 1991b: 21)

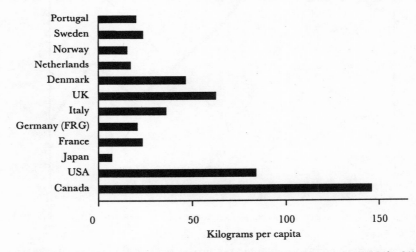

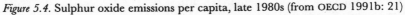

Figure 5.4. Sulphur oxide emissions per capita, late 1980s (from OECD 1991b: 21)

sulphur oxides (SO_x) as an important example, using as an illustration our twelve countries from the OECD. From Figure 5.3 the problem is very obvious. The G7 countries, with the exception of Japan, are the obvious culprits, with the United States as the pre-eminent offender. If we went outside the OECD and found comparable data, others would be privileged to join this group, notably the former Soviet Union and Eastern Europe, plus other emerging industrial economies such as Brazil, Mexico, India, and China. For

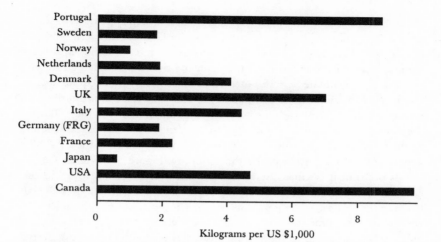

Figure 5.5. Sulphur oxide emissions per GDP, late 1980s (from OECD 1991b: 21)

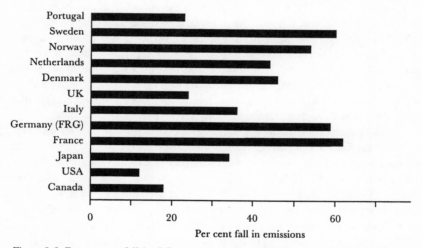

Figure 5.6. Percentage fall in SO$_x$ emissions from 1980 to late 1980s (from OECD 1991b: 21)

the moment, let us consider the implications of the OECD figures.

To the extent that countries vary enormously in size of population and size of economy, they are statistically comparable only in a very limited sense. Elsewhere in this book there is some discussion of per capita rights to pollute, that is, to use some portion of the global sinks, especially the atmosphere and the ocean. Figure 5.4 shows the quantity of sulphur oxides emitted per capita for each of the twelve countries. Now it is Canada which appears as the heaviest polluter, followed by the United States, the United Kingdom, and (perhaps surprisingly) Denmark. Does this indicate some deficiency in terms of Canada's use of the environment, or can the figure be explained away in terms of a cold climate, vast distances, and an economy that is quite dependent on smelting sulphide ores, especially to recover nickel? It is interesting to note that Japan, the world's most dynamic major economy in the 1980s, has the lowest per capita figure of this group. One might also expect emissions to be correlated with the value of the gross domestic product, the total of all goods and services produced by the economy (Figure 5.5). Again Canada stands out, but it is joined by Portugal, which suggests that lower-income countries may tend to be relatively inefficient producers of wealth in the earlier stages of industrialization. This has very important implications for the economic development of the South, in that its economic growth will probably be accompanied by significant increases in pollution, on the present technological trajectory.

If we were to use these kinds of figures to examine pollution-control policies, we might be tempted to think of rewarding not necessarily the cleanest producers, but the most improved. Figure 5.6 shows that the four relatively 'green' countries performed best in the 1980s, along with France and (what was then) West Germany. It is notable that the three least-improved in the group – the United States, Canada, and the United Kingdom – are the ones with the highest per capita emissions (Figure 5.4), which would suggest that their environmental deficiencies are long term.

Should legislation then target the biggest or the dirtiest operations? Perhaps, when the data become available, it will be seen that one country can be held to be both the biggest and the dirtiest in Europe – the former Soviet Union (*Economist*, 4 November 1989: 23–6.) As a whole, Eastern Europe produced 150 kg of SO_2 per head (in 1984), compared with 62 kg in the European Community (*Economist*, 17 February 1990: 54, 56). However, most international discussions on pollution reduction have been confined to the OECD, to which the republics of the former Soviet Union and East European countries do not (yet) belong.

From this preliminary inspection it would seem that there are pitfalls in basing environmental policies simply on current national-emission levels, or on per capita 'rights,' or on economic efficiency when based on such simple criteria. Certainly these are somewhat ambiguous conclusions, even within the relatively homogeneous world of the OECD. So where do we go from here, in terms of North–South relations?

So far, the acidification debate has been conducted in the context of the OECD – the rich industrial North – and even within this privileged club no consensus has emerged. What rules should be applied to the restructuring economies of Eastern Europe and low-income countries of the South – those which are already industrializing rapidly (like India, China, Mexico, and Brazil) and those that hope to become middle-weight industrial countries soon (like Egypt, Zimbabwe, Thailand, and Indonesia)?

Those who believe that 'the market' could correct all environmental evils would simply propose the imposition of a tax per ton of emissions per firm. In national terms, this would put the burden on the biggest economies, such as Germany, Japan, and the United States; however, as we have noted, some of them could point out that they have already done much more, in one sense, to reduce pollution than certain other countries. Furthermore, it is one thing to propose such a tax and another to implement it. Thus, there are many difficulties in settling the emissions problem by international legislation. For the European Community, change will eventually come from community-wide regulations, devised in Brussels, directed at the individual firm.

Despite the difficulties in finding an equitable means of employing market forces to reduce the impact of acidification, the trend to do so appears to be strong. However, the engineering dictum that 'the solution to pollution is dilution' has gone the way of the traditional micro-economic approach to categorizing costs not borne by the firm as 'externalities.' Both viewpoints must give way to the physical forces of system closure which insist that dead lakes, blighted trees, reduced crop yields, damaged buildings, and the as yet unknown impacts on human health are costs that must be accounted for as 'internal' costs from a global perspective.

Acidification in the South

Acid deposition is usually considered almost exclusively as a problem of the old industrial world. Given that the offending particles do not stay very long in the atmosphere, it might be expected that this is not a problem for the poorer nations. However, there are at least four aspects of the problem that affect the poorer countries of the South, even though they do not have the misfortune to lie downwind of the dirty North. First, a percentage of the emissions (perhaps as high as 10 per cent) does travel global distances. It is estimated that about 10 per cent of North America's emissions falls on Europe, and a smaller percentage of East Asia's falls on North America. So, some must fall on those developing countries closest to the industrial North, even if they are not directly in the path (e.g., Mexico, North Africa, South and East Asia). However, as mentioned above, the net deposition is likely to be that of the South on the North, rather than vice versa.

Second, at least one large developing country is already suffering from serious acidification because of its own coal-burning activities, namely China (IIED/WRI 1987: 153). Third, there are other developing countries which have soils that are very sensitive to acid deposition (being naturally acidic, low in cation exchange, and high in aluminum), and which are generating damaging levels of emissions, from bush burning and/or from industrial output. These critical regions include Venezuela, southern Brazil, Nigeria, western India, the Gangetic Plain in northern India, and parts of southeast Asia. In some parts of southern Brazil the deposition of SO_2 (measured in grams per square metre) already reaches the quantities recorded in Sweden (Rodhe and Herrera 1988: 269). Nearly three-quarters of the surface of Venezuela is regarded as highly sensitive to the effects of acidification. In Nigeria there are sensitive soils adjacent to the oilfields from which all the gas is still flared off. Other significant contributing sources in Nigeria are paper mills, a sulphuric acid plant, petroleum refineries, vehicle exhaust, and bush burning (Rodhe and Herrera 1988: 311–14). In these regions acidification will have a twofold negative impact – on agricultural productivity and on human health. Both will reduce the ability of the countries of the South to support their still rapidly growing populations, with all the implications this has for relations between North and South.

Lastly, there is the question of technology transfer from North to South. As in the case of reducing CO_2 and CFC emissions, the technology for the reduction of SO_2 and NO_x is being developed in the rich industrial countries. Under what circumstances will this technology be transferred to the newly industrializing world? These three atmospheric issues – global warming, ozone depletion, and acid deposition – are very closely linked, both in terms of their physical interaction and in terms of the economic and political development of a solution. Under what organizational framework can human beings develop a cooperative, sustainable approach to the use of natural resources?

Steps towards clean-up

Much could be done to reduce the problem if economic incentives, such as a tax on emissions, were put in place. One of the advantages of the relatively short lifetime of the acidifying particles in the air is that some improvements to air quality and plant growth might be seen almost immediately if emissions were reduced. However, the longer-term problem of the lifeless lakes and the acidified soil and groundwater would remain.

Emissions could be reduced by cleaning the coal of sulphur before burning and by improved coal-burning techniques, such as fluidized bed combustion, coal gasification, and coal liquefaction. Scrubbers can be put on

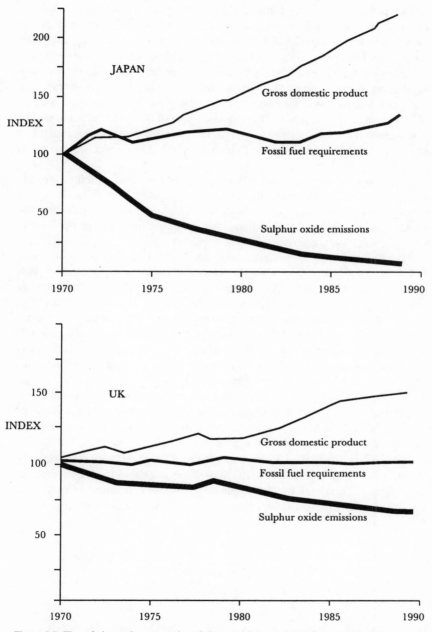

Figure 5.7. Trends in anthropogenic sulphur oxide emissions (from OECD 1991a: 37)

smokestacks to retain the sulphur. The sulphur would still need to be disposed of, but at least it would not be free on the wind. Demand could be switched to low-sulphur coal. NO_x emissions could be reduced by improved emission controls on vehicle exhausts. The practicality of emission reduction is clearly illustrated from the OECD data (Figure 5.7). Japan is, beyond any argument, the most successful national economy over the past twenty years, and yet it has achieved high rates of economic growth without increasing its use of fossil fuels and while reducing emissions of SO_x. (True, some of this was achieved by using nuclear power.) This trend is present, but much less strongly, in the United Kingdom (which also shifted to nuclear power in this period).

Emission-reduction technology is costly in capital terms, and it evades the basic problem that was identified in Chapter 3, global warming. The real solution is to move out of the early chemical age, as quickly as possible. We need to reduce demand and change over to non-polluting (or less-polluting) energy sources – solar, tidal, wind, and geothermal.

The acid-deposition problem is not one that has drawn the North and South into conflict yet, because deposition is a more localized effect than global warming and ozone depletion. However, the question of technology transfer is still paramount. The sustainable growth of the economies of the South is a prerequisite for stabilizing the world population. If the North does not help with the best available technology, then widespread acidification of the major economies of the South is only a matter of time. Then, truly, the Swedish attempts to rehabilitate their dead lakes by pouring in crushed limestone will become the labour of Sisyphus.

The acidification problem may help to avoid a strictly North versus South confrontation on global environmental issues in that it is some countries of the North (such as Canada and the Scandinavian countries) that were the first transboundary victims of our careless technology. Yet it is other Northern economies (the United States, southern Europe, and Japan) that are likely to suffer next from the acid deposition of the emerging industrial economies of the South. This break-up of a simple North–South confrontation may open up avenues for a more global, cooperative approach to the problem.

6

Management of the Ocean

The Argentine fishing lobby has frequently accused the Soviet side of failing to keep within the catch limit. Its worry is that the domestic Argentine fishing fleet ... will soon become extinct if maximum catch levels are not properly policed.

They point to the sobering example of Peru, which has dropped from being the world's number one fishing nation in 1970 (with 20% of the catch total) to 14th today (with 2%), a direct result of uncontrolled exploitation of its resources. (Gary Mead, 'Moscow pays up for Argentine fish,' *Financial Times*, 27 March 1990: 38)

The role of the ocean in human affairs

The last three chapters have dealt with the environmental implications of the changing composition of the atmosphere due to human interference with natural bio-geochemical cycles. It has been difficult for the nations of the earth to address these problems through traditional forums because until this century the atmosphere was regarded as a 'free good,' belonging to no person and no nation. Only with the invention of aircraft did the notion of national airspace emerge. The development of telecommunications brought in further need for management of the air.

Humankind has had much longer experience in regulating the rights of nations to the world's oceans, especially for navigation and for fishing. These rights have evolved over hundreds of years, although consensus has never been achieved, as illustrated by the opening quotation to the chapter. In the past thirty years we have seen the emergence of 'exclusive economic zones' up to 200 miles off national shorelines. Through the efforts of UNEP we have seen cooperative attempts to manage 'regional seas' and to develop an international Law of the Sea (of which more is said later). Although the concept of ocean management is thus not unfamiliar to people and their national representatives, it is still at a very early stage of elaboration. Concerns have been limited to traditional rights to transportation and fishing – the latter focused on a few readily exploitable species. In this century concerns have broadened to include offshore mining, principally for petroleum, but with a growing interest in seabed mining for metallic minerals. The ocean has always been a handy 'sink' for sewage and other human wastes; recently this has extended to incinerator ash, nuclear-weapons testing, and nuclear- waste disposal. A handful of nations use the sea as a source of desalinized water.

This ad hoc approach to ocean management is now changing under the pressure of the environmental crisis, which means nothing less than system closure at the global scale. Although many of the above uses of the sea by human beings are expected to continue, the viewpoint now required is much broader. Probably the fundamental role of the ocean in human affairs today is that of a climatic regulator, a global thermostat and a sink for excess carbon dioxide, for example. Right now we urgently need to know much more about the interaction between air and sea. The limitations of our knowledge are clearly exposed by our difficulty in explaining the El Niño phenomenon, described below. All the unknowns associated with global warming, sea-level rise, and the vulnerability of fish and phytoplankton to ultraviolet radiation can be analysed only with the help of much more knowledge of the evolution and resilience of the ocean. The second change in human attitudes relates to the more traditional concern regarding human access to ocean resources – only now we attach the adjective renewable to those resources. It has often been said that so far people have simply hunted in the oceans, whereas now we need to farm them. As will be seen later, our ability to reason in these terms is still very limited. So how can we change our traditional view of the oceans from being a cheap means of transport, source of fish, and cheap dumping ground to being valued as a climate regulator and a properly managed, long-term asset?

The next sections of this chapter consider the role of the ocean in the natural bio-geochemical cycles and the impact of human waste on these cycles, especially near the shoreline.

The role of the ocean in bio-geochemical cycles

Although the ocean covers 70 per cent of the earth's surface we know far too little about it. Some scientists think that the ocean's great capacity to absorb carbon dioxide will save us from global warming; others see the chemistry of the deep ocean as the key that flips the climate back and forth between glacial cycles. In order to use the ocean wisely we need to know far more about its chemistry and its physics; most important, right now, we need to know more about how it interacts with the atmosphere, particularly with regard to the exchange of carbon dioxide. We should also learn more about the ocean's capacity to absorb the solid wastes that we deposit directly into it – like petroleum, sewage, and radioactive waste. Some of the solid waste dissolves harmlessly, but some of it accumulates.

In a number of ways the ocean operates as an environmental pathway in a fashion analogous to the atmosphere. Surface ocean currents run parallel to the prevailing winds; gases are deposited on the surface; then they are mixed, ingested by biota, and cycled through various life forms. Some are then returned to the air and some are deposited on the ocean bed. However, beyond the generalities, the specific interactions are even more difficult to measure than they are in the atmosphere.

The ocean acts as a sink or repository for material from the atmosphere and from the land. For example, the ocean is estimated to hold about 70 per cent of the carbon in the world, compared with only 1 per cent in the atmosphere, the balance being on land or in sedimentary rocks. What we do not know is how much more carbon the ocean can absorb. As we are pumping additional carbon into the atmosphere every time we burn fossil fuels and as we are reducing the biosphere's carbon-recycling capacity every time we reduce the forest cover, this unknown absorptive capacity of the oceans becomes a factor of crucial importance. This is true not only for the carbon cycle but also for all the other major bio-geochemical cycles, like nitrogen, oxygen, and sulphur.

The answer is not likely to be a simple one of 'so many tons of carbon is the maximum the ocean can hold.' The interchange of chemicals between air and ocean is highly dynamic. From the perspective of humanity, the important question is not so much the ultimate quantity of carbon that the ocean can hold, as the rate at which the ocean can absorb the extra carbon that we are continually releasing from fossil fuels. It is quite possible that, in the shorter term, the amount of CO_2 in the atmosphere will increase rapidly and that this will seriously disrupt climatic patterns. Yet, in the longer term, this excess CO_2 might be absorbed easily by the ocean. However, as noted in Chapter 2, the 'longer term' might be too late for humanity.

The extent of our ignorance about the role of the ocean in the life of the planet was illustrated by the irregular recurrence of the El Niño–Southern Oscillation, or ENSO, events. Every five to eight years a weakening of the trade winds allows the equatorial counter-current to bring warmer water from the western Pacific to the Peruvian coast. This surface layer of warmer water reduces the normal upwelling of nutrient-rich colder water on which the anchovy and other fish rely for their diet of plankton. Apart from the fact that the resultant reduction of the fish supply (already overfished) had a cata-strophic impact on Peru's economy, the warmer surface temperatures brought damaging torrential rain to the coast. However, what is even more alarming about these ENSO events is the evidence of systematic linkages be-tween this unpredictable oscillation and disruptions in the normal pattern of rainfall around the world. These associated disruptions are known as teleconnections. The evidence remains only at the level of statistical associa-tion, not causal linkage. For example, Laban Ogalla notes: 'results may be loosely interpreted as suggesting that El Niño is linked to drought in southern Africa and high rainfall in eastern Africa' (1987: 57). Glantz, too, is cautious in interpreting these apparent teleconnections: 'The 1982–83 ENSO event, which was the largest of the century, and the previous major ENSO event (1972–73) coincided with a spate of major droughts worldwide, including drought in the West African Sahel and in the Horn of Africa' (1987: 63). After thirty years of intensive study, interpretations of the wider impacts of the phenomenon are still incomplete (Glantz, Katz, and Krenz 1987: passim; Firor 1988: 57). This example shows how our knowledge of the behaviour of the ocean is quite limited once we need to predict the evolution of the envi-ronment in this age of human-induced change on a global scale.

The second factor to note is that it is of very limited use to know the average characteristics of the ocean. As a medium it is less fluid than the at-mosphere, and its contents are mixed less homogeneously. This is especially true of the shoreline where nearly all the wastes produced by human society remain, in suspension or deposited on the seabed. These are wastes that run off the land in rivers, that seep from sediments, and that are deposited from ships. In 1982 UNEP was said to have given the deep ocean a 'fairly clean bill of health,' but that said nothing of the condition of the shoreline, and espe-cially the condition of nearly enclosed bodies of water like the Mediterra-nean, the Baltic, or the Persian Gulf (UNEP 1987b: 2). As was noted in Chapter 3, over 60 per cent of the world's population lives within 80 km of the shoreline (UNEP 1987b: 1). The human use of the ocean as the ultimate garbage dump therefore has fairly immediate impacts on human health and the quality of life.

The ocean as a sink for wastes

Most of the deposition from the air to the ocean is invisible. We tend to see the results only as pollution on the beaches and in analyses of the pollutants that bio-accumulate in the food chain, especially in crustaceans. Not only may the chemical characteristics of the ocean be changed (analogous to the change in the presence of trace gases in the atmosphere), but these changes may lead to changes in the ability of the ocean to act as a global sink. Unfortunately we will not know when the ocean's absorptive capacity has been exhausted until after it has happened, by which time it will probably be irreversible. We have some direct knowledge of what happens out of sight of land just from rough calculations of waste dumped by ships. This is estimated as an annual input of 6.4 million tons of general shipboard litter, plus 136,000 tons of plastic, nets, lines, and buoys and 22,000 tons of plastic containers from fishing boats (IIED/WRI 1987: 128). What follows is a brief review of the various forms of dumping that may have, or already have had, a significant effect on the ocean's continued ability to act as the globe's major buffering agent.

The substances that have been multiplied in quantity, or been invented, during the chemical age and that may have harmful side-effects may be assigned roughly to four main groups: nutrients, toxic metals, hydrocarbons, and radioactive materials. All the chemicals used as fertilizers, herbicides, and pesticides in modern agricultural systems flow through various environmental pathways. Some evaporate; some remain a long time in the soil; but a great many flow through streams into the ocean within a matter of days or weeks. The latter pathway is important because most agricultural areas are associated with major river systems, like the Po, Rhine, Ganges, Mekong, and Mississippi. Nutrients encourage the growth of algae. In a sense they intensify the natural eutrophication process, whereby protected bodies of water, like bays and deltas, are gradually filled in by biomass, such as plant litter, sewage, and agricultural run-off, to the eventual exclusion of aquatic life forms. The northern Adriatic has become particularly susceptible to 'red tides' caused by algal blooms, mainly in response to excessive inputs of phosphorus in detergents. In 1988 an algal bloom in the Venice lagoon led to 'an invasion of insects and the release of hydrogen sulphide with extremely disagreeable consequences for the population and the tourists' (Grenon and Batisse 1989: 254).

So far, the impact of chemical-based agriculture is most clearly seen in the industrialized economies of the North. However, higher agricultural productivity in the South is expected to come from increased use of chemical inputs; this is one of the cornerstones of the green revolution. If this process continues, then we should expect to see harmful algal blooms in the deltas of the Yangtze, Ganges, Nile, and Niger. (I have never seen a cost-benefit analysis of a fertilizer-using agricultural project that included this negative side-effect.)

The second group of substances – toxic metals and compounds – have caused concern for some time, especially since the Minamata case of mercury poisoning in Japan in 1953, when at least seventeen people died and many more were permanently disabled. (The claims of some of the victims are still being heard in Japanese courts.) The main substances to cause concern are lead, mercury, cadmium, aluminum, and polychlorinated biphenyls (PCBs). These materials enter the pathways as residuals from industrial and mining activities. Some are put directly into the ocean by incinerating dangerous wastes at sea, which is a common practice around the shores of North America, Japan, and northwest Europe. These, the most advanced industrial countries, determined that this was a safer practice than burying such wastes on land, even though by incinerating at sea these potentially dangerous substances were injected directly into the food chain. No practice more clearly illustrates the 'out of sight, out of mind' attitude than our view of the ocean as the ideal global garbage dump. However, some account is finally being taken of these extraordinarily self-destructive practices. The United States Environmental Protection Agency has supported the Mussel Watch program to sample mussels at American coastal locations to measure their uptake of PCBs, DDT, copper, cadmium, and other heavy metals. As the unhappy bivalves have no choice but to ingest our rubbish along with their normal diet they become ideal 'cumulative indicators' of our careless distribution of toxic materials.

Hydrocarbons are the ocean-polluting substances that have received the most persistent coverage in the media, probably because of the spectacular nature of spills from oil tankers that run aground. Here the public can see the sea birds drowned in oil and the angry fishermen, hotel owners, and coastal residents. The public can see the problem and the villain is only too visible; the media can haul in the guilty owners of the vessel and the negligent captain of the ship. Drama is not lacking in these cases. Whether you are doing a thirty-minute feature or a clip for the evening news it is quite easy to present the issue in a way that the viewing public (and the newspaper-reading public) can understand. This is very different from the loss of stratospheric ozone or even from monitoring metal uptake in the lowly mussel.

Yet, it would probably come as a surprise to most readers to learn that only 22 per cent of the hydrocarbons deposited in the ocean, from marine sources, come from tanker spills. Another 2.7 per cent come from oil platform accidents, while 16 per cent come from natural seepage from hydrocarbon-rich sediments open to the ocean. The remaining 59 per cent come from the routine flushing of oil-tanker holds! The practice is banned, but it continues without interference. (For a commentary on this situation see OECD 1985a: 83.) Furthermore, an almost equal quantity of hydrocarbons is deposited from the atmosphere or run off the land.

Perhaps the ultimate example of the ocean as the dump of last resort is the ocean disposal of radioactive waste. Until 1983 European countries like Britain, Belgium, Switzerland, and the Netherlands dumped their radioactive waste near Cape Finisterre, in northwest Spain. It seemed suitable because the water was 4,000 metres deep, and at that time it lay within 'international waters.' The potential impact on the coasts and fisheries of Spain and Portugal was presumably considered to be unimportant. Today the United Kingdom Atomic Energy Authority is developing a disposal site, off the coast of Cumberland, for the radioactive waste from the notoriously unsafe Sellafield nuclear-power station. The coastal seabed has been selected. The only question is whether the horizontal mine shaft to the disposal chambers will be permanently sealed, or will be left open so as to be accessible for retrieval and safer disposal of the waste, if and when such techniques become available.

To add to these serious problems we must consider the practice of dumping municipal wastes in the sea. Liquid and semisolid wastes are often sent out through very short pipes (sometimes less than 100 metres) into the ocean. Other solid wastes, such as compacted sewage and household, industrial, and hospital waste, are often bundled up, put in barges, and simply dumped in the sea at a point where it is assumed that the problem will disappear. The London Dumping Convention (first signed in 1972) curbed some of these practices, but it did not end the idea that the ocean was ultimately the best final resting-place for humanity's most problematical waste. People are beginning to understand that the problem does not disappear; it is passed on to an unsuspecting party. (Other aspects of waste management are examined in Chapter 10.)

The filth that washes up on beaches is only a small part of the problem, although it is the one that has the most visual impact on sensitive sectors of the international economy such as tourism. UNEP estimates that we put about twenty billion tons of waste – sewage, agricultural run-off, industrial waste, and sludge from dredging operations – into the ocean every year (see Figure 6.1). About 90 per cent of this remains near the coast. Yet, the coast also provides about 90 per cent of humanity's fish catch. Shellfish are especially prone to pollution because of their fixed location close to shore. Other heavily threatened coastal environments are coral reefs and mangrove forests. In brief, not only do we rely on the ocean as our principal garbage dump, we deposit most of this waste in exactly the places from which we take an important part of our diet. On the scale of the individual or the family such behaviour would be considered bizarre, to say the least.

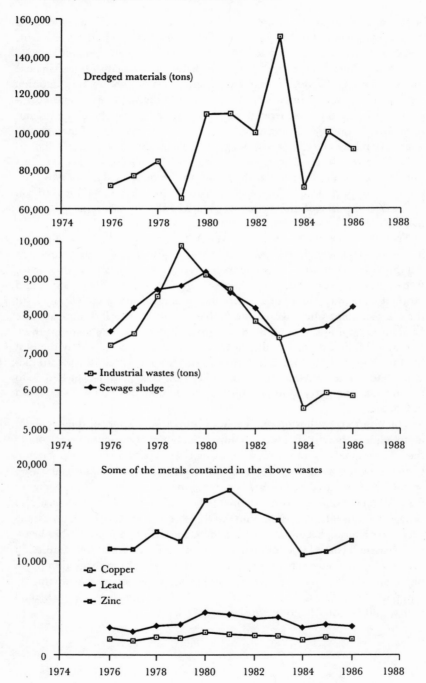

TABLE 6.1
Ten countries with the largest fish catch, 1982

North	South	Catch (1,000 tonnes)
Japan		10,760
USSR		9,450
USA		3,922
	Chile	3,673
	Peru	3,452
Norway		2,463
	India	2,400
	Korea, South	2,281
	Indonesia	2,020
Denmark		1,907

Note: On the North–South dichotomy used here this would assign about 28 million tons to the North and 14 million tons to the South. Note that the 'Northern catch' does not include those Northern ships that operate under flags of convenience, like Panama and Liberia.
Source: taken from IIED/WRI, *World Resources 1986*: 143, based on FAO reports

The ocean as a source of food

There are four main ways in which people's activities affect the ocean to the detriment of their life-support system. The most direct is the propensity to overfish the most desirable species of fish, crustaceans, and mammals to the point of extinction. Some fisheries (like North Sea herring, haddock, Alaskan pollack, and Peruvian anchovy) have already been reduced below the level of commercial viability or have begun to decline. The haddock catch in the northwest Atlantic fell from 250,000 tons in 1965 to 20,000 tons in 1970. The drive to overfish is a response to steadily rising demand for fish, part of which comes from the growing population of the South, especially from those countries for which fish are a major source of animal protein – countries like Senegal, Thailand, Indonesia, and the Philippines. But, paradoxically, the greatest part of the increase in demand comes from the North's intensification of its demand for meat (Table 6.1). Almost one-third of the global fish catch is now processed into oil, fish meal, and fertilizer. Fish meal is a high-protein feed supplement for pigs, poultry, and cattle; the fertilizer is for grains, of which a significant portion goes as feed for livestock. As noted in Chapter 2, the higher up the food chain you eat, the less efficiently you use the protein and other nutrients that are potentially available.

Figure 6.1. Wastes and metals dumped in the North Atlantic (from World Resources Institute 1990: 341)

People inflict indirect damage to their food supply through the accumulation of pollutants in the food chain from plankton, to plankton-eating fish, to fish-eating fish, and in a parallel fashion through crustaceans. We have already noted the appearance of giant algal blooms in nutrient-enriched coastal zones like the northern Adriatic, which is supplied by the sewage of the cities, industrial waste, and the fertilizers of the Po Valley. Apart from their lack of aesthetic appeal, and their immediate impact on tourism, these blooms are inimical to most of the fish and crustaceans in the human diet (*European*, 12–14 July 1991). Lastly, as noted in Chapter 4, the loss of stratospheric ozone will probably result in radiation damage to fish in the larval stage and to plankton, the very basis of the marine food chain.

The disappearance of commercial species like the North Sea herring promoted concerns that led to the concept of a maximum sustainable yield (MSY) for a fishery. Logically, such a point must exist. Beyond this point fishing exceeds stock recruitment and the fishery will die out. The first difficulty lies in estimating the MSY before it is reached. Even fish that shoal close to the surface, like herring and tuna, are difficult to count. Somewhat less of a problem is found with marine mammals, especially whales, which is probably part of the reason why some agreement was reached to halt whaling in the early 1980s (except for scientific purposes). More difficulty has been met in reducing the unwanted catch of porpoises, dolphins, and other mammals that are caught up in giant drift-nets designed for fish and shrimps.

Even if the MSY can be estimated, the problem of enforcing quotas on fishing fleets remains. This is a particularly vexing problem for North–South relations as some of the world's richest fishing grounds lie off the coast of low-income countries; yet these countries rarely have the equipment to exploit their coastal waters. They also do not have a Coast Guard capable of enforcing quotas on foreign ships, most of which come from the rich North. The establishment of 200-mile Exclusive Economic Zones by the International Conference on the Law of the Sea in 1982 did nothing to change this situation. Competition for available fisheries is an extremely contentious issue among countries of the North – witness the perennial struggle between Canada and the United States and the European Community, intense struggles within the European Community, and struggles between the former Soviet Union and Japan (by far, the two largest fishing nations) and coastal states throughout the world. Without some better agreement on the rules of ocean fishing, what does the North have to offer the South other than further exploitation of their vulnerable stocks?

Finally, we must also consider the provision of drinking-water from sea water through desalinization. This is practised extensively in only a few countries, like Israel and Saudi Arabia. However, with the increasing cost of providing clean water from the land, and with the improvements in the efficiency of desalinization, it would seem to be only a matter of time before we have a process that is affordable for low-income countries (Richmond 1988: 82; *Economist*, 16 May 1987: 89–90; CEEC 1988: passim). Perhaps, when desalinization has become more widespread, there will be more active concern about dumping raw sewage and other untreated wastes into coastal waters, as the heavier the level of contamination, the more costly it is to provide water of potable standard.

The ocean as a source of minerals and power

Coastal mineral and fuel deposits have been mined for centuries, from tar in the ancient world to the sea coal of Northumberland and Durham. Wastes from these operations go directly into the sea. A new era opened when oil drilling moved from strictly coastal operations such as those of Louisiana, Venezuela, and the Caspian Sea to ocean-based operations on the scale of the North Sea oilfields developed in the 1960s. As noted in the previous section, oil-platform and -tanker accidents account for 25 per cent of hydrocarbons deposited in the sea from marine activities. These ocean-based oilfields all lie within national territorial waters. Although disputes occur, they can be settled through the International Court in the Hague.

Some metallic minerals are already extracted from territorial waters, such as uranium off Japan, polymetallic sulphide ores off the coast of Oregon, and manganese nodules off Tahiti. Associated with the manganese nodules are iron, nickel, copper, cobalt, molybdenum, and vanadium. However, there is no territorial basis for allocating rights to mining the seabed under international waters. In all the major oceans, mining companies expect to find commercially viable manganese deposits as soon as the Law of the Sea has been extended to permit exploitation. Currently it has been ratified by only thirty-five countries; notable absences include the former Soviet Union, the United States, and the United Kingdom.

Whereas seabed mining promises to unleash a new set of waste problems, the ocean also offers the possibility of providing renewable, non-polluting energy. These possibilities include kinetic energy based on tides and waves as well as thermal energy which exploits the temperature gradient between different depths of water. It has been proposed that the variation in temperature could be used to drive a turbine by alternately evaporating and condensing water in a column. The biggest temperature differentials are found in the tropics. However, as long as the full cost of burning fossil fuels is ignored, these renewable, non-polluting energy sources will appear to be too expensive to justify commercial exploitation.

TABLE 6.2
Annual inputs of pollutants into the Mediterranean (tonnes)

Nitrogen	800,000
Phosphorus	320,000
Mineral oil	120,000
Detergents	60,000
Zinc	21,000
Phenols	12,000
Lead	3,800
Mercury	100

Source: UNEP 1987b: 2

Regional examples of ocean mismanagement

The problems of ocean mismanagement appear to be much more pressing on a regional scale whether the example is taken from the North Sea, Tokyo Bay, Jakarta Bay, or the coastal oilfields of Venezuela, Mexico, or Indonesia (Bower and Koudstaal 1986; Koudstaal 1987; Dekker, Bower, and Koudstaal 1987). The Mediterranean, still the favourite holiday destination for wealthy Europeans, has been the focus of a great deal of concern, regarding both the impact of pollution on recreation and the impact on shellfish. In the summer, approximately one hundred million tourists are added to the year-round coastal population of 130 million. The fish harvest exceeds a million tons per year. Yet, despite this intensive human dependence, it is estimated that 80 per cent of the waste entering the sea is either untreated or is treated inadequately (UNEP 1987b: 5). It is estimated that water, and other material, in the Mediterranean circulates for seventy to eighty years, on the average, before it escapes to the Atlantic Ocean (OECD 1985a: 83). The immediacy of the danger was brought home to Naples in 1973 when many people died from cholera which was thought to have been caused by contaminated mussels. Table 6.2 shows some annual inputs into the Mediterranean. Here, in the heart of the rich North, the problem is one of the health risks of an industrialized, fish-eating, leisure-seeking society.

In Senegal, West Africa, the mix of problems is rather different, although tourism is still an issue. In an average year there are 230,000 foreign visitors to Senegal; three-quarters of them come from Europe (République du Sénégal 1984b: 367). Tourism is the third-largest earner of foreign exchange. However, oil, sewage, and other wastes are a problem; if they are not better managed they will certainly affect the tourist business. The more pressing issue, though, is access to the rich fishing grounds off the coast. The 1970s saw a rapid increase in the Senegalese fishing catch based on traditional boats, augmented by outboard motors, which remained close to the shore. Fish are an important part of the local diet. Dried or smoked fish are transported to inland towns, including some in Mali and Mauritania. When agriculture was depressed by drought in the 1970s and 1980s the fishery was the only buoyant economic sector. However, Senegal's access to its rich offshore fishery potential has remained very tenuous. A local ocean-fishing company, set up in the early 1970s, collapsed financially after a few years. Traditionally the fishery has been exploited by fleets from France, Spain, and Portugal. Since the 1980s, however, an increasing percentage of the catch has been going to Russian boats operating from a factory ship which processes the fish on the spot. Complaints about Russian fishing within territorial waters were sent through diplomatic channels, but they went unanswered. The situation sounds remarkably similar to the problem reported between Russia and Argentina, at the beginning of this chapter.

In this situation we encounter the full irony of North–South relations at a time of environmental crisis. A low-income country, faced with desertification on land, cannot gain access to its rich potential harvest in the ocean. This situation is typical of all of West Africa, where local nations have increased their fishing capability, but their percentage of the total fish catch declines as the ships of the North increase their catch even faster. By the time the Senegalese have the equipment to take a significant share of the offshore catch they could well find that the fishery is exhausted.

Options for the redevelopment of the ocean

The United Nations has taken two separate approaches to improved ocean management. One is through the continuing conferences on the Law of the Sea, which deal with problems of chronic pollution, overfishing, response to emergencies, and seabed mining. Progress has been slow. Indeed, it took fifteen years to negotiate the limited agreement that some nations signed in 1982 (MacNeill, Winsemius, and Yakushiji 1991: 113). In principle, these ocean-wide agreements require the signature of the governments of all countries, or at least of those that have an ocean coast or other maritime interests. Thus, as long as there are perceived conflicts of interest the problem of holdouts remains. Specific issues such as ocean dumping, drift-net fishing, and whaling have received some useful attention.

The second approach, spearheaded by UNEP, has been to set up programs for 'regional seas,' focused on partially enclosed portions of the ocean. Here, the group of nations that is being encouraged to cooperate is smaller and the nature of the problems is much more obvious. So far, programs have been set up for the Mediterranean (1974), the Red Sea and the Gulf of Aden

(1976), the Persian Gulf (1978), the Caribbean (1981), West and Central Africa (1981), East Asia (1981), the South-East Pacific (1981), the South Pacific (1982), East Africa (1985), and South Asia (1988). These programs attempt to guide the signatory nations through a progressive commitment going from action plans, to conventions, to protocols, to treaties, and finally to financial support for monitoring and implementation (UNEP 1987b: 5). However, although the total of 130 signatory nations is impressive, the programs so far have received only $20 million from UNEP and a further $43 million from other donor agencies. Given the size of the problems it would not seem inappropriate to call the sums invested derisory.

Certainly the regional-seas programs, with their emphasis on the coastal problems of pollution and the health of the fishery, are starting in the right place. However, serious problems also lie in the deep ocean – our last buffer against the impact of our many environmental follies. Until we have better monitoring of what is happening to the chemistry of the deep ocean, the era of ocean management can hardly be said to have begun. As far as the ocean is concerned our involvement is still at the hunting and gathering stage of our distant ancestors. This is highly unfortunate for, as we shall see in the next chapters, land-based resources are under very severe strain, worldwide. By default, the ocean is probably our best hope for increased access to sustainable resources for the global community.

7

Land for Food and Energy

The report said rising demand for food, water, land, firewood and other natural resources had further aggravated an already precarious ecological balance in many countries [of the Third World]. It said a new class of displaced persons has emerged in these countries in the 1980s − 'environmental refugees': 'Growing human pressure on the natural environment has either rendered ecosystems more vulnerable or triggered off a self-reinforcing process of natural degradation, or both. As a result, more people are affected by natural catastrophes such as landslides, cyclones, earthquakes and flood than before.' ('Poor Nations to Get Poorer, UNCTAD Report Says,' *Globe and Mail*, 27 March 1990: B28)

The complexities of the atmosphere and the oceans are unfamiliar to most people, being remote from their everyday concerns. The use of land, however, has direct daily consequences for everyone, whether a commuter in the North or a street-vendor in the South. Thus, it is the land issues that provide the most immediate problems for resolution between the North and the South. How much land does a family need to support itself? In the rich countries of the North this is a difficult calculation to make beyond the immediate allocations for a home, place of work, school, transportation, shops, hospitals, and recreational facilities. The provision of food, energy, and water requires huge regional, and even global, networks − all of which require land. At the other extreme, the peasant farming family in the South would be lucky if it had two hectares of poor land susceptible to unpredictable rainfall to provide all its material needs. In the cities of the South many families have virtually no space they can call their own.

   Until now the physical distance between the people of rich and poor countries has usually been adequate, at least in peacetime, to keep this highly unequal situation in the background of the conduct of international affairs − at which meetings the representatives of the South, almost invariably, are people whose lifestyle resembles that of their Northern counterparts rather than that of their compatriots. However, system closure is making it increasingly difficult to ignore the global land-use issue. Two significant pressure points are emerging.

First, as noted in the UNCTAD quotation at the beginning of this chapter, there is a swelling number of 'environmental refugees.' Some are the product of dramatic catastrophes like earthquakes and floods, but an increasing number are the victims of what the UNCTAD report refers to as 'natural degradation,' which presumably includes soil erosion and drought. Until recently, many of the most desperate of the poor were held in check by repressive political systems, which effectively helped to keep the pressure off the frontiers of the North. Now that some of these repressive systems are weakening, their citizens are voting with their feet (Tickell 1990). It is unlikely that they can all be contained in refugee camps in the North. Eventually many, if not most, of them will participate in the Northern way of life, commanding a commensurate share of worldwide resources.

Second, representatives of the North and the South must discuss the longer-term land allocation issue, even though this was virtually ignored at the 1992 United Nations Conference on Environment and Development (UNCED) in Rio de Janeiro. As noted in Chapter 1, the North and South have different, and diverging, priorities in the environmental crisis. For the North the major issues are the unknown, potentially disastrous, consequences of the changing chemistry of the atmosphere and the sustainable development of land and marine resources. These they see as being threatened by the continued rapid growth of the population of the South, as well as by the North's use of resources. For the South, the issues are poverty and access to the technology, capital, and markets of the North. There is very little overlap in the two lists of priorities.

An active commitment to effective family planning programs by the South was implicit in the Northern agenda for UNCED, because even a more 'conserving' version of the Northern lifestyle is not physically feasible for the world's present population of five and a half billion, let alone for the optimistically projected stable number of ten billion. Thus, the population issue will certainly be a priority from a global perspective. Yet for the South to focus on this issue would be politically suicidal, even apart from the cultural and logistical difficulties, under the present conditions of entrenched poverty and crumbling ecosystems. When the population issue was raised, obliquely, at a preparatory meeting for the Rio conference a delegate from the South retorted that his country had no intention of limiting its population in order to provide 'empty gardens' for the North. A poignant phrase.

The land-based environmental issues are unlike the remoter problems of stratospheric ozone depletion and the carbon-absorptive capacity of the ocean in that some of the land issues are well understood by many people;

they hinge on people's daily access to their physical means of support and on all the inequities involved in that access. These inequities run throughout all our societies, between male and female, young and old, ethnic groups, classes and castes, and new settlers and indigenous people.

This book is not intended to analyse all these persistent problems. What it should do is examine some aspects of the physical reality of the human occupancy of the planet from the perspective of national interests and ecological sustainability. Such an examination should clarify the policy options. Even a cursory look at the figures underlines the folly of the status quo. The 'population problem' must have a prominent place on the environmental agenda. However, the North is not going to abandon very much of its comfortable lifestyle, nor is the South likely to implement a China-style policy of the one-child family. To clarify what options do exist it is useful to return to the ecosystem approach outlined in Chapter 2.

The underlying question is: from the land available, globally, how can the human population extract sufficient energy to maintain itself? Of course, food is energy too. It provides the somatic energy used by biological systems, such as human beings. 'Energy' is used in the title of this chapter to refer to extra-somatic energy − the fuels we burn, like wood, coal, oil, and gas − to provide mechanical energy to produce heat, smelt ores, and move our transportation systems. Extra-somatic energy also includes hydroelectric and nuclear power.

When the human population was less numerous than it is now, people set land aside for wood lots, and later for coal-mines, to provide their extra-somatic energy. Often the land used for these energy activities was not of good enough quality to be used for pasture, let alone for crop production. As cities became bigger and more dependent on industry their fuel needs outgrew the local hinterland and huge distribution networks were built to provide the power they needed. These networks became global in extent as the first industrial cities appropriated hinterlands all over the world.

The continuing increase of the human population and its growing need for additional resources have now brought us to the realization that the world is one closed system. And now hard choices must be made. Many of them seem to come down to a straight choice between using land to produce food and to produce extra-somatic energy. Should a productive agricultural valley be flooded to produce hydroelectric power? Was Brazil right to plough up its food crops to produce sugar- cane to be converted to ethanol to power motor vehicles? Should Senegal commit land to grow peanuts, in order to export them to pay for imported petroleum; or should that same land be used to produce millet and beans to feed the population? If Malawi needs wood lots to produce charcoal for the towns, should maize fields be converted to this purpose? These are the kinds of choices brought on by system closure.

Forests, soils, and land-use change

The perspective of this chapter is an areal one – patterns of land use from a bird's-eye view – as this is the way in which choices between land-use alternatives can be seen most easily. In later chapters we look at the related questions of water consumption by farms and cities, and the production and disposal of wastes, all of which add complexity to the simple areal viewpoint of this chapter.

The major land-use change associated with the human occupancy of the planet is deforestation, to clear land for agriculture and to provide wood fuel in the first stage of the energy transition. The North has almost completed this phase, but in the South the pace of deforestation is still rapid. We have seen how the atmosphere and the oceans have been despoiled by our growing demand for material goods and the careless way in which this demand has been satisfied, yet it is on the land that we see the most obvious signs of the cost of this heedless drive towards material accumulation. It is the land that directly supports food crops, fibre crops, and livestock; and it is the land that supplies wood, which is still the principal fuel for nearly half the world's population.

Before concentrating on the changes that are visible today it is helpful to look at a longer time span than humanity's brief tenure on earth. Earth's history is one of slowly changing distribution of land and sea, and slowly changing climates. Deserts shrink and grow; at times the land is covered by the sea, and then it emerges as new sediments millions of years later. Soils form when conditions for the breakdown of chemical nutrients permit the establishment of organic matter, which then decays and allows plant and animal communities to develop. The forces of erosion – water, ice, and wind – break up the soil horizons and deposit their nutrients downstream and downwind, where they may form again into soils on the land, or they may be deposited in the sea. Generally the soils in today's temperate climatic zones are deep where the bedrock is not exposed. By contrast, most tropical soils are highly leached as a result of exposure to high temperatures and/or heavy rainfall, and, in the tropics, 80 per cent of the nutrients are locked up in the trees and plants. Hence, when tropical forests are clear-cut, the nutrients remain available on the surface only briefly; once the roots have rotted or been pulled out by farmers the entire soil horizon washes away. It is true, however, that there are some rich tropical soils, such as those that are formed partly by volcanic ash and those that combine elements of sand and clay. (For a fuller picture of the impact of erosion on the productivity of tropical soils see Lal 1984.)

Throughout the history of the planet, since life evolved, the soil formation process has waxed and waned at different rates in different places. When the forces of erosion are stronger than the sources of soil formation, then there is a local loss in soil productivity. What we are seeing today, in the combination of activities that characterize our increasingly demanding tenancy of the planet, is a heavy thrust on the side of soil erosion relative to the rate of soil formation. Let us briefly consider the current trends in deforestation, desertification, and soil erosion.

It is estimated that 10,000 years ago forests and open woodland covered 6.2 billion hectares (60 per cent) of the dry land; today this is only 4.2 billion (40 per cent) (Brown 1988: 83–5). This might still seem like a lot of forest land, except that a certain balance is required to maintain carbon dioxide at the current level. The nitrogen–oxygen–trace gas balance, which makes up the breathable atmosphere and maintains the temperature levels within which humans and other organisms evolved, developed as a function of this forest cover factor (among others). The question of an adequate quantity of forest cover, then, cannot be determined by looking simply at patterns of human food and energy needs, but rather at the dynamics of the atmosphere. We already know that 40 per cent cover is not enough to stabilize the balance of trace gases (such as carbon dioxide) in the atmosphere, even at the current rate at which we are releasing extra carbon dioxide from the combustion of wood and fossil fuels. In fact, no amount of forest cover can absorb this additional, anthropogenic output of carbon dioxide at current levels of emissions.

We need to change our view of the forest, just as we need to change our view of the ocean, from that of a resource to be used, to that of a part of the biosphere which is an essential component in the maintenance of the habitability of the planet for the human species. As we are already going out of balance it would seem prudent to reverse the current rate of deforestation, which annually amounts to a net loss of tropical forests of eleven million hectares. As 0.26 per cent of the present forest cover this may not sound like too much; however, it must be remembered that the loss of a tropical rain forest with its rich genetic diversity is irreversible. The need to maintain the earth's biodiversity is now emerging as a key issue. There are also moral and aesthetic reasons for preserving genetic diversity because many indigenous people depend on the forest for their cultural survival. There is also the weight of caution. As we do not fully understand the ecological links between all species it would seem unwise to continue to remove species without adequate reflection on the consequences. On a simple, practical note, a large percentage of modern pharmaceuticals are derived from vegetal matter, and yet we have analysed only a small number of the plant species that are believed to be available in tropical forests. In terms of the potential for the acquisition of useful knowledge it is as if we had burned down a unique, unread library without even bothering to glance at the books. If only for pharmaceutical reasons, apart from the consequences for food production, the stability of the atmosphere, and moral reasons, this unrelenting process of deforestation is a self-destructive step on the part of humanity.

Coniferous and deciduous forests are easier to replant than tropical forests, and some countries (mainly European countries of the OECD) have actually increased their forest cover in this century (OECD 1985a: 123). However, the health of temperate forests is now threatened by acidification and pollution by gases such as tropospheric ozone. It is reckoned that between 20 and 30 per cent of northern and central Europe's forests are seriously affected. Similar levels of damage are found in North America and parts of China. It was the die-back of their forests that persuaded the people of West Germany to join with Scandinavian countries in calling for tougher emission standards for factories and power plants in the 1970s. (For a description of the levels of damage in Germany, see OECD 1985a: 85.)

The stock of agricultural land

The other massive land-use change that has been taking place this century is the spread of desertification. Estimates have been made that an additional six million hectares of new desert appear every year, while an additional twenty million hectares of land become too degraded to support even low-intensity grazing (Brown 1989: 21). The causes behind this conversion, other than natural climatic change, are deforestation, overgrazing, and over-cropping. The American Dust Bowl of the 1930s was a sharp lesson that had enormous impact on the farmers and the government of the United States regarding conservation policy. It did not, however, deter the Russians from committing exactly the same error: extending crop cultivation into areas of insufficient rainfall, in Kazakhstan in the 1950s and 1960s. The irrigation water taken from the rivers feeding the Aral Sea to support this expansion has ruined that sea as a fishery (Brown 1989: 26).

Deforestation and desertification show up plainly on a land-use map, especially now that we have frequently updated, satellite-based imagery, some of which is designed specifically to monitor environmental change. What is more insidious and less visible than these land-use changes is the steady process of soil erosion. The general type of land use may stay the same, but the natural productivity declines. This decline can be measured by taking samples of the quantity of plant nutrients and soil moisture (Rijsberman and Wolman 1985: passim), or it can be estimated more crudely by measuring the amount of topsoil that is blown away. The latter quantity was estimated at twenty-six billion tons worldwide in 1982, with two billion tons in the United States alone. As mentioned at the beginning of this chapter, a certain amount of soil loss is natural. The question is: What is the impact of the process, on balance?

Responses to soil loss in rich countries have included legislation and subsidies to take land out of cultivation, to build wind-breaks, and to use chemical fertilizers to make up the nutrient loss. In poor countries such alternatives are not so available as there is already a domestic food deficit, so the government can hardly advise its farmers to take land out of production. Wind-breaks, on a scale to change the balance, will require a colossal effort, sustained over at least twenty or thirty years. The use of chemical fertilizers has greatly increased in the postwar period, but Latin America (in terms of kilograms per hectare) uses only one-third as much as North America, and Africa uses only one-tenth. Not too much should be read into this kilogram/hectare application figure, as the benefits of chemical fertilizer application are a function of soil, climate, and agricultural management. In general, while the reduction in the total world cropland and pasture land may not affect the rich countries initially, it is already affecting the economic well-being of the South.

An avoidable negative land-use change is the loss of agricultural land to non-farm uses, such as urbanization and transportation (OECD 1985a: 99). In high- income, highly urbanized countries with a very restricted area of arable land such a conversion is scarcely credible. Yet it is progressing uninterruptedly in Canada and Australia, where agricultural land is much more limited than in Europe or the United States. The loss of valuable agricultural land to virtually uncontrolled urbanization is also widespread around the major cities of the South. Examples abound. One need think only of Kano and Ibadan in Nigeria, Khartoum in the Sudan, and Kinshasa in Zaire. There have been some interesting reversals of this process in those countries where the rural economy has deteriorated and the cities have become homes for the landless unemployed. Agriculture is taken up on urban plots as a matter of survival. Home-grown small livestock, especially goats and chickens, become an important part of the family diet (Stren 1986). Home-grown food supplies have been estimated at 15 per cent of the food consumed in Khartoum (Whitney 1981). Given the intense pressure under which the urban poor live, such developments are not surprising.

Despite these changes, after 150 years of a fairly steady increase in the output of food production, worldwide, there has developed an ingrained optimism, in rich countries, about the earth's ability to produce ever-increasing amounts of food, fibre, fuel, and minerals. Optimists may recognize that the inequitable distribution of this wealth remains as problematic as it did in the Ancient World, but they view distribution as a political problem, not a technical (or environmental) one. Hence, there are huge food surpluses in Western Europe and North America. These surpluses are expensive to store, and they are heavily subsidized by the government. The Americans blame the Europeans for this development; the Europeans blame the Americans. The surpluses are disposed of when possible at subsidized prices to Eastern Europe and to countries of the South. Some financial papers reported that the 1988 North American drought was a very good thing, in that it helped to clear out the costly goods in storage! The forced growth of agriculture in the hothouse of EC subsidies has produced some amazing reverses in patterns of production and trade. Perhaps it was quite predictable that a subsidy system that is designed to support a marginal hill farm in the Cévennes or Calabria will produce some remarkable results on the larger, mechanized farms of Holland, the Ile de France, and East Anglia. With surpluses of sugar-beet and sunflower oil, Europe has less need for tropical sugar, groundnuts, and oil palm. Britain now exports some timber, although it is still a net importer. Western Europe, once Canada's number one customer for wheat, now exports twenty-two million tons of grains. In 1986 the Canadian Wheat Board closed down its London office for lack of business. This rich-country cornucopia of agricultural output may indeed suggest that the earth as a whole is well able to feed the growing population, if only the global (income) distribution problem could be solved.

It now seems possible, however, that the 1988 North American drought was not just an anomaly which helpfully cleared out the overloaded storage silos. It could well have been one of those maddening 'externalities' from the market system that was now insisting on being internalized into our accounting system. If indeed, as most experts now think, it is prudent to assume that global warming has begun, and if one of its most probable effects will be to reduce precipitation in the continental (grain-growing) heartlands of North America and Ukraine, then other changes in global land-use patterns become distinctly alarming. Of world exports in grains in 1988, over three-quarters came from North America (see Table 7.1). A significant reduction in productive capacity there would have serious repercussions for the importing regions, such as the South and the former Soviet Union, especially as the latter would probably find its own production reduced by global warming as well.

Agricultural productivity

Civilization evolved only when people assured themselves of a reliable food supply based on domesticated crops and animals. This surplus above minimal

TABLE 7.1
World grain trade, 1950-88 (million metric tons; − = net import; + = net export)

Region	1950	1960	1970	1980	1988
North America	+23	+39	+56	+131	+119
Latin America	+1	0	+ 4	−10	−11
Western Europe	−22	−25	−30	−16	+22
Eastern Europe and Soviet Union	0	0	0	−46	−27
Africa	0	−2	−5	−15	−28
Asia	−6	−17	−37	−63	−89
Australia and New Zealand	+3	+6	+12	+19	+14
Total traded	27	45	72	150	155

Source: Lester Brown (ed.), *State of the World 1989*: 45, based on data from the FAO and U.S. Department of Agriculture

daily needs became substantial enough to support cities and a complex division of labour only when irrigation was used to boost the output of those early domesticated crops. By this innovation not only was water assured for the critical periods of growth, but furthermore the plants were able to benefit from the nutrients (phosphorus, nitrogen, potassium, etc.) carried and deposited by major rivers like the Nile, Tigris, Euphrates, Indus, and Huang Ho, on the banks of which the first civilizations flourished.

In selecting these river banks and deltas the early farmers had inserted themselves into a very rich niche in the natural cycle of soil formation, soil erosion, and the transportation and deposition of soil nutrients. The annual flood of these major rivers naturally recharged the nutrients taken out by the domesticated plants. Other early farmers found themselves less fortunately situated on the forest margins. Here they made use of the soil/nutrient cycle on a sustainable basis by farming the same patch for two or three years until the nutrients were exhausted, and then moving on, leaving the land fallow and waiting fifteen or twenty years for the secondary forest to replace what they had used. Even when the forests were cleared permanently from the early agricultural regions of Italy and France, for example, the open fields of the manor, which were planted to grains, would still be left fallow for at least one year in three.

In this way, people relied for their sustenance on what the natural cycle of soil formation and nutrient availability would provide. From this they derived the somatic energy to keep them and their animals available for work. For extra-somatic energy they used wind power (for pumping water and for sailing), water power (for grinding grains), and the combustion of wood (for heat for cooking and smelting minerals). In using wood for smelting they found that they outgrew the natural resources, especially in places where there was additional demand for wood for the construction of buildings and ships. Iron smelters were forced to relocate once the local woods had been exhausted. It is estimated that, before the advent of agriculture and smelting, about 80 per cent of the surface of present-day France was covered by forest. By 1789 it was down to 14 per cent (Brown 1988: 84). Today it is back to 25 per cent.

In the agricultural world of Europe in the late Middle Ages, innovations came slowly. Drainage techniques, pioneered by the Dutch, opened up wetlands to ploughing in the Po Valley, southwest France, the Fenlands of England, and the estuaries of all the major rivers of northern Europe. While the enclosure movement drove thousands of people off the land, it encouraged those that remained to experiment with new techniques of crop and animal breeding. Later, innovation and investment were encouraged by the introduction of new crops and animals from the Americas, improved storage, and mechanically planted seed. With the establishment of fenced land, controlled mixed farming became possible, so that the animals' manure could be used to return nutrients to the soil. By these means, agricultural pioneers in the North had, by the end of the eighteenth century, discovered how to sustain high-yielding crops without relying on additional river-borne nutrients or 'shifting agriculture' in the forests or leaving the open fields fallow and thereby susceptible to wind erosion. Having no new frontier lands to exploit they sustained a growing population by the continuing intensification of agriculture.

However, the rapid rise of population in Europe and North America and the explosive growth of the industrial revolution required ever greater output from the agricultural sector. This was made possible by the incorporation of agriculture into the chemical age. Henceforth, the evolution of modern agriculture responded to the demands and possibilities of an increasingly urbanized and industrialized world. Cities no longer evolved as a result of what the agricultural sector made possible. People living in cities decided what they needed, and then they determined how agriculture would make the necessary contribution.

America took the forefront in agricultural modernization in the twentieth century. Average yields of corn, per hectare, rose from 1.5 tons in 1900 to 6 tons in 1970. Farm holdings were many times bigger than even the biggest in Europe. Mechanization was applied, and the number of workers required to farm one hundred hectares steadily went down. The family farm began its long demise. Today only 2 per cent of the American labour force is required to operate the most productive agricultural economy the world has ever seen. It is productive according to the following criteria: the highest yields per

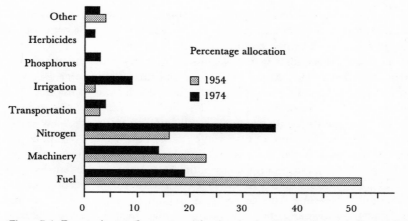

Figure 7.1. Energy inputs for corn production in the United States (adapted from Smil, Nachman, and Long 1983: 152)

hectare, the highest yields per labour input, and the lowest monetary costs per ton. As far as the efficient use of land, labour, and capital are concerned, the American agricultural system is an unqualified success. However, the productivity depends on very large quantities of energy inputs. These energy inputs are low in monetary cost because of America's abundant supplies of low-cost oil and gas. Although the source of energy inputs has changed in the past thirty years, the quantity of energy required remains very high. Note from Figure 7.1 that the increasing efficiency of the system has been accomplished by a relative decline in dependence on mechanization in comparison with a much greater increase in the importance of fertilizers, especially nitrogen.

If we look further afield into the production of livestock and poultry, the same pattern is evident. Americans can afford to, and do, eat more animal protein than anyone else. But this human acquisition of animal protein is very costly in terms of energy inputs. It is estimated that 'one calorie of grain-fed beef requires 10 or more calories of grain; one calorie of battery chicken, 12 calories of grain' (Myers 1985: 37). In other terms, 40 per cent of world grains are produced to feed livestock. In the United States, the figure is 90 per cent, and it requires forty million hectares of land. Now there is an expanding reach for rangelands in Latin America to produce even more beef for America. Much of this rangeland is being carved out of tropical rain forests. In the past twenty years there has been an increasing amount of research into the energy aspects of production systems in modern, industrialized economies. The results indicate that, although the (monetary) cost and yield (tons/hectare) figures look very impressive, they are being obtained by methods that, overall, are not energy efficient, particularly when the dependence on irrigation is taken into account.

Increased yields from irrigation are always impressive; after all, that is how civilization began. However, over the four millennia since Sumer the equation has changed somewhat. What the Sumerians did was to use nutrients and water that were delivered 'free.' The farmers' impact on the delivery system (river, rainfall, soils) was negligible by modern standards. New irrigation systems today are not of that 'run of the stream' variety. We build expensive dams which first flood productive river valleys and then eventually silt up, if the headwaters of the contributing streams are eroded after deforestation. Yet, water users are hardly ever charged the full production costs of this water. Furthermore, the energy used for pumping the water, for making the cement for the dam, and for building the machinery for the farm is produced by fossil fuels. Lastly, the heavy reliance on chemical inputs, such as fertilizers, herbicides, and pesticides, requires heavy fossil-fuel inputs and leaves us with the problem of some potentially harmful residues, as well as the health problems that may be caused by inappropriately applying them.

In summary, we are left with two fundamental problems. First, this modern agricultural production system – this rural by-product of the early chemical age – entails enormous externalities. Second, this 'path to progress,' if transferred to the South, would multiply those very externalities four- or fivefold. These are global problems. Our chemical- and energy-based agriculture is contributing to carbon dioxide build-up, ozone depletion, acidification, and marine pollution. We need to change this approach, not transfer it as it is.

The North is trying to apply modern agricultural technology to the South in a piecemeal way through the international and bilateral development agencies. Success has been very limited for many reasons, including the fact that the technology is not always physically appropriate for tropical ecosystems in the South. In the more marginal areas of the South, with poor soils, uncertain rainfall, and a great variety of pests, farmers have developed risk-reduction strategies such as multicropping and the minimal disturbance of the soil. In these same lands experts from the North have recommended ploughing with tractors and mono-cropping, because capital-intensive specialization was the formula that had worked for them. After a long period of trial and error experts are now recommending multicropping and minimal tillage.

Furthermore, modern agriculture requires a broad and deep transformation of traditional society. In the North the agricultural revolution was already well under way before the death rates came down. By the time it became common in Europe or America for a family to include ten or more living children the percentage of the national population working on the land was already falling quickly and the industrial revolution was in full swing. Jobs were available for much of the surplus labour displaced from the mechanizing farms. What makes the situation in the South so difficult today is that very high population growth rates are occurring without the support of either an agricultural or an industrial revolution.

Some traditional farming systems were sustainable in certain favoured localities in the South (especially in southeast Asia) or in less-favoured regions that had a low enough population density to allow shifting cultivation. As population increased new land was cultivated where available, and the more favoured areas intensified their means of production. In the wake of decolonization and the emergence of technology transfer through international 'aid' it was apparently assumed that variants of Northern agricultural technology could be used to raise yields in the South. This transfer has met with mixed results, and a growing food gap (see below) has emerged in many countries of the South. In addition, it is now realized that although the North's technology can produce high yields, it is not sustainable at the global level of environmental accounting because of its high energy requirements.

Agricultural policy in the South

Before new initiatives are considered, the present policy and production situation in the South should be briefly reviewed. As always, conditions vary greatly from one country to another. The following summary is typical of sub-Saharan Africa, and applies to some countries in Latin America and Asia. First, policies have not been developed with the *problématique* of global warming and sustainable agriculture in mind. At best, low-income countries have tried, with the encouragement of the development agencies, to follow the Western path to increased industrial productivity. For example, irrigation produces one-third of the world's food on less than one-fifth of the total arable land and, thus, irrigation has been pursued as the obvious route to increased yields. Other elements of the Western agricultural package include the application of high-yielding crop varieties (HYVs), the provision of agricultural extension agents, and the application of fertilizers. The rest of the World Bank's 'Basic Service Package,' to take one development agency example, includes the provision of rural feeder roads and agricultural credit. Together these inputs provide the main components of the 'green revolution' which successfully increased crop yields in southeast Asia in the 1970s.

In macro-economic terms the purpose of this re-emphasis on agriculture among the development agencies in the past twenty years was to promote 'export-led growth.' In recognition that family incomes were too low to support 'effective' (i.e., cash-backed) demand for increased agricultural production, the emphasis has been placed on export crops. In this role the World Bank and other agencies found themselves financing the rehabilitation of colonially founded plantations for bananas, pineapples, oil palm, tea, coffee, cocoa, cotton, and sugar. Complementary to this drive was a concern for 'food security,' especially after the famine which followed the Sahel droughts of the early 1970s. However, even this food-security approach was based on the perceived food gap at the national level, the national difference between the amount of food produced and consumed, whereby a deficit affected the balance of payments and undermined the value of the national currency on international markets. Many of the food security plans were aimed primarily at attempting to provide food for urban dwellers from domestic rather than imported sources.

None of these approaches had much to do with the reality of smallholder farming in a low-income country, particularly in a country with low rainfall as well. The irrigation schemes suffered from salinization and poor management (see Chapter 8). Often, because they had been developed on the best soils, smallholders were first displaced before larger irrigated holdings could be established. The subsidized fertilizer passed through the political distribution system so that party supporters got the lucrative job of storing the fertilizer before distributing it to the peasants (at a higher cost). Agricultural extension agents were poorly trained, poorly motivated, and left without any means of transport to cover vast territories. In some societies, where women are kept secluded from non-family males, they would be unable to speak to half of the farmers because half of the farmers were women and almost all of the agents were men. As governments tended to keep down, by decree, the prices paid to farmers (in order to mollify urban dwellers) they had no freedom to market their produce. Worse, the government sometimes did not announce the prices for the crops until after planting had begun, and, when payment came, it might be in the form of unusable government scrip.

This is a familiar litany which has been well documented elsewhere (see, for example, Lawrence 1986; Mortimer 1989; Somerville 1986). Its relevance to the present argument is this. Through political reform, more-sensible policies could be put in place which would encourage the farmer to produce more, both for the farmer's own family and for the market. If prices were liberated and if inputs could be channelled through means other than through a one-party government distribution system, then this too would encourage smallholders to produce more. Few would now argue that a 'market-oriented' approach could be worse than the state-controlled system that many poor countries instituted after independence. In some African countries it might also help if small farmers could sell their land, thus permitting the aggregation of larger, more efficient farms. These political reforms are badly needed. In Africa the communal approach to land management is difficult to modernize, while in Latin America the dominance of large landowners is a key factor in the perpetuation of inequality.

As noted above, the modernization paradigm itself is, however, not sustainable. 'Getting the prices right' will not usher in an age of sustainable agriculture in low-income countries. If a solution is to be found at all it will be found on the smallholder's farm, at least for the next generation, by which time other forms of landholding may evolve, and different farming systems may become appropriate. However, the answer is not to be found in trying to emulate what happened in Europe in the nineteenth century or to force the pace by exporting the technology of the early chemical age, which is destroying the planet anyway.

The solution will vary from place to place, even within the same country. The following is a brief list of examples of practices that have been found useful, where appropriate to the local culture and physical environment:

1 *Agronomic practices*: small-scale irrigation; fish farming; village woodlots, (for fuelwood); minimum tillage; multicropping (several crops in the field at the same time); preservation of local varieties of crops along with the new varieties; pest control by biological, not chemical, agents

2 *Distribution of products*: improved storage facilities in the village; village-based cooperatives for purchasing, marketing, and (sometimes) production; free market prices for products and inputs

All of the above should be considered only in a longer-term framework of fifteen to twenty years at least (Bingen 1985: 120–3).

These approaches have been tried successfully on various scales, although they have not yet become the norm. The tendency is still for the development agencies to go directly to the government for an agreement, even though they expect the work to be done by the peasant. The emphasis is still on maximizing yields rather than on determining, first, what is sustainable on both local and global scales. The farmer is still seen as the cog in the politician's macro-economic machine. What we have, partly as a result of this export-led, chemical-based approach, at a time of rapid population growth, was discussed at the beginning of this chapter: continuing deforestation, desertification, and soil loss.

Energy sources

The use of the land for food production cannot be divorced from the use of the land for energy supply, especially in those regions where fuel wood and charcoal remain the principal sources of domestic, extra-somatic energy. Throughout history we can trace a transition from dependence on one kind of energy to another. The environmental impact of the early phase of dependence on fuel wood depends on the cutting/replanting ratio. If cutting exceeds replanting we know that this could contribute to a carbon dioxide imbalance in the atmosphere and could accelerate soil erosion. Thereafter follows a rapid change to coal and oil, with far greater consequences for carbon dioxide build-up, but, at the same time, relieving pressure on the forest as a source of energy. Over a longer span of history we can see variations in this transition. In the Ancient World almost all energy came from somatic energy (the muscle power of people and animals), the use of running water for grinding grains, or wind power for sailing. Later, windmills enabled the Dutch to drain the reclaimed wetlands of northern and western Europe. The industrial revolution began in England with the use of water power for mills and fuel wood for the early smelters. As seen in Chapter 3, it was the rapid spread of the advanced form of industrial revolution, based on coal-fired steam, that completely changed the balance, leading to the problem of carbon dioxide build-up that we are experiencing today.

The situation in the South as regards the energy transition is quite varied. Some of the newly industrializing countries have followed the European and American pattern and have become heavy users of fossil fuels and some hydroelectric power, with a small (recently frozen) percentage of the total energy coming from nuclear sources. Brazil is perhaps a case apart. It has little in the way of oil production or coal and has switched its automobiles to ethanol, derived from cane sugar. However, this policy has not been without problems. In order to persuade motorists to change to ethanol the government promised to keep the price below the price of gasoline. In the 1970s that did not seem too difficult a promise to keep. In the early 1980s, however, as the oil price fell, the government, crippled by the problem of foreign-owned debt, was forced to cut subsidies to the sugar-cane farmers (*Economist*, 3 March 1990). The farmers, in turn, switched from sugar-cane to soybeans and maize, mostly to provide feed for American and European livestock. This is an example of how one country's attempts to avoid the fossil-fuel trap have run into difficulty.

For the poorer countries of the South the energy transition has barely begun. Fuel wood and charcoal still dominate the energy budget. In the Sahel these provide over 80 per cent of extra-somatic energy (Viaud 1984: 53). In none of these countries is replanting even close to the level of consumption. Dumont and Mottin reckoned that for every tree planted in Senegal in the 1970s, fifty were cut down (1982: 19). Government-directed plantations have had very limited success, and even where successful in terms of survival rate

TABLE 7.2
Government energy research and development budgets in some OECD countries, by
energy source, 1986 (million dollars)

Country	Fossil fuels	Nuclear	Renewables	Efficiency	Total
Japan	310	**1,801**	99	78	2,311
United States	294	**1,134**	177	275	2,261
Italy	4	**658**	30	48	761
West Germany	122	**352**	66	21	566
United Kingdom	20	**271**	16	43	378
Canada	138	**144**	11	34	336
Sweden	9	12	17	**29**	79
Greece	3	2	**10**	0	15
Denmark	5	0	3	**5**	14
Total OECD	990	**4,503**	484	622	7,133

Source: Lester Brown, *State of the World 1988*: 37. Based on the International Energy Agency,
published by the OECD. The major energy sector for investment is indicated by bold type.

of seedlings and protection from people and animals they remain far too small
to keep up with the demand for fuel wood.

Two big questions remain. First, would it be possible to keep up with the
growing demand for fuel wood and charcoal if a new approach to planting
were adopted? The favoured approach is village wood lots and farm forestry,
whereby the onus for planting and maintenance passes from the national
forestry department to the villager and the farmer. Many such schemes have
been implemented, and the results are encouraging (White 1990: 157–8;
Anderson 1987: passim). No one is yet confident that this approach can be
expanded to the point that it could produce a surplus for export to the cities,
although this is not unimaginable.

Second, is it necessary to encourage a transition from fuel wood and charcoal to fossil resources like kerosene, oil, gas, coal, and fossil-derived electricity? Or, is it possible to encourage an energy transition in the South from
fuel wood and charcoal directly to renewable sources, like biogas, and solar
or wind power? There have been some successful projects involving the use
of biogas, in India, for example. But, generally, research into practical forms
of renewable energy has been limited, despite the evident potential for the
application of solar power in abundance, especially in some of the poorer
countries, like those of the Sahel, North Africa, and the Horn of Africa. This
is not really surprising given the limited role of renewable energy research
even in the rich countries, as shown in Table 7.2.

It is possible that the nuclear dominance shown in figures of research
expenditures reflects an era which closed with the Chernobyl disaster – a

disaster that served to crystallize all the public doubts and fears that have surrounded nuclear power since its inception. These doubts have been reinforced by incidents such as leaks from Cadarache (France), Windscale/Sellafield (UK), and in 1979 the meltdown at Three Mile Island (USA). Even if the production technology is made much safer, nuclear energy – based on conventional plant design – costs billions of dollars per plant just to produce the energy, without including the costs for disposing of the waste and decommissioning the plant. Governments and utilities are finding it increasingly difficult to justify these expenditures in the face of public scepticism and outright opposition. Even in Canada, with its great expanses of thinly populated granitic shield, this is a highly contentious issue. Certainly, it would be hard to present nuclear power as a panacea for the North, let alone for the South where the necessary technological and budgetary support are even less evident. From Table 7.2, however, it would appear that if even only half of government nuclear research budgets were spent on renewable energy then the returns from that might be more promising, whether for use in rich or poor countries.

A coherent land-use policy

At this moment human activities are wasting away the soils on which terrestrial food supplies depend. This is happening as a result of overpopulation of the desert margins, the inability of the poorest people to find sources of energy other than the last remaining trees within daily walking distance of their village, and the reckless cutting of timber to provide ranch lands for the export of beef and other rich-country needs. Our combined assault on the forest and on the soils throughout the world is beginning to have marked effects. Meanwhile, in some countries, like Canada and Australia, we are letting our cities sprawl over the best farmland we have. The causes for this include the desperate situation of the poor and the blind exercise of the individual profit drive among the rich.

Our twentieth-century response to declining soil fertility is to apply more fertilizer. Now this remedy is being called in question because of the accumulation of unwanted chemicals in the food chain and the probable impact on global warming of burning fossil fuels to produce and apply the fertilizers. The usual policy in those rich countries that do have options has been either to concentrate on short-term political advantages, such as subsidies to oil and gas companies, or to invest in grandiose schemes to subsidize nuclear power. In order to take a wider view of the situation we need to go back to the energy basis for human existence and the expansion of the species. We need a renewable basis for agriculture, one that is renewable without significant

recourse to manufactured chemical inputs. Renewable energy and soil conservation should be the first point on the decision-makers' agenda. Without
this as a priority the old appeals to 'export-led growth' and 'closing the food
gap' will remain as superficial slogans.

There are some signs that a new policy consensus is emerging. For example, in Malawi the old idea of a forestry program has been replaced by an
integrated energy program in which all forms of biomass used by people –
whether food crops, fuel wood, or construction material – are considered at
the same time. As the problems are happening simultaneously, the solutions
will have to operate simultaneously too. Also the policy focus will have to
shift. The environmental crisis, on both global and local scales, dictates that
we abandon prescriptions based on short-term development projects designed to maximize output or meet short-term political needs. Not only do
such projects usually fail in their objectives; they also entrain hidden environmental costs. The basic policy challenge in the poorest countries of the
world is to find ways to enable small farmers to feed their families. To do this
we have no need to invoke the national food gap or the national balance of
payments.

We must also recognize that modern agricultural techniques have contributed, via fossil fuel use, to carbon dioxide build-up, with its as yet unknown
consequences. The North no longer has a successful agricultural model to
export, if, indeed, it ever did have. A related critical problem is the availability of water.

8

Water Supply

In a period of twenty-five years would it be practicable to improve the water
supply for those populations now inadequately served, so as to provide water
supply and sanitation with low or insignificant health hazard to 95 per cent
of the human family? I am taking the time period of a generation as the
maximum that a major world effort might be expected to accept in dealing
with a matter of vital and universal concern. (Gilbert F. White, *Domestic
Water Supply: Right or Good?* 1973)

Sources of water and uses of water

Globally, there is no shortage of water per se. The problem is the cost of
making water available at a particular place. Figure 8.1 illustrates the difference between absolute water supplies and available (or potentially available)
water for domestic and agricultural use. Roughly, of the world's total water
only 3 per cent is fresh, and of that 3 per cent less than 1 per cent is available
at the surface; a further 22 per cent is groundwater (i.e., underground water),
some of which can be drawn up or pumped up for human use. Of the water
that is available at the surface, about half is cycling through the atmosphere,
through the soil, and through biological systems. The other half is on the
surface in rivers, lakes, and swamps.

Through all of these locations water continually cycles, moving quickly
through some places, such as rivers, more slowly through others, such as the
atmosphere, and resting without movement for very long periods in others,
such as fossil (or unreplenished) groundwater aquifers. These movements are
known collectively as the hydrological cycle (Figure 2.3). The surface water
is usually the most available source, meaning deliverable at reasonable cost.
However, in theory, people may avail themselves of water from almost any
point in the cycle. For example, they may desalinize salt water, collect rain-

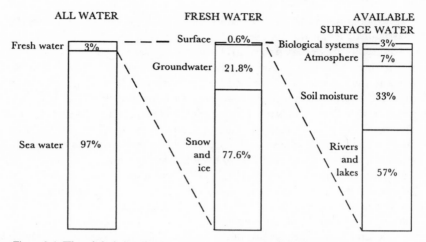

Figure 8.1. The global distribution of water (adapted from UNEP 1988: 2)

water, melt glaciers, or even collect moisture from low-lying clouds (as is being done experimentally with nylon nets in Chile). In practice, costs vary enormously. The *Economist* recently quoted the following costs per acre-foot, delivered to Los Angeles: from Mono Lake in the Sierra Nevada, $70; from California's Central Valley, $250; from desalinized ocean water, $2,000.

Generally people measure only part of what is used, principally for irrigation, industrial use, and urban water supply. The equally important usage by livestock and rain-fed plants can be estimated, as so much per livestock unit or so much per ton of crop produced. However, these unmeasured requirements are often ignored when an urban water supply company or an irrigated farm puts in a bid for available water. When water supply becomes constrained the various users quickly come into conflict. Such conflicts are increasingly common now as population increases; also environmentalists in the North question whether we really need new water supplies when we make such wasteful use of what is already available. The most controversial projects are those that involve dams for water retention or for water diversion and those that pump the groundwater in excess of the recharge rate.

In the North it was in the drier parts of North America and the Soviet Union that the largest dams were built, especially in the immediate postwar period in the 1950s and 1960s when there existed a veritable competition between the superpowers to build the biggest dams. This was at an age when the size of a project was considered synonymous with efficiency. The Americans could boast that the Colorado River was 'fully allocated' – that is all the water in the stream was used for hydroelectric power generation, irrigation, and urban and industrial purposes, so that by the time the river reached the coast, in Mexico, it was reduced to a muddy trickle.

Reservoirs are designed to control water temporally: they retain the water so that it can be used to generate electric power and/or released later for irrigation when rainfall is not available. In this way, land which produced only one harvest per year might produce two, or even three harvests, and perhaps with higher yields than those dependent on rainfall. Other dams and diversions are used to control water spatially by redirecting the flow into another river system where there is a potential for greater use to be made of it. Again, in the postwar period, just from looking at a map, this seemed like a good idea in those regions where rivers flowed 'wastefully' to places where people could not use the water. The American southwest could make good use of Canada's Arctic-flowing rivers. Similarly, Russia planned to harness the Ob, Lena, and Yenisei to redirect their flow to the parched lands of Soviet Central Asia. Throughout the European colonies dams and diversion schemes appeared to promise a major boost to agricultural productivity and industrial output. The Russians financed and supervised the construction of the Aswan Dam on the Nile, the British built the Kariba Dam on the Zambezi, while the French and Belgians had plans to divert the flow of the Congo River northwards to the Lake Chad Basin.

When these projects are viewed simply in terms of the delivery and use of water they often make economic sense: 'wasted' water is being made available for productive human use. In the case of the Aswan Dam, the Sudan was able to grow more cotton, while Egypt boosted its electricity supply for its growing industrial base. As northern Sudan had no rainfall and Egypt had no coal the advantages appeared incontrovertible. Now the situation is seen to be much more complicated as various hidden, or ignored, costs have been revealed. Costs upstream of the dam include the immediate loss of agricultural, grazing, and hunting land that would be flooded and the relocation of the inhabitants. Ghana's Volta River Dam put nearly one-sixth of the country under water, and the new lake entailed major cuts in the national transportation network. If areas around the new lake are not well drained there is increased risk from malaria. In general the upstream costs might be expected to be justified by downstream benefits. However, there are costs downstream as well, such as the disruption of the existing economy, which might include fishing and flood-recession agriculture. For the workers in the downstream irrigated fields, in the tropics, there is increased risk from schistosomiasis and other water-related diseases (see below). Apart from the physical costs there are distributional impacts on income as such schemes generally disrupt the most marginal members of society, while potentially bringing benefits to those with capital to invest in more intensive forms of agriculture or in industrial and commercial activities that can benefit from hydroelectric power. Projects that divert water from one drainage basin to another bring the additional problem of disruption of the ecosystem by introducing different fauna and flora.

In response to concerns such as these, planners are much more circumspect now in recommending large dams for retaining or diverting rivers. Major developments, such as the second phase of the James Bay project in Quebec and the Three Gorges project in China, are now on hold while a more careful examination of the true costs and benefits is being made. Once again, while a short-term analysis of limited areal extent may indicate net benefits from such Northern technology, a broader analysis identifies longer-term and more extensive costs. Similar caution is also being applied to the practice of groundwater pumping in excess of the recharge rate now that the effects of the fall in the water-table become visible (see 'Water and human health,' below). Beyond the question of the costs and benefits of a particular project designed to make more water available for human use there is the issue of the efficiency with which currently available water is being used. In no sector is the question of efficiency more pressing than in that of irrigation.

Water for irrigation

In these times of increasing water shortage there is every reason to require those users who can afford it to pay the full cost of their water supply, including the cost of cleansing it of all impurities after use so that it can be reused. Water is no longer a free good, or even an almost-free good. As noted in Chapter 7, civilization evolved in Sumer, Egypt, and the valleys of the Indus and the Huang Ho based on irrigation. Agriculture is still in operation in those four cultural and economic hearths, more than 4,000 years later. Meanwhile irrigated agriculture has spread around the world, pushing out the agricultural frontier into areas without rain, and doubling or tripling yields in places that also support rain-fed agriculture. Figures 8.2 and 8.3 show the total irrigated area and the percentage of cropland that is irrigated in certain countries; over 60 per cent of the world's irrigated land lies in five countries – India, China, the former Soviet Union, the United States, and Pakistan. Table 8.1 shows the enormous increase in irrigated area since the Second World War.

This era of rapid expansion is now coming to an end. As a measure of this we can compare the peak year for development agency funding for irrigation 1977, with $1.5 billion, and the 1980s with an annual average around $800 million (Postel 1989: 11). Clearly this reduction does not mean that potential demand for irrigated products has diminished, in the sense that

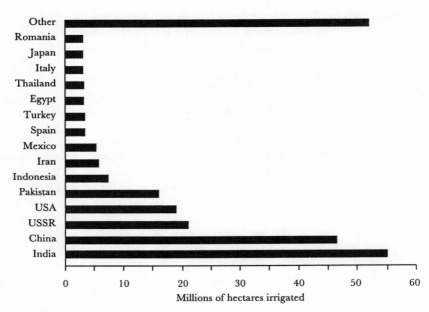

Figure 8.2. Total area irrigated, by country (from Postel 1989)

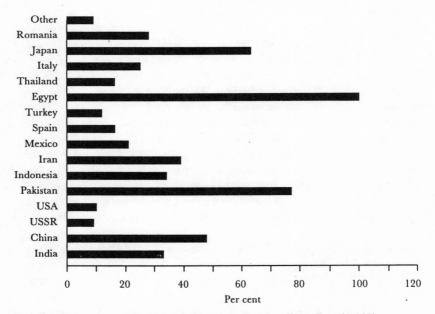

Figure 8.3. Percentage of farmland irrigated, by country (from Postel 1989)

TABLE 8.1
World irrigated cropland

Year	Hectares irrigated (millions)
1800	8
1900	48
1950	94
1989	250

Source: Postel 1989: 7

there are fewer hungry mouths to feed. On the contrary, the potential demand, as measured in terms of hunger, not income, steadily increases. What the slow-down reflects is that we appear to be reaching, simultaneously, various limits to expansion: ecological, managerial, and economic. Irrigation technology, on which early civilizations were based, cannot be boundlessly extended under current conditions. The ecological limits are complex. One of the major ones is inadequate surface-water management, which may result in waterlogging or salinization. The latter occurs when rapid evaporation leaves salt encrusted on the fields. Figure 8.4 shows how widespread this problem is in the five leading countries (as identified from Figure 8.3). Inadequate drainage is also a widespread problem. The second important ecological limit relates to those irrigation schemes that rely on groundwater and have pumped in excess of the natural recharge rate. This results in a draw-down of the water-table, as has been extensively monitored in the United States. The phenomenon is reported elsewhere, especially in Mexico, India, and China. In many areas the draw-down due to pumping for irrigation is added to by urban water demands. This is critically so in the North China Plain, which contains the cities of Beijing and Tianjin. The water supply for Mexico City has been undercutting upstream agriculture for many years.

The managerial difficulties are many. For example, in the United States ownership of land confers use of underground water. This was not a problem as long as natural recharge exceeded the amount pumped out. Once the equation reverses, however, the operator with the biggest pump begins to draw water from under the neighbours' fields. Is this theft or efficient exploitation? The lawyers may argue about it, but in environmental terms the question is irrelevant. Draw-down is draw-down, and it is not sustainable. Across the Rio Grande this becomes an international problem, as American industries pump out the water from under Mexican fields. Spatially, this process has some elements in common with the acid-deposition problem (Chapter 5). The effects are visible on a regional scale. You can identify the victims and the culprits, although you cannot always match them up in pairs.

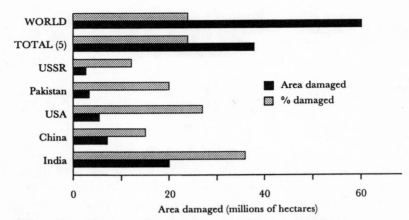

Figure 8.4. Irrigated land damaged by salinization (from Postel 1989)

In political terms, this is an interesting problem: you have one group of producers undermining the environmental basis of their own production system and the production system of their neighbours. Yet, so far, redress of this obvious injustice eludes us.

The managerial and social limits to the further expansion of irrigation are perhaps even more complex than the ecological limits. Most of the world's irrigated land still depends on the original distribution force – gravity. Under this system those farmers nearest the water source are in a privileged position, literally. Whatever rules may have been worked out for the fair distribution of the water, nothing can alter the fact that the farmers nearest the input point are first in line. If water supply falls short of projections, which it must do for half of the time if the distribution projections are based on average conditions, then these privileged farmers will be supplied, but not those further down the system. This factor will exacerbate social and economic distinctions in a society very quickly. Added to this potentially destabilizing factor are the capital requirements for irrigated agriculture, relative to those for rain-fed agriculture. Again, this requirement emphasizes economic and social distinctions. The general observation is that irrigation brings disproportionate benefits to the richer farmers and further marginalizes the poorer. These problems are not solved by state ownership of the scheme, as the state's agents may form their own client relationships among the dependent farmers (Bingen 1985: 117–23). Large-scale, gravity-fed irrigation projects are difficult to manage in low-income countries simply because the technology differentiates between the poor and the very poor farmer. Technical innovation implies social change. However, if other opportunities do not exist, elsewhere, for those who are further marginalized by their relative lack of security, then the impact on the society as a whole may be negative.

Lastly, there are economic limits to irrigation. The economics, especially for the gravity-fed irrigation projects in low-income countries, are often obscured by low-interest loans from development agencies and underpriced water distributed to farmers. Government priorities, such as employment generation and national food security, tend to discourage a rigorous examination of the costs and benefits. However, it has been calculated that it is hardly ever economical to irrigate cereals, unless the cropped area is naturally floodable (Engelhard and Ben Abdallah 1986). Once even small distribution pumps are involved the cost of the energy inputs added to the other costs outweighs the value of the crop.

Now that we are facing system closure on a variety of environmental fronts, such as water-table draw-down and pollution, we will have to begin to count the full (replacement) cost of all the inputs into agricultural technology. At this time, we have to re-evaluate the technology and the social implications of irrigation. Until now, as water has been widely treated as an almost-free good, there has been little incentive to improve operations. Now, the operational improvements are serious enough to force that reconsideration, given that, for example, as much as 60 per cent of the world's irrigated land requires rehabilitation and that salinity already cuts American irrigation productivity by 25 to 30 per cent. The underlying reason for these problems is that much of today's irrigation is still being carried on more or less as it was 4,000 years ago, when people were few in number in relation to the available water. Today we cannot afford to let 70 per cent of the available water seep away through unlined distribution channels, which is why in the rich countries, like the United States and France, irrigation water is now delivered by pipes and overhead sprinkler systems. Even more efficient systems drip the water directly to the stem of the plant, further reducing the losses to evaporation. Such systems are more expensive to build and to operate, but they are more cost-effective than the traditional flooding techniques.

Another expensive, but highly cost-effective, solution to a water-shortage problem has been proposed by the City of Los Angeles, which is in fierce competition with farmers for water from the Colorado River. To ease the problem the city has offered to pay $115 million to line the farmers' delivery channels if the city is allowed to take 100,000 acre-feet annually for the next thirty-five years. This quantity is less than the amount saved by lining the channels. The city will also pay $3 million annually in management costs. This is the kind of calculation that could be made in North China, Pakistan, and everywhere else where cities and farmers are competing for access to a resource which all have liberally squandered until now.

Improved management of irrigation water is essential to global water management because it accounts for over 70 per cent of human usage. This is where the big economies must begin. With better management – and a lot more capital and widespread social changes – we can produce the same yields with less water. We can also release grain for human consumption by changing from a meat-intensive diet in the North. If we feed less grain and oilseeds to livestock, then we may find we need less irrigated rice and wheat. Perhaps we do not need so much irrigated cotton, or so much irrigated sugar for our rich Northern diets. The same cannot be said for the supply of water for domestic uses: drinking, cooking, washing, and the evacuation of sewage. All of these require quantities of water which are much more difficult to reduce.

Water and human health

The consequences of having too little water for these domestic purposes are quite well known. Where water supply and water treatment are deficient, human health status is low, life expectancy is low, and infant mortality is very high. Table 8.2 gives the ways in which diseases travel along water-related pathways: water-borne diseases are transmitted when water containing a pathogen is ingested; water-washed diseases are those whose incidence will fall when increased quantities of clean, although not necessarily pure, water are used for drinking and hygienic purposes; water-based diseases are those in which a pathogen spends part of its life cycle in an intermediate aquatic host or hosts.

The distinction should be made between quantity and quality of water. Human health specialists argue that, at least in rural settings, quantity of water is a better guide to human health than is quality. That is, in low-income countries you can go too far in insisting on very stringent potability standards, thereby tying up a lot of money that would be better spent providing dependable quantities of water to villages. Even in industrial countries the debate has rarely been decided as to whether cities should have two qualities of piped water: one for human ingestion, the other for such less-vulnerable consumers as steel mills and municipal gardens. However, it should be noted, even at this level of generalization, that water-quality issues spread further than human ingestion – poor-quality water can damage output from industry, agriculture, and construction. Even so, the water-quality issue of immediate relevance to most people is the provision of potable water and the proper treatment of waste water.

As human beings cannot live without water its supply must be viewed as the single most critical variable in the current global crisis. For example, an adequate supply of clean domestic water is the most important factor in

TABLE 8.2
Pathways for water-related diseases

Pathway	Disease
Water-borne or water-washed	Cholera, typhoid, diarrhoeas, dysentries, amoebiasis, infectious hepatitis, poliomyelitis, intestinal worms
Water-washed	Trachoma, skin infections, leprosy, scabies, louseborne typhus
Water-based Penetrating skin Ingested	Schistosomiasis Guinea worm
Water-related insect vectors Biting near water Breeding in water	Sleeping sickness Malaria, yellow fever, onchoceriasis

Source: IIED/WRI, *World Resources 1987*: 19, based on David Sanders 1985: 20

bringing down infant mortality rates in the South. The treatment of used water is equally essential to improve health conditions; indeed, it has been argued that increasing the supply of water without simultaneously improving water-treatment capacity will worsen the health situation by encouraging the spread of water-related diseases.

Despite widespread agreement on the importance of improved water supply and water treatment, progress is slow, and in some places conditions are deteriorating. Today, 1.7 billion of the world's five billion people are still without adequate water supply and three billion are without adequate sanitation (UNEP 1988: 1). Almost all of these people are in the South. Despite the WHO's leadership in establishing the International Drinking Water Supply and Sanitation Decade in 1981 to 'provide water for all by the year 2000,' 'there is now no chance that this goal ... can be achieved' (UNEP 1988: 4). In some countries, like Ethiopia, village water-supply systems are actually falling into disuse faster than new ones are being established (Mangin 1989).

Conditions in the major cities of the South may be worse than in the countryside because of the concentration of contaminants of both human and industrial origin. (This situation is discussed in more detail in the subsequent chapters on Urban Management and Waste Management.) Some coastal cities, like Dakar, Jakarta, and Manila, suffer from the additional problem of the saline intrusion of the aquifer. In others, like Mexico City and Bangkok, overpumping of the aquifer has led to subsidence and, in the case of Bangkok, frequent flooding (Anton 1990: 5). Although groundwater is initially better protected from pollution than is surface water, it is much more diffi-cult to rehabilitate once it has been contaminated. The consequences of the failure to provide adequate water are dramatic. In places of endemic poverty malnutrition and diarrhoeal diseases are the largest killers and are believed to account for 4.6 million children's deaths annually (UNEP 1986: 8). Another two million children are estimated to die of malaria each year.

In the face of this apparent impasse Wolman and Wolman observed that: 'While the rhetoric giving water supply top priority among the needs of de-veloping countries is well intended, and the need heartfelt, there is a ten-dency for the resolve to melt in the face of the large sums of money that appear to be needed – and more importantly, upon recognition of the ad-ministrative or institutional demands of such efforts' (1986: 9).

These authors rightly put the emphasis for failure on social and political factors, because the technical problems of delivering water to human settle-ments are rarely insurmountable. Furthermore, the financial cost of provid-ing rural water supply could be quite modest and is at least partly recoverable from the users. As we will see, it is not the potential availability of water that is the constraint. The constraints are lack of determination among the gov-ernments of rich and poor countries alike to deal with the social and political implications of universal access to adequate water supply and treatment. What is needed to rectify water-supply deficiencies is very well known. The World Bank and other development agencies have rooms full of manuals on project design. (For a typical example see Frank Lamson-Scribner and John Huang, *Municipal Water Supply Project Analysis: Case Studies.*) This is not a sci-entific mystery like discovering a cure for AIDS; nor does it pose baffling technical problems like removing the CFCs that have drifted up into the stratosphere. Yet progress is imperceptible in most of the world's poorest countries, because, despite the rhetoric (as noted by Wolman and Wolman), the political commitment is not there. Universal water supply is simply not a priority.

Why has progress been so disappointing, if the technical requirements for solution are understood? Part of the answer lies in the fact that public health policy cannot be changed without changing almost everything else in a soci-ety, from the physical means of communication (like the roads and the tel-ephone) to the distribution of power between rich and poor, between female and male, and between all other divisions in society. Current efforts to im-prove urban and rural water supply in low-income countries have been highly dependent on development-agency funding and on pretending that the main dimensions of the problem are technical. It was assumed that these technical problems could be solved by good engineering, 'getting the prices right,' and good management, and that it could all be done in the five-year time horizon

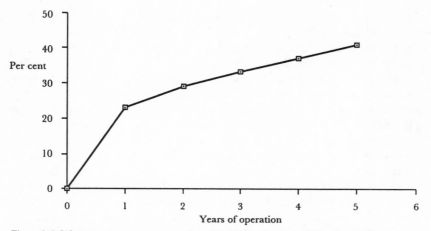

Figure 8.5. Water systems non-operational in Ethiopia (from Mangin 1989)

which is convenient for development-agency projects. Later, when it was seen that most projects did not work well in rural areas, a budget was added for 'training for maintenance.' Yet the results are reflected in Figure 8.5. Admittedly, Ethiopia may be thought to be an extreme case, but the results are fairly typical of the lowest-income countries, where water supply is most deficient. In a recent report from Ethiopia Mangin noted that: 'Almost 30% of water systems broke down within the first two years of operation. After five years in operation, more than 40% ... do not yield any water. The results would be even worse if unsanitary water systems were included in the figure below' (1989: 8). He concludes: 'The establishment of adequate maintenance procedures and facilities presents a much more difficult task to a developing country's administration than the construction of water systems. Successful organisation and maintenance (O & M) require extensive and recurrent interaction between rural society and the state. The demands of an O & M agency go beyond routinely inspecting a few pumps and boreholes and tightening a bolt or two' (1989: 9).

The failure to apply so much well-known and important knowledge about basic health care is the responsibility of both the North and the South. The rich countries, through the development agencies, persist in the convenient (but highly inaccurate) assumption that they need only provide the five-year effort to install the system, so long as a 'training component' is now included in the project. The governments of poor countries, for their part, accept the projects on these terms although they resist the social transformation that is required in order to provide 'adequate water for all.'

Yet history shows that rapid results can be achieved. At the time of the

1890 census, malaria was the leading cause of death in the United States. The southern states reported 7,000 malaria deaths per 100,000 people, compared with 1,000 deaths in the northern states (Meade, Florin, and Gesler 1988: 80–1). By 1930, even in the South, the rates were down to 25 malaria deaths per 100,000 people. Improved drainage, land-use controls, screened houses, antimalarial drugs, and the managed fluctuation of water levels in reservoirs brought about this rapid decline. It is true that tropical ecosystems provide a more difficult and varied environment for control and eradication, and therefore such rapid results should not be expected. However, the ecological differences should not obscure the fact that the main problems are social and political – and there is nothing as political as water. A Ghanaian engineer who supervised the installation of 2,000 village boreholes in northern Ghana in 1979 told me that what he wanted to do next was earn a doctoral degree in political science, using as data the files from the project. Even he, a citizen of the country, had been amazed by the intense conflicts that had been aroused by the installation of a limited number of boreholes in a place of very great need: a need that could nowhere near be met by one five-year project, however well designed and implemented.

Water and wildlife

The discussion so far in this chapter has considered only the immediate needs of human beings, yet more and more people believe that the survival of the human species alone is an inadequate objective. They believe that for moral, aesthetic, and practical reasons it is important to preserve global biodiversity, and therefore we should halt humanity's relentless drive towards the extinction of other species, whether deliberately or by neglect. Each time that we take water for direct human use, for our crops and livestock, or for industrial and recreational purposes, we are usually denying the use of the water to other animals and plants. This is particularly true of wetlands which are a refuge for endangered animal species and migratory birds.

Nowhere is the conflict better illustrated than in the case of Spain's Doñana National Park in the estuary of the Guadalquivir River, which is the home of '250 species of migratory and domestic birds, including Spain's few remaining Imperial eagles and 60 animal species, including the last Iberian lynx. It is Europe's most important biological station' (*Financial Times*, 18 July 1991: 2). Despite the unique importance of the park, the provincial government of Andalucia has continued to support the competing water claims of a nearby irrigation project (covering 10,000 hectares) and a huge coastal resort. The irrigation project is overpumping the groundwater on which the park depends, and it discharges pesticides fatal to geese and ducks. The 32,000-bed tourist complex abstracts water also, and discharges sewage along the beach.

It should not be impossible in such a situation to manage the water resource in a sustainable fashion with the use of only organic fertilizers, adequate sewage treatment, and the recycling of water. It will cost more in the short term, admittedly, but it should be possible to preserve a unique resource. The issue goes much further than preserving endangered species, however, in that it also relates to the sustainability of human activities. Neither the irrigation scheme nor the resort complex is 'sustainable' under the present management system. In such a situation good ecology is also good for business. The threat to the park simply makes the need for better management more apparent. On a wider scale in the Mediterranean basin unwise irrigation projects and the profusion of coastal resorts have contributed to the desiccation of one-third of Spain, half of Italy, and all of Greece (*European*, 12 July 1991: 5).

Water for all?

Water of adequate quality is an increasingly scarce resource. As the world's population and the world's economy continue to grow, that scarcity will become critical. In some cases it has already led to widespread violence. In Mexico one state is dumping waste into a lake which flows into another state which depends on it for its principal source of water. In Senegal a large, modern hotel complex on the coast was designed with its own water supply, pumped from its own grounds; unfortunately it is pumping in excess of the recharge rate and is drawing down the water-table underneath the nearby villages. If it continues this activity it will bring in sea water, which will seep into the fresh groundwater on which the hotel and the villages depend. In Morocco there is some regret that the country's tourism strategy concentrated on five-star hotels for the wealthiest travellers; it has now been found that there is a linear correlation between the number of stars earned by the hotel and the number of litres of water used per bed of hotel capacity. It is about 100 litres per star. So five-star luxury hotels are using 500 litres per bed per day, whether occupied or not, mostly to fill the swimming-pools and water the gardens. Around Marrakesh the hotel owners are now in competition with farmers who are growing irrigated wheat.

The examples are countless, but the conclusions are fairly clear. Even with existing knowledge, drinking water could be provided for all, and the present irrigated land, industries, hotels, and hydroelectric-power stations could be supplied. But the social and political problems are very complex. Identification of the already existing improvements in the technology has been done; avenues for research are already mapped out. What is needed is a joint recognition by the North and the South that the commitment must be long term and comprehensive. This is not just a matter of more ribbon cutting for new dams; it is, literally, a matter of life and death. In the quotation at the opening of the chapter, Gilbert White, in 1973, set us a period of twenty-five years to provide adequate water supply and sanitation for all the world's people. Today it would be difficult to argue that the situation is any better than it was then.

9

Urban Management

The weak economic position of most developing nations makes the 'global environmental debate' somewhat of a luxury. The environmental issues are reduced to visible consequences particularly in cities ... The environmental question is perceived in terms of the poor living conditions of the majority of urban dwellers – the lack of rudimentary housing, water supply and sanitation. (Kadmiel Wekwete 1992)

Urbanization in the North

In Chapter 1, urbanization, industrialization, and the increase in population were identified as the driving variables behind human-induced global environmental change. As we have seen, the residuals from urban-industrial society have changed global bio-geochemical cycles. In other chapters we have seen just how widespread those impacts have become, stretching far beyond human settlements (which are the sources of change) to the ocean depths and the polar deserts. Why has our civilization evolved in this way, and how well equipped are we to reverse the negative side-effects of our global expansion? To understand the dynamics behind these processes we must look in some detail at the evolution of cities and at the role they play in shaping our options for the redevelopment of the planet.

This chapter focuses on the impact of cities on the environment, especially in the South, because it is there that the negative consequences of environmental change are most difficult to control. From the policy perspective, urbanization is a complex process with many negative side-effects in that it pollutes the local environment and demands a large share of public investment. At the same time it is a key to the completion of the demographic transition and to economic growth. Thus, the urbanization process produces both negative and (potentially) positive effects together.

Until the past one hundred years or so, the demographic impact of cities was very different from what it is today. Death rates tended to be higher than in rural areas. Neither rural nor urban environments provided much in the way of health care – the death rate differential came from the greater exposure to communicable diseases experienced in cities, which, until modern times, depended on rural migration for demographic growth. Public health and improved water supply appeared in the more-advanced cities, in the nineteenth century, as a belated by-product of the industrial revolution. The impact of these improvements was reinforced by free public education, at least through the primary grades. These developments were partly the work of enlightened philanthropists and partly the recognition by decision-makers that a healthier and better-educated population was a more productive one (Goubert 1989: passim).

The demographic impact of the cities and rural areas was reversed. Improved access to these new services lowered death rates in the cities below the level found in most rural areas. This was not a simple, unidirectional process – a gradual improvement of urban conditions, a decline in fertility, and a transformation to demographic stationarity. On the contrary, for some time after the introduction of improved water supply, health, and education, other indicators of the quality of life continued to deteriorate. In most cities households and industries continued to rely on coal as their principal source of energy. At the turn of this century there was a steady growth in the use of hydroelectricity and natural gas, especially in North America, but in most cities the absolute demand for coal continued to grow. The environment around cities suffered from subsidence, air pollution, and water pollution. Around major cities like London and Paris the water-table was drawn down (Goudie 1990: 169).

Only since the Second World War have the early industrialized cities begun to emerge from a steadily deteriorating ambient environment. The turning-point occurred at different times in different places. In Britain the impetus for the 1956 Clean Air Act was partly due to the London smogs of 1951 and 1952, which were responsible for about 400 deaths. In British cities smoke emissions are estimated to have fallen in the 1970s to one-tenth their level in the 1950s (Goudie 1990: 269).

Apart from greater environmental concern, other factors aided the process. The heavy industries of Europe and North America declined rapidly in importance after the Second World War. This was partly because of competition from the rising industrial economies of East Asia and partly because the first industrialized countries were moving into higher-value-adding activities. Most of the industries that remained in North American and Western European cities consumed electricity or oil rather than coal. Many moved out of the city centre to dispersed industrial parks. More efficient transformation processes required fewer energy inputs. Car ownership went up, but there was a gradual improvement in pollution-abatement devices, although there is still a long way to go. In general terms, the first industrial cities were passing into a postindustrial age in which new jobs came from the service sector rather than from industry.

The urbanization process was highly dynamic, multifaceted, and difficult to control by legislation. Some success was achieved in regulating land use, such as preserving green spaces and directing economic growth to less-congested locations. Control was partial, however, and what occurred was possible only because the rate of population growth was much slower than what we witness in the South today.

Urbanization in the South

At the most general level, three features differentiate the urbanization process in the South from that of the early industrialized countries of Europe and North America. First, cities in the South are growing faster. Second, in absolute size, some already surpass New York and Tokyo, and more soon will. Third, they are poorer. Or, more succinctly, their experience is one of rapid growth, unprecedented size, and vast poverty. Some continue to industrialize (Seoul, Sao Paulo, Calcutta) while in others industry stagnates (Kinshasa, Lagos, and Addis Ababa).

Three diagrams illustrate some of these factors. Figure 9.1 shows that, following current projections, most of the world's remaining population growth will come from the urban population of the South and that by the year 2010 the urban dwellers of poor countries will be the largest population of the four-way split (urban-rural, rich countries and poor). Figure 9.2 shows that both rich and poor countries will continue to urbanize, but the poor will do so at a much faster rate. Figure 9.3 tracks the populations of the six largest cities as projected for the year 2000. It predicts continuing rapid growth for Mexico City, Sao Paulo, and Calcutta, which may reach populations of 25, 24, and 17 million, respectively, by the year 2000. Rapid growth, immense size, and poverty, separately, would pose enormous problems for urban management. In conjunction they have virtually overwhelmed existing management institutions.

By comparison, Toronto, Canada, which grew rapidly in the 1960s, even by North American standards, probably peaked at 5 per cent in one year, with an expansion of 3 or 4 per cent per annum in the rest of the decade. Many cities of the South have surpassed 5 per cent growth every year for over a decade; some are completing their second decade at this rate. Some

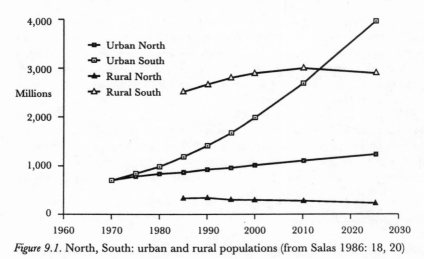

Figure 9.1. North, South: urban and rural populations (from Salas 1986: 18, 20)

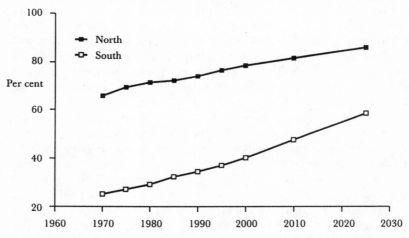

Figure 9.2. North, South: percentage urbanized (from Salas 1986: 17)

have grown at 10 per cent for several years (Stren and White 1989: 2–7). The case of Dakar, Senegal, is not extreme. At independence in 1962 it was a well-planned and well-managed colonial city of 250,000. At the time of the first national census, in 1976, it had reached 900,000; at the next census, 10 years later, it had doubled to nearly 2 million. For the year 2005 official projections vary from 2.5 to 4 million. Its administration still continues to function, albeit with difficulty.

In many cases, urban growth has simply outstripped the institutional

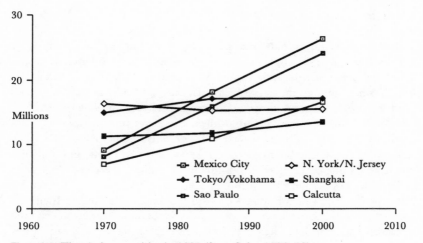

Figure 9.3. The six largest cities in 1985 (from Salas 1986: 20)

capacity to adapt. As Donatus Okpala explains in the case of Nigeria: 'society as of now largely works not through institutions but rather through personalities. Although the laws and regulations may be there in the books, personalities tend to be more powerful than the institutions, regulations and even the laws' (1984: 82). For a time most urban governments tried to control illegal squatters by destroying their homes and expelling the people from the city. Most authorities have now capitulated to the inevitable. Similarly, although governments used to clear sidewalk hawkers and small businesses, and such sweeps still occur, many urban governments now welcome any form of employment even if does not conform to municipal regulations. This preoccupation has also led to the tolerance of industrial pollution. Tawanchai Xoomsai wrote of Bangkok: 'laws to compel firms to minimise pollution by their factories exist but enforcement is not vigorous. This is partly due to fear of alienating industry, which is seen as an engine of growth' (1988: 21).

Size poses its own problems, such as the difficulty of devising a form of government to serve an increasingly heterogeneous settlement, the management of commuter traffic (the sudden concentration and deconcentration of millions of vehicles), and the widening search for water and for waste-disposal sites. With the extension of these catchment areas (commuters, water, and waste) the cost-per-unit begins to rise again, having previously fallen because of scale advantages. We read a phrase such as Kinshasa 'extending over an area a third the size of Belgium,' and the imagination must strain to absorb the very idea. Yet, as Figure 9.3 suggests, we are still far short of the probable maximum size of these immense settlements.

Urban finance and urban management

Rate of growth and absolute size pose evident problems, but it is poverty that poses the greatest challenge. In Europe and North America the nineteenth-century industrialization process suffered many setbacks with recessions, business failures, industrial accidents, wars, and epidemics. The overall trend, however, was one of economic expansion. Central governments invested in interurban infrastructure, while urban governments financed intraurban investment through property taxes and municipal bonds. The contribution of businesses to the tax base was crucial. Public utilities were established, some of which were self-financing. Schools were built to absorb the growing population of children, and in many countries public housing was built for rental at subsidized rates to low-income families. Much was deficient (and still is, as shown by the resurgence of homelessness in even the richest countries of the North) but, in general, the situation was one of improving urban quality of life, even as the cities grew at (then) unprecedented rates.

The current situation in most of the giant cities of the South is completely different, even though the range of experience is very broad, running from Singapore at one end of the scale to cities like Lagos at the other. Except for some of the cities at the top end of the scale, the governments of these giant cities have failed to collect the potential property tax created by a large urban system. In most African cities the concept of property taxes is difficult to apply, since the myth of nationalized land has replaced customary tenure systems based on usufruct. Where a property tax would be feasible in modern cities like Nairobi and Abidjan, it is resisted by the governing class. Even in cities where the concept of property tax exists it cannot be applied to those 'illegal' (i.e., not officially recognized) squatter settlements, even though they include the majority of the inhabitants in most cities in the South. The flood of new arrivals has been so great that no coherent land-survey and -valuation system could be prepared in time. In hardly any case does the government have a revenue-collecting system that allows it to finance urban infrastructure. This means that there is not enough money to maintain existing services, nor is there money to provide new ones.

It is in this context of a very difficult management situation that we must return to two major, intertwined questions. The first comes in two parts: 'what capacity do cities, in both the North and the South, have to reduce their own negative impacts on the biosphere – pollution of the land, sea, and air – and what capacity do they have to protect themselves from external environmental impacts, such as marine pollution and an increasingly uncertain climate?' The second question is: 'can the cities of the South maintain a high enough quality of life for their inhabitants to bring death rates down and thereby contribute to the speediest possible transition to demographic stability?'

Quality of life may be measured by many variables. Morris D. Morris convincingly argues for an index based on infant mortality, life expectancy at one year of age, and adult literacy (Morris 1979: 3–4). Certainly, freedom from physical oppression would probably be first on most people's list, though it could be argued that this will be closely correlated with the variables Morris has used. Income (size and distribution) is also widely used as a key indicator. For the environmental and urban-management perspective adopted here, an emphasis on physical variables is chosen: specifically, the provision of water, food, and energy and the management of industrial risks. Water, food, and energy are the basic physical inputs for the urban population. (The topic of waste management, including urban waste management, is dealt with in Chapter 10.) Risk management is included because of the catastrophic impact of major accidents in large, poor cities, as was seen tragically in the cases of Bhopal and Mexico City. Industrial risk reduction is also closely related to the introduction of low-waste technology (a requirement for reducing the biospheric impact of industrialization) and occupational health, which links back to the quality of life.

When we take into account the three problems of growth rate, absolute size, and poverty, it is hard to be optimistic about most of the cities of the South. However, there are some management alternatives that are more promising than others. These will be examined from an intra-urban perspective, taking examples mainly from Dakar, Senegal, to show how one city attempts to provide the basic goods and services required by its inhabitants.

Urban water supply

As Dakar expanded it overran and polluted the local groundwater supplies; also the overpumping of the local, basalt aquifer resulted in salt-water intrusion. As the local aquifer became inadequate, supplies were drawn from sedimentary aquifers eighty kilometres distant. Later, as these were unable to keep up with demand, water was drawn from sediments even further north. As these too were surpassed, a pumping station was established in the Lac de Guiers, a shallow reservoir created in a fossil river valley, 200 kilometres from Dakar (Wane 1983, 1985). By 1978 Lac de Guiers was providing approximately 20 per cent of Dakar's water supply, although the figure varies greatly according to the amount of water in the lake. Furthermore, pumping is sometimes curtailed because of the lack of purifying chemicals, itself occasioned by the lack of foreign exchange to buy them. The lake is contaminated by

TABLE 9.1
Water demand in Senegal projected for the year 2005

	Region of Dakar	Urban population outside Dakar	Rural population
Inhabitants (1,000s)	3,000	3,480	5,620
Litres (pc/pd)	175	60	25
Daily demand (m^3)	572,000	209,000	140,000

(The comparable figures for Dakar in 1981 were: inhabitants 1,100,000; litres pc/pd 108; daily demand (m^3) 119,000.)

Source: République du Sénégal 1984b: 299
pc/pd = per capita, per day; m^3 = cubic metres.

irrigation water that drains into it from sugar plantations in the Senegal Valley (Cogels and Gac 1983; Gac and Cogels 1986).

As Dakar has grown, like many big cities it has had to reach further and further afield for sources of water. In the late 1970s plans were made for the doubling and tripling of the capacity of the water pipes from Lac de Guiers to Dakar (République du Sénégal 1983a). The money was never found to finance these schemes. Now, they are inadequate anyway. A much larger plan is on the drawing- board, to bring water from the southern end of Lac de Guiers by an open canal, known as the Canal de Cayor. Compared with some African cities Dakar does not yet face a serious lack of water, although the prognosis is not good. On the distribution side, the government – at the instigation of the World Bank – has reduced the number of public stand-pipes and encouraged the installation of private taps in household compounds, in an effort to recover more of the costs (Ngom 1989). Table 9.1 illustrates the implications of increasing population growth and increasing urbanization, based on current water-consumption patterns. The money needed to build new sources of supply far outstrips the revenue that is recovered from consumers. Bills to some public consumers, such as the university, remain unpaid, yet the agents from the Water Supply Corporation quickly shut off the taps of any private consumers who do not pay. It is interesting to note that virtually no water is recycled; it is widely believed that there would be serious cultural objections to a proposal to do so. An important effect of the overall lack of water is that the sewage and waste-water canals and drains are inadequately flushed. In summary, in the search for an adequate water supply Dakar has had to go further and further afield. In the past ten years the proposed solutions have exceeded the financial capacity of the city and the national government, and the difference between needs and supply has now reached a critical point.

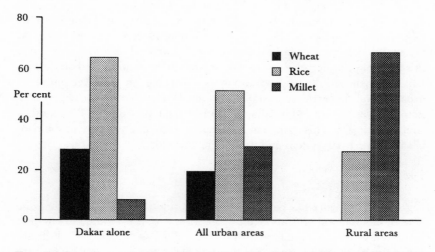

80 ─

60 ─

Per cent

40 ─

20 ─

0 ─

■ Wheat
▨ Rice
▨ Millet

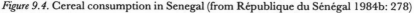

Dakar alone   All urban areas   Rural areas

Figure 9.4. Cereal consumption in Senegal (from République du Sénégal 1984b: 278)

Urban food

In a healthy regional economy city and village interact symbiotically to meet one another's needs, with exchanges outside the region to balance the differences. In an unhealthy regional economy a city may drain the countryside of resources until no more can be extracted. This is the case in Senegal.

Two processes operate in the Dakar situation which make it very difficult for the city to maintain a healthy relationship with its region, which encompasses all of Senegal. The first of these processes is the old policy problem which has become known as 'urban bias' (Lipton 1977). Senegal is a classic case of a government which controlled the prices of essential goods and services in order to control the rise of the urban cost of living (République du Sénégal 1984a; O'Brien 1979; White 1990). This holding down of the price of almost all crops, livestock, and fuel helps the urban dweller only in the short term. Gradually the peasant producer withdraws from an unprofitable market and produces mainly for the family and local barter. If there is a surplus it is more likely (in Africa at least) to be smuggled over the nearest profitable border than it is to be delivered to a marketing agency. The best that one can hope for is that official figures underestimate the amounts actually produced, consumed, and traded.

The second process is an individual response to urban life. As urban life usually requires women to spend more time outside the home, there is less time spent on food preparation. Hence, as the pounding of traditional cereals like millet and sorghum is more difficult to do and is inconvenient in a city, prepared cereals, like rice and wheat, are more likely to be consumed. As Senegal already imports large quantities of rice, and as it cannot grow wheat, this tendency has negative impacts on the regional economy and on the balance of payments. What we see in Figure 9.4 is an example of the impact of urbanization on cereal consumption habits. (This is part of the diet transition that was introduced in Chapter 2.) When people come to the city they change their diet. This change may have important implications for the symbiosis of the urban system and its rural hinterland.

Urban fuel

A great deal of work has been done on the transition in demand from one kind of fuel to another (Onibokun 1989: 97–106). As explained in Chapter 7, the energy transition reflects the processes of urbanization and industrialization. It also changes over time as different fuels become available. The transition can be very difficult. Toronto, which now has every appearance of a twentieth-century city, underwent a 'fuel-wood crisis' in the middle of the nineteenth century. At that time the supply of fuel seemed to be a serious constraint on further urbanization. London, in the late nineteenth century, had become heavily dependent on horse-drawn transport (like Paris, New York, and similar cities). The result was severe traffic congestion, unsanitary waste accumulation, and many accidents. It was not clear how a modern city could evolve from such a point. In both of these cases a new fuel was produced to break the bottleneck (natural gas in the first case, steam and gasoline in the second), and the cities continued their growth. In Dakar today it is even less clear how a transition can be made. The dominant household fuel is charcoal, which is cheap and convenient. Unfortunately demand now outstrips the domestic supply. There is no convenient source for imports, and, in any case, any potential exporting country in West Africa has its own fuel-wood/charcoal crisis.

Two solutions have been proposed to reduce urban demand for charcoal in Dakar. The first was the government's 'butanization campaign' in 1974–5. The government subsidized the price of bottled gas (butane) as a cooking fuel (almost all household energy consumption being for cooking). A survey three years later showed that only the relatively wealthy classes were using the cheap bottled gas (République du Sénégal 1982). The poor, the vast majority of the people, did not have an indoor kitchen, could not afford to buy a stove, or even to pay the price of the subsidized bottles of gas (Tibesar and White 1990).

TABLE 9.2
Implied elasticity of demand for charcoal in Dakar
(The table shows the percentage of people responding positively to the questions: 'Would
you switch to a source of energy other than charcoal if the charcoal price doubles ... etc.?'
For each income class the most common response is shown in bold type.)

Price change	Class 1 (poorer)	Class 2 (middle)	Class 3 (richer)	Total
1. Charcoal price doubles	14	40	**54**	28
2. Charcoal price triples	**22**	15	13	18
3. Would use other source only if charcoal not available	**64**	**45**	33	**54**
Total percentage	100	100	100	100

Source: Tibesar and White 1990

The second solution remains at the policy-discussion level. It is promoted
mostly by economists in the development agencies who feel that the true price
(i.e., the replacement price) should be charged for goods such as charcoal,
and the proceeds could then be used to ensure a sustainable supply of the
product. One of the assumptions behind this proposal is that an increase in
the real price of charcoal will cause a diminution in demand. This assumption was tested in a household survey of which the key results are given in
Table 9.2. These results (based, albeit, on intention rather than action) suggest that a doubling or tripling of the charcoal price might persuade some
wealthier households to change to other energy sources (bottled gas, electricity), but that the poor would continue to use charcoal. The conclusion from
a follow-up study, carried out in one district of Dakar, was that there was no
immediate alternative for poor people except to continue to burn charcoal
(Gasherebuka 1985). This has two implications. First, a serious reforestation
program must be undertaken, so that wood fuel becomes a truly renewable
resource. Second, the efficient use of charcoal should be encouraged by the
serious diffusion of an urban variant of the improved (energy-efficient) stove,
along with other conservation measures. Whatever improvements occur in
the consumption of fuel in Dakar, there are no easy options. From the government's perspective there is a grand plan to bring hydroelectric power from
the Manantali Dam on the Senegal River (600 kilometres away in Mali). It is
difficult to imagine how this would reduce the low-income demand for charcoal as a household cooking fuel. Longer-term alternatives for the city are
the development of wind and solar power. Passive solar heaters for hot-wa-
ter supply are found in some modern houses.

The management of urban risks

It is difficult to extrapolate from the present management situation in the cities of the South as they will be operating under more and more stressful conditions. One way to anticipate some of the new problems is to investigate the most stressful events of the present and the recent industrial past (Lagadec 1981). Stress exposes the hidden weaknesses of a system whether on the scale of the individual or the city (Perez-Trejo and White 1991: 263). Nowhere was this more clearly illustrated than in the tragic case of Bhopal. We can call such events accidental in the sense that they are (usually) unintentional, but they are not really unpredictable in a statistical sense. Probabilities for such a disaster can be computed from the conjunction of events in the past. In this particular case there was even documented concern that such an accident could occur. Two years before the event a local journalist wrote three articles to warn residents about the dangers posed by the poor management of the plant (Pandey and Bowonder 1987: i).

The fatal leak of methyl isocyanate from Union Carbide's fertilizer plant at Bhopal (a rapidly growing town of 700,000 people 650 kilometres northeast of Bombay) killed about 2,000 people between 2 and 4 December 1984, and another 1,600 have since died. Over 500,000 people were seriously injured. Yet, eight years later, the government of India and the Union Carbide Corporation have not reached agreement on an interim settlement to the victims. A detailed study showed how the dangerous situation built up from the initial process of site selection, falling sales of the product and consequent neglect of staffing requirements, failure to carry out a routine maintenance task, failure to warn the population or the authorities once the accident occurred, and the complete lack of availability of diagnostic information to help treat the wounded. Errors can be classified in a variety of ways; however, according to my count, there were thirty-nine independent errors of judgment that led up to the accident (based on Pandey and Bowonder's description of events).

One can argue from statistics that this was an extreme event and should not be taken as an important piece of evidence of the inadequacy of the management of industries in such cities. Yet the extreme event tells us a great deal about the probability distribution of which such an event is, admittedly, the tail. With this dreadful happening in recent memory, we must ask again the question: In what circumstances can these cities reduce their adverse impact on the global environment and ensure a decent quality of life for their inhabitants? The circumstances must include the active cooperation of the multinational corporations that play such a significant role in the economies of the South. Because the supporting infrastructure (such as transportation and communications) is weaker in poor countries than in rich ones, it would seem that even greater efforts are required by a company working in the South to promote safety on the job than would be the case in the North. The South's need for jobs and for foreign exchange cannot be used as an excuse to reduce safety and environmental standards.

Cities and global change

The emphasis in this chapter has been on a city's ability to assure its own inhabitants of an acceptable quality of life while not operating to the detriment of the rural hinterland – what we might classify as local impacts and regional impacts. However, as has been noted throughout this book, it is the very nature of urban, industrial society that is responsible for the global impacts which we can now measure, such as the build-up of carbon dioxide and other greenhouse gases, the production of CFCs, the global circulation of acidifying compounds like sulphur dioxide, the pollution of the ocean, and deforestation. Recently it is urban governments themselves that have begun to examine and rectify these impacts (Climate Institute 1991). The first step in this urban intervention in global environmental politics was the banning of CFCs by several cities in support of the Montreal Protocol on Ozone Depletion. Although it was national governments that signed the protocol, cities highlighted the issue for the public by enforcing a ban within their areas of jurisdiction. However, it is their commitment to the CO_2 issue that promises to have the most far-reaching impact on urban management because it links into so many of the basic characteristics of modern urban life, founded as it is on the lavish consumption of fossil fuels. For cities that are still growing in population and spatial extent to reduce their CO_2 production major changes in lifestyle and politics will be required.

Some cities have already produced detailed programs showing just how they intend to meet this goal (City of Hannover 1991; City of Toronto 1991). Most of the proposals involve waste reduction and energy conservation, to make the cities ecologically more efficient. It has been demonstrated many times that it is more efficient for modern cities to reduce their demand for energy than to provide additional supplies. Public transport is much more energy efficient than the private automobile, and yet for years city governments of the North, especially in North America and Australia, have encouraged the dispersion of their urban populations to low-density suburbs. It is this trend that the committed cities are now trying to reverse by encouraging compact housing and improved public transport.

Another important set of proposals concerns the 'greening' of cities, especially with shade trees (Gordon 1990). This will increase CO_2 uptake capacity while reducing the need for air-conditioning in the summer. In recognition of the fact that CO_2 uptake capacity is a global issue, the City of Toronto is also proposing to plant trees elsewhere in the province of Ontario and in Central America. This is the beginning of a trend towards each city becoming responsible for its own 'CO_2 budget' and taking steps to bring it into balance. In this way the CO_2 issue links into existing concerns for the urban heat-island effect, whereby dense urban buildings, the removal of vegetation, and the residuals from fossil-fuel consumption combine to raise the temperature between 3° and 5° Celsius in city centres in the summer (Akbari, Rosenfeld, and Taha 1989). It thus appears possible that the threat of global warming and other potentially disastrous types of environmental change may finally have stimulated some governments to do what they had many good reasons to do anyway, in order to improve local air quality, and reduce the demand for new landfills, new highways for commuters, and so on.

Prospects for improved urban management

Given the intensity of the global environmental crisis we are now past the time for making lists of things to do, with priorities and weights and separate budgets and responsibilities. In its present form, the list of proposals from the World Commission on Environment and Development is difficult to make operational. It would be nice to have green space and urban wood lots and to legalize squatter settlements – but how do you manage these potentially conflicting goals concomitantly? (See Brundtland Commission, *Our Common Future*, 218–32 for industry, 243–58 for urban systems.) One way we might manage them together is by treating the system as a whole, to see how one policy impinges on another using a dynamic systems approach. We need rural and urban development. We need rural development to increase agricultural output and to lessen the pressure to migrate to the city; we need urban development to improve the quality of life, generate more employment, reduce the urban death rate, reduce the urban birth rate, and encourage the demographic transition.

However, we must recognize the current inability of the national and municipal governments of the South to provide adequate urban services, although we can also recognize the willingness of some urban dwellers to pay for services were they actually to be delivered. The solution is much more difficult, however, than simply espousing privatization of urban services. How can you link the needs and means of the richer members of the community to the needs (and lack of means) of the poorer to provide services for all? Cross-subsidies among consumers became the solution that evolved in the nineteenth century in Western Europe and North America. Along with privatization the other popular slogan in the aid agencies has been decentralization. Many developing countries have ministries or departments of decentralization. What was found in a recent comparative study in Africa was that the concept was passed through the legislature, but it was not carried through on the ground, for reasons that seem obvious in the conditions described above (Ngom 1989; Koffi 1989). The decentralization on paper was not supported by a financial decentralization or by a political decentralization, whereby the new decision-makers could be made answerable to a local electorate, and whereby local taxes could be raised to pay for local services.

It is now time for us to abandon the easy watchwords and go for the physically observable and practical changes, whether this is to be achieved by the private or the public sector, whether by central or local authority. First, as has been recognized by the World Bank, the South should drop the subsidies of urban food and services that are ultimately paid for by the peasants. This practice has contributed to overurbanization and has impoverished the peasants. The city must, more or less, pay its own way. Second, the Bank's (rather belated) call for true prices for water and other environmental goods is a step in the right direction. Similar principles rapidly follow. All environmental goods that can be recycled should be recycled – including water. This will be difficult in many developing countries, for cultural as well as technical reasons. We need a serious commitment to research and the application of renewable energy. Until now this has been just a political slogan and an occasional interest of diversified energy companies. It must become the energy priority. We should always ask the question: 'why is the energy we are using for this procedure not from a renewable source?'

All of these steps require a radical departure from traditional approaches to urban management. Is it reasonable to assume that such steps might be taken? It might become reasonable because one of the paradoxes of the environmental crisis is that the increasing visibility of a host of interconnected problems is one of the consequences of system closure on a global scale. The links between the problems are becoming clearer as they become more acute. It is daily becoming more evident that rural and urban systems are intricately linked, that the process of urbanization is affecting the global environment as well as local air quality, and that the future of the North is inextricably linked to that of the South. In the City of Toronto's program for reducing carbon dioxide it was duly noted that: 'Carbon dioxide emissions from the

Third World could have a greater effect on our own climate in the long run than emissions from the entire industrialized world if the Third World does not receive adequate development assistance' (1991: vol. 1, 3).

Once a city begins to evaluate its own CO_2 budget, it is a short step to conducting a materials balance audit – a measurement of all the physical flows in and out of the city (Basta and Bower 1982). At that point many environmental objectives should point the city in the same direction, toward a more efficient ordering of its activities – less waste, less pollution, and less uncertainty. System closure is forcing this new perception of events on urban managers. If the global warming predictions are correct, most cities will grow even warmer, adding to the additional warmth they already receive from the local heat-island effect. This will raise the demand for air-conditioning and refrigeration, increasing the demand for CFCs if substitutes are not readily available. The hotter the city centres become, the less willing will people be to live and work there, and the greater the pressure for dispersion, thereby making public transport less efficient and private automobiles more attractive. This tendency will be re-enforced if the cities are obliged to 'internalize' more of their own wastes, in the face of growing hostility from their rural neighbours. Waste management is the subject of the next chapter.

10

Waste Management

The tipping fee for a tonne was $2.50 in 1986; this year it should average
$45 per tonne ... The average price-earnings ratio for [waste management
companies trading in the United States] is 28.2 times earnings. In other
words, investors have been paying a healthy premium to buy into waste
management companies in the prospect of big earnings down the road.
(Edward Clifford, 'Money and Markets,' *Globe and Mail*, 20 June 1990)

In earlier chapters we reviewed agricultural and industrial processes which
produce residual material that is potentially harmful to human beings, either
directly or through the food chain, or that constitute a more indirect threat,
like ozone depletion and carbon dioxide build-up. Many of these residuals,
such as carbon dioxide, sulphur dioxide, CFCs, and so on, have entered the
global bio-geochemical cycles and have begun to modify them. Decisions to
control the growth of these by-products can be resolved only by international
agreements.

Other toxic wastes, such as heavy metals and PCBs, have a more localized
impact and can be controlled, to some extent, by national legislation;
although in federations like Canada and Malaysia federal legislation may be
impeded by lack of support at the provincial/state level. Also there is a global
impact from some of these wastes through long-term atmospheric deposition, as is shown by the build-up of lead and PCBs in wildlife in the Arctic and
Antarctic. Yet, whatever higher-level decisions are taken concerning the production of such residuals, the burden of the task of waste disposal has been
largely the responsibility of local government – rural, urban, and metropolitan councils. Today we are witnessing the globalization of waste-management issues. National governments are taking a more active role; but, for the
moment, it is the local authority that has the job of moving the visible wastes

from human settlements. Thus, this chapter is focused on the local scale.

Wastes are materials that have no further value for human society; therefore, what is considered waste varies greatly over time and from one place to another. You will see very little waste paper, plastic, or metal in low-income countries because these materials all have a reuse value for construction and other purposes. Archaeologists excavating ancient cities, such as those of Egypt and Sumer, concentrate on the waste heaps on which successive stages of the city were laid down. In those days waste was simply put outside the house or sometimes buried in pits by the house wall. This still happens in many low-income settlements today. If the density of population is low enough and if the economy is based on agriculture and handicrafts, powered by water, wind, and animal energy, then such casual disposal methods may suffice, especially if one is prepared to accept periodic outbreaks of cholera, plague, and typhoid as 'natural.'

The factors that destabilized this equilibrium between people, their wastes, and diseases are twofold. First, population numbers have greatly increased, thereby increasing the density of polluting wastes in water, air, and land. Second, the nature of the wastes has become steadily more varied, and potentially more deadly. The industrial activities of the early chemical age have introduced a wide variety of potentially harmful elements into the biological cycles on which people depend for a healthy existence. These include hydrocarbons, aluminum, arsenic, heavy metals (such as cadmium, mercury, and lead), artificial compounds like DDT, PCBs, and PAHs, hospital wastes, and, lastly, radioactive materials.

Despite the obvious health implications of inadequate waste disposal, the actual number of deaths directly attributable to inadequate waste management have been few enough to keep concern at a low level throughout most of human history. It is only the accumulation of accidents leading to deaths, miscarriages, birth defects, and prolonged illness that have led to widespread concern. In Japan there were the Minamata Bay mercury poisoning incidents in the 1950s and 1960s (many deaths and many permanent, disfiguring injuries). In Italy there was the cholera outbreak in Naples (1973, 33 deaths), followed by the release of dioxins from a pesticide plant in Seveso (1976, 193 injured, no known deaths). In North America the landmark case was the exposure of the Love Canal landfill (1977) for which courts in the United States eventually made the historic decision (1980) that held the person or company who dumped the dangerous wastes responsible for their handling, whether or not they had subsequently managed to sell the site to someone else. (The decision was 'historic' in the sense that it overturned the previous assumption of 'buyer beware.') Gradually it has been realized that these potential threats to health have a probability of affecting any individual in the vicinity. From this has developed the 'not in my backyard' (NIMBY) syndrome which used to be dismissed as an irrational objection to any waste-management facility, however well managed. (It may be irrational, of course, except in the case of your own backyard.) Public confidence in the possibility of proper waste disposal is now extremely low. Above all, it is the management of nuclear power stations and nuclear waste that people fear the most.

Thus, waste management has become an intensely personal issue, hitting both one's own health concern and one's own wallet, as the cost of providing improved management increases. (The introductory statement for this chapter quoted a nearly twentyfold increase in tipping costs in the United States in a five-year period.) This personal interest is passed up the political ladder from the city to the central government and sometimes to the international court. As an international issue some aspects of waste management have already been encountered in Chapter 6. For example, we have seen how ocean dumping engenders international conflict, whether from oil-tanker discharge, dumping radioactive waste on the sea floor, or the incineration of toxic materials. In this chapter, with the focus on local authority decision-making, only two international issues are analysed. The first is the appropriateness of the waste-management technology that is sold by the North to the South; the second is the export of wastes in the same direction. But, first, let us briefly consider the differing practices of waste management in North and South, beginning with the North – generator of most of the waste and purveyor of most of the technology.

The management of household wastes in the North

Countries of the industrial North are suffering from increasing problems with waste management, with respect to both quantity and composition. In this chapter, as we are most concerned with local response to the waste crisis, we will concentrate on municipal wastes and, within that category, on household solid waste (i.e., that which is collected at the door) and sewage.

North American and Australasian consumers produce much more waste per capita than anyone else within the OECD (Figures 10.1 and 10.2). The quantity of waste is closely correlated with per capita income, although there are some important cultural distinctions. In general, Europe and Japan produce less waste than North Americans at the same income level. However, if incomes continue to rise, worldwide, under present conditions, we should expect the quantity of waste to increase also. This development is a direct result of a cultural and economic view of life which promotes sales for the company and consumption for the individual, at virtually any cost to the environment or to the individual's health. This has been critically observed

Figure 10.1. Municipal waste per capita (from OECD 1991: 45)

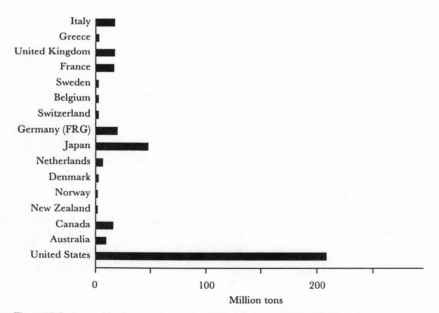

Figure 10.2. Annual quantity of municipal waste (from OECD 1991: 45)

TABLE 10.1
Type of waste and treatment

	Type of waste	Treatment
A	Food waste Garden waste	Composting
B	Glass Metal	Recycling
C	Plastics Paper	Incineration or recycling

since the 1950s. The leaders in this drive are the Americans, whom everyone else attempts to emulate to the fullest possible extent. What happens to all this waste we produce?

Of the 175 million tons of non-durable consumer goods produced in the United States every year, only 15 million tons (9 per cent) are recycled and only 7 million tons (4 per cent) are saved and reused. The rest is thrown out. Nearly half of the household waste is made up of packaging. It is estimated that the average American discards 300 kilograms of packaging every year; packaging accounts for 10 per cent of the grocery bill. Now that the environmental and financial costs of this material obsession are becoming evident, we are engaged in some modest attempts to slow down and reverse the trend. At this point we run into some paradoxes regarding the disposal of the rich waste stream we have created. Broadly, the four options that might be available for municipal waste management are landfill, dumping at sea, incineration, and recycling (including composting). Different materials in the waste stream are more readily channelled to one destination or another (Table 10.1).

Group A in Table 10.1 provides the least problem because the sorting and composting can be handled by the household itself, if the household has access to a garden, which would obviously be the case for the garden-waste producers. The items in Group B are relatively high in value and, if efficiently sorted, can be recycled economically. Better still, many of the artefacts can be cleaned and reused, and therefore held back from the waste stream. Group C provides a difficult choice for waste managers if they are committed to energy production from waste incineration, because these materials – paper and plastic – have the highest combustion value. However, paper is the most easily recyclable material, although it has been difficult to persuade paper producers to invest in the required de-inking and rerolling facilities because of the initial uncertainty of the quantity of used paper that can be supplied. A simulation model for Toronto has demonstrated the conflict that emerges between recycling and incineration for the paper component of the stream (Laikin, Jones, and Whitney 1985). A further problem with plastic is the potential health risk of the gases released into the atmosphere from the incinerator stack.

Generally, northern Europe (especially Germany) has been ahead of North America in reducing municipal waste through product legislation (for example, reducing the quantity of packaging) and efficient recycling. In Germany about 50 per cent of glass bottles, 70 per cent of drinks packaging, and nearly 50 per cent of paper are recycled. The targets for 1995 are 80 per cent for plastics and papers and 90 per cent for glass, tin, and aluminum (*Financial Times*, 14 August 1991). German standards for environmentally approved products are now being introduced to the European Community against the protests of France and Britain, who claim that these kinds of environmental regulations are a non-tariff barrier to Community trade, as only German producers can currently satisfy them (*Financial Times*, 30 November 1990). Legal difficulties have arisen from environmental regulations for packaging and recycling. If supermarkets, for example, agree among themselves not to stock environmentally unfriendly products, such an agreement would breach anticartel laws. Where municipalities or states set targets (such as 80 per cent recycling of plastics and paper) there is the problem of allocating the 80 per cent saved and the 20 per cent wasted among producers, as the more efficient allow the less efficient to travel as 'free-riders.'

Reforms in North America have been more tentative, although municipalities and taxpayers are becoming aware of the cost of inaction. Over the past ten years the cost of removing household waste in a medium-sized North American city – for collection, transport, tipping fee, and landfill management – has risen from about $10 per ton to about $140 per ton (i.e., much higher than the costs quoted in the introduction). In Toronto it has been estimated that the charge to the householders for garbage collection could go from its current $25 per annum to $150 (*Globe and Mail*, 1 November 1989). Even at the higher prices, planning for the timely provision of landfills has fallen seriously behind in many municipalities, mainly because of the political implications of the NIMBY syndrome. In Metro Toronto, despite several years of active political debate on the shortage of landfill sites, a solution is not yet on hand. The plan for rail haulage of the garbage to an empty mine at Kirkland Lake (600 kilometres to the north) was abandoned after local residents complained that they were being treated 'like people in the Third World.' As the new provincial government had also ruled out incineration and as surrounding municipalities remained unwilling to provide new landfill sites, the options appear to be rather limited. Most cities in the industrial world are either in this sort of situation already, or soon will be.

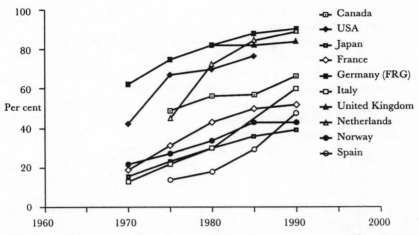

Figure 10.3. Percentage of people served by waste-water treatment (from OECD 1991: 29)

American enthusiasm for waste incineration is on the wane now that it is difficult to find sites to bury the remaining fly ash and residents are complaining about lead, zinc, and other airborne residuals. Canadians are suing in the American courts against a giant new incinerator that has been built in Detroit, just across the international border.

Even if the solid-household-waste problem can be reduced significantly by better waste-management practices, the problem of adequate sewage disposal remains. As cities have grown larger, our essentially nineteenth-century technology for the removal and treatment of human bodily wastes has become more evidently inadequate. There are four main problems. One is the connection between overflow storm-water drains which flow into the sewage drains when, at times of heavy rain, the floodgates are left open (to prevent backing up of the storm water) and sewage is flushed out, untreated, with the storm water into open bodies of water. The second problem is that only about half of the population in the OECD – including the richest countries of the world – are served by waste-water treatment facilities at all (Figure 10.3). Third is the problem of industrialists dumping prohibited materials (such as PCBs and heavy metals) into the sewage system, because it is convenient and relatively cheap for them to do so, even if they are occasionally prosecuted and fined. These dangerous materials then end up in the food chain whether the dried sewage sludge goes to a landfill site, where the materials would escape with the leachate, or whether the sludge is applied to the fields as fertilizer. The fourth problem is that inadequately treated human wastes contain bacteria, such as coliforms, which, if they re-enter the food chain, can cause intestinal diseases.

Better-designed treatment systems can take care of these problems, but until now it was assumed that for smaller communities the natural dilution of human wastes in the surface-water system, or filtration through septic tanks, was adequate. For the larger settlements the cost of new treatment plants would greatly increase the cost of the service for the consumer. At the municipal level, where the politician is relatively close to the voter, there is a reluctance to face this costly reality. However, those consumer-voters will soon have to choose between their health and their wallet.

The management of household wastes in the South

Worrisome as these problems are, they are manageable compared with the waste-management problems faced by the low-income countries of the South. As the cities mushroomed in size the old village-scale waste-disposal methods became dangerously outmoded. Waste cannot simply be heaped by the roadside and left to decompose, dry out, and blow away, without entraining serious health consequences. Yet, in many poor countries, that is what happens to most of the waste. This practice is euphemistically referred to as 'above-ground disposal' in Shanghai, where in 1988 there was a serious outbreak of hepatitis that killed hundreds, hospitalized thousands, and brought the city to a standstill.

In most countries of the South even the waste that is picked up by the municipality and trucked to a waste-disposal site is rarely treated adequately. Sanitary landfill sites are very few and far between. Bulldozers may push the waste into place, but daily coverings of earth are rare and virtually nothing is known about the leachate plumes under the dump, or whether the plumes contaminate the groundwater. City managers are too preoccupied with the visible problems to worry about the invisible ones. Yet, unless these problems are dealt with, we lose another key entry point (along with the provision of potable water) to lowering infant mortality and bringing an end to the demographic transition.

Sewage and semiliquid waste are usually the first to become problematical in a tropical urban system, resulting in increased coliform counts, beaches closed for swimming, and reduced catches from the inshore fishery. In 1986 the Senegalese Department of the Environment put into operation its new water-quality laboratory. It carried out coliform counts for the beaches around the city and published the results in the national newspaper alongside seasonal warnings regarding storms and dangerous tides. The results were appalling. For some samples the coliforms were too numerous to count, yet the safety limit is just ten per litre. The problems of industrial wastes are only just being recognized in Senegal. There is no treatment facility, and it is very difficult for the Department of the Environment to monitor the abuses. Although an Environmental Law has been enacted, the department (like similar departments all over the world) does not have the means to monitor and curtail abuses (République du Sénégal 1983b). Out of necessity, the department has adopted a joint strategy with the industrialists to monitor and improve industrial production techniques (République du Sénégal 1985, 1986). Meanwhile the combination of household and industrial wastes has polluted the coastline, and algae growths have killed off the local inshore fishery (Kornprobst 1983: 70). Few local fishermen have the means to fish much further from the shore. The dumping of household wastes collected by the garbage company (contracted out by the Municipality of Dakar) is done in the traditional fashion. The garbage is picked up, trucked out of town, and dumped. (In this respect, it should be said that Dakar is managing better than many African cities.) The dump site is not a sanitary landfill, and the leachate drains into an area of intensive market gardening crucial to the city's food supply.

What prevents municipal authorities from improving their waste-management system? It is believed that the higher-income groups would pay the full cost of waste removal, while a token payment could be collected from even the poorest households in the poorest countries. Then, why is it difficult to set up and manage improved waste-management systems, at least to the level of the technology that is currently being applied in higher-income countries? Like the supply of potable water, the problem of waste management is closely linked to all the other socio-economic problems of low-income countries. It is hard to change the management of one activity without changing many other aspects of the socio-economic system. First, just on a physical level, it is difficult for garbage-collection vehicles to gain access to pick-up points, because city streets are often narrow with buildings close together and garbage in the streets. In Ibadan, in 1984, the garbage in the main streets became so dense that vehicles were reduced to single file! Planners can, and do, designate communal pick-up points. However, the further these are from the household, the less frequently people use them and the more garbage is dropped along the way when they do, especially as this task is often the responsibility of children who are too small to reach into the garbage skips. Waste-management agencies of the typical cities of the South are low on the stretched priority list when it comes to budgets. They are understaffed, in both quantity and quality. Vehicles are few in number and in poor repair; landfill sites are usually overfilled and surrounded by dwellings. Foreign exchange is inadequate for the purchase of fuel and spare parts. It is not unusual for this unenviable responsibility to be delegated in turn from one branch of the government to another in the vain hope that a new administrative structure will remedy the defects (Onibokun 1989: 94). Privatization is an answer only in the richer suburbs, a small percentage of the typical city in the South. Efforts to improve the status quo by recycling may be met with hostility by that section of the population that supports itself by scavenging, although recovery and recycling technology is well known in the South (Lohani 1982). Garbage sorting provides many jobs, and so an attempt to improve the system by the purchase of modern vehicles might do more harm than good.

Most improvement efforts have been based on the transfer of Western technology, which is not only expensive in the context of a low-income country but often physically inappropriate as well. The inappropriateness stems from the difference in the waste composition between rich (generally temperate) lands and poor (generally tropical) lands. The poor-country waste stream has a smaller percentage of paper, glass, metal, and plastics, and a higher percentage of food wastes and other organic matter. In some countries waste includes large quantities of sand from uncovered streets and sidewalks. These factors mean that the compactor trucks that rich countries use for curbside collection are less efficient, having few boxes and cartons to crush; in their place they have wet vegetable matter and sand. Conversely, the tropical waste stream is lower in combustible material, so incinerators are not as efficient either. These physical facts have not stopped aid agencies and private Western companies from supplying municipalities of low-income countries with expensive compactors and incinerators that very soon break down.

A more insidious threat to the quality of life in low-income cities is the inadequacy of the sewage and waste-water treatment system. The percentage of households with water-mains and flush toilets is very small, usually much less than 10 per cent. Perhaps 50 per cent have access to private or communal septic-tank systems. For the rest there is nothing. Again, the problem is not amenable to a simple, frontal assault. Septic tanks are inappropriate in large cities anyway, because the groundwater is likely to become polluted from the leaking and rarely emptied tanks. In general, such systems worked well for the small, elite colonial population for which they were originally constructed. However, the mushrooming of cities has completely overwhelmed the infrastructure, both physical and managerial. Once a critical size is surpassed, pollutants accumulate in the ground and contaminate wells, boreholes, and sources of surface water.

The management of an adequate sewage disposal system can be further complicated if there is either a dearth or an overabundance of water, or if one condition alternates with the other on a seasonal basis. In water-short cities like Dakar, Kano, or Khartoum, there is generally inadequate water to flush through the sewage system. Even if the system is sometimes adequately flushed the material is usually ejected, untreated, at the river bank or on the beach. If the electricity supply is sporadic this further reduces the effectiveness of pumping stations. For cities located in areas of plentiful rain and plentiful surface water it might be expected that some of these flushing problems could be handled. However, a city with a high water-table (like Kinshasa, Manila, or Bangkok) will probably face even greater problems in ensuring adequate drainage of sewage and waste water. In some cases a quantity of sewage waste may be turned into energy by the installation of biogas digesters, in which microbes break down waste-plant material and human and other animal wastes to give off methane, which can be burned to produce electricity. This technology has been successfully installed in Asia, especially in rural India. It poses some health risks associated with transferring the wastes to the digester; however, this can be done by pipes from communal toilets. What is clear is that the technology of the modern industrial city, inadequate as it is in its own setting, cannot be transferred, unmodified, to low-income tropical countries even if the money were available to cover the cost of installation.

The export of waste

In the late 1980s, the municipal problem of waste management suddenly appeared at the global scale, thus affording a dramatic example of the implications of global system closure and the demise of the North's 'throw-away society.' This sudden transformation appeared through the media exposure of a few extraordinary export adventures. One began with the prosaic shipment of municipal wastes by an ocean-going barge from New York to North Carolina. The other uncovered a newly developed export business of shipping highly toxic industrial wastes from America and Europe to Africa – to escape stiffening environmental regulations and disposal costs at home. Underneath all the heated exchanges and counter-offers involved in these incidents lies an important moral question: 'is it acceptable for a rich country or city, newly aware of the environmental concerns of its citizens, to make a deal with a poor country, or American state, to export its filth, because the poor country or state does not have any better economic prospect on the horizon?' The answer, from the perspective of this book, is a solid no. The rationale for the no is that the waste problem is very deeply rooted in our production system and must be solved as an integral part of improvement of that system. Exporting the unwanted residuals just puts off the day of reckoning.

Traditionally we make a distinction between municipal wastes (80 per cent of which originate from households) and industrial waste. It is generally assumed that all the hazardous wastes (corrosive, ignitable, toxic, and so on) originate in industry. However, this distinction is less valid now that both sewage sludge and household wastes contain a greater variety of chemical residues, which, when concentrated, can be hazardous. One paradox of improved waste-disposal standards is that hazardous wastes are now more concentrated in incinerator flue ash, in material trapped by filters on incinerators and other smokestacks, in dried sewage sludge, and in leachate seeping from landfills. Because of the great complexity of the modern waste-management process it often happens that attempts to improve one part of the system simply relocate the problem chemicals to another part of it.

It was in the United States and Western Europe that many of these new problems first surfaced, forced by the very volume of industrial production, the multiplicity of jurisdictions involved, and a widening concern for improved environmental standards. Even at the, supposedly safer, level of municipal-garbage disposal it has been evident for some time that old practices would have to change. New York City was the most obvious case in point. Once the largest population concentration in the world, short of nearby land for disposal sites, yet surrounded by the sea and conveniently close to very deep water, the disposal solution seemed to be obvious. Since 1924, and until very recently, most of New York City's garbage – including dredge spoil, sewage sludge, and waste chemicals – was simply put in barges and dumped at sea. In the 1980s the quantity reached ten million tons per year (Clark 1989: 25–7). But not all garbage sinks, and much of what floated came ashore on the expensive property of Long Island. So much garbage accumulated on the beaches that local protesters forced the authorities to find other disposal methods. Congested municipalities like New York signed contracts with less-populous states, like North Carolina and Mississippi, to accept some of their sewage sludge and municipal waste. However, even in these less densely populated states such imports are no longer acceptable, as was demonstrated by the frustrated voyage of the *Break of Dawn*, a barge loaded with 3,000 tons of New York garbage destined for North Carolina in March 1987. The barge was refused permission to unload in North Carolina, and over the next few weeks the rejection scene was repeated at other American ports and some in Mexico and the Caribbean islands. After three months, the *Break of Dawn* returned ignominiously with its load to New York (*Globe and Mail*, 28 April 1987).

The problems arising with hazardous wastes are more severe than those associated with (supposedly non-hazardous) municipal wastes. It is estimated that about 80 per cent of hazardous wastes in Western Europe is disposed of on site, another 10 per cent is transported locally for disposal, and the remaining 10 per cent crosses a national border. The reason for the border crossings is that not all countries possess the specialized disposal facilities for certain wastes, or there are economies of scale. Britain and Belgium have developed waste-disposal facilities to handle specialized wastes, although that era may be coming to a close. In 1989 Quebec tried to export some of its troublesome PCBs for disposal in Britain, but dockers in Liverpool and Southampton refused to unload the (Russian) ship. The ship returned to Montreal, where, again, dockers refused to unload it. Finally, it was unloaded, under armed guard, at Baie-Comeau – the prime minister's own riding at the mouth of the St Lawrence. The circle of disposal options is obviously closing.

The problems are still far from being solved, however. In December 1989 an enquiry into hazardous wastes in Quebec exposed the absence of most of the information needed to even monitor the production, transportation, and disposal of the estimated annual production of 410,000 tons. Of this estimated production, less than half could be accounted for. Provincial regulations exclude companies with fewer than twenty employees or which produce less than five tons of hazardous wastes per year. Of the 4,300 companies which should file reports, only 800 had done so. Also exempted from toxic-waste regulations are 'agriculture, pulp and paper residues, mining waste, biomedical waste and sludge from municipal sewage treatment plants' – in other words, the bulk of the Quebec economy. Furthermore, the province's Ministry of the Environment 'needed three weeks to produce a list of companies authorized to transport and store hazardous wastes in the province' (*Globe and Mail*, 14 December 1989).

The lack of monitoring in Quebec illustrates the current difficulties in improving hazardous-waste management. In these circumstances one can see how easy it was for companies to dispose of their wastes by exporting them to low-income countries. This scandal broke, like the American municipal-waste scandal, largely over the voyage of a single ship. In this case it was a an Italian waste transporter who paid the owner of a Nigerian construction company, Mr Sunday Nana, $100 per month to 'store' about 2,500 tons of toxic industrial waste in his yard. (Some of the drums contained PCBs, and the government later stated that some of the waste was radioactive.) The Nigerian government reaction to this was swift; they commandeered other Italian vessels – the *Karin B* and the *Deep Sea Carrier* – to take the drums away, and they arrested local representatives of the Italian company. There were calls in the Nigerian press for the death penalty. The story did not end there. Like the *Break of Dawn*, the Italian ships experienced great difficulty in disposing of their load. They were refused entry in Britain, the Netherlands, West Germany, and France; the last even refused them permission to take on fuel. Eventually they had to return to Italy to face rioting people and squabbling between various levels of government, all anxious to avoid any responsibility for the wastes.

Interest in this story, and the negative impact it had on Nigerian-Italian relations, soon exposed the fact that such toxic-waste export deals had recently become widespread in Africa. More than twenty countries were affected, through either official channels or individuals who were prepared to circumvent the law. One feature they all shared was the very low price being offered. The government of Guinea was offered $50 per ton, Guinea-Bissau $40 per ton, Benin $2.5 per ton – all of them just one-time payments. These fees compare with $4,000 per ton for legally disposing of toxic wastes in the United States. Once the scandal broke these and similar agreements were hastily cancelled. An international meeting took place in Luxembourg to lay down new guidelines which would make it the responsibility of the exporting country to ensure that any exported hazardous materials would be properly handled at their destination. What these events clearly illustrate is a callous exploitation of the poverty of the poorest countries of the world, whether by governments or individuals. It is hard to see how this behaviour can masquerade as an 'economic opportunity if properly handled' even though it has been presented as such. Indeed, in an internal memo (12 December 1991), later defended as intended only to stimulate discussion, Lawrence Summers, chief economist of the World Bank, wrote: 'Only the lamentable facts that so much pollution is generated by non-tradable industries (transport, electrical generation) and that the unit transport costs of solid waste are so high prevent world-welfare-enhancing trade in air pollution and waste' (*Economist*, 8 February 1992: 82). His argument was based on the fact that in the South 'forgone earnings from increased morbidity and mortality' are lower, and therefore the measurable impact (i.e., based on earning power) of pollution on health would be lower. He concluded in the same memo: 'I think the economic logic behind dumping a load of toxic waste in the lowest-wage country is impeccable and we should face up to that.' Such arguments are reminiscent of the defence of slavery, the slave trade, and child labour in the coal-mines.

When the earth was more lightly populated and before industrialization became the main motor of national wealth, people could solve their waste problems locally, or be prepared to suffer the consequences of their own management deficiency. (This generalization ignores the cases of diffusion of plagues far from their unhygienic place of origin.) Today, although most aspects of waste management are still the responsibility of local authorities, these authorities no longer have the resources to manage the huge quantities of waste that the proliferation of industry, material wealth, and human numbers has produced. We can see the stirrings of some concern to control the waste problem by the recycling of household and industrial waste materials in the wealthy North. However, the more-expensive disposal problems posed by hazardous wastes have still not been addressed in a holistic way. The exposure of the international toxic-waste trade amply demonstrates that market forces will always seek the cheapest solution, even if that solution creates a potentially lethal risk for someone else, preferably in a poor country a long way away.

Such loopholes will continue to exist as long as the problem is tackled piecemeal as a disposal problem, rather than as a production problem, at source. Yet, as early as the 1972 Stockholm conference on the environment it was recommended that there should be a centrally kept register of hazardous chemicals. In 1976 the newly created United Nations Environment Programme set up just such a centre in Geneva: the International Register of Potentially Toxic Chemicals (IRPTC). Its data files are linked with those of the European Community's Environmental Chemicals Data and Information Network (ECDIN); it cooperates with the World Health Programme's International Programme on Chemical Safety (IPCS). It issues guidelines (e.g., the Cairo Guidelines on the transportation, handling, and disposal of hazardous wastes, 1985), and it responds to requests for information on the handling of potentially hazardous materials, especially from Third World countries, where no other source of information may be available. However, its staff remains very small, and it has no legislative power.

It is a start. Nevertheless, what is required is a comprehensive international agreement on the verification of transportation manifests, higher penalties for non-compliance, more education on waste management, and, finally, a holistic approach to the problem which examines the whole life cycle of a product: from production, to consumption, to the final disposal of all waste materials. In January 1989 a conference called 'Product Life: the Overall Design – Life-cycle Engineering: The Key to Risk Management, Safer Products and Industrial Environmental Strategies' was held in Zurich. The holding of such a conference might be interpreted as a recognition that system closure encompasses all kinds of human activity from the scale of the earth itself to every product we, as individuals, create or use.

11

The Environment and International Relations

The accelerating impact of human activities on earth's resource and environmental base has become the decisive factor determining a nation's potential for development, its economic health, and its security. Properly approached, within the context of promoting sustainable development, the issues of climate change, ozone depletion, deforestation, the spread of deserts, and the allocation of shared water and other resources could force a new spirit of international co-operation, and fresh thinking about multilateral approaches to other issues. (Jim MacNeill, 'The Greening of International Relations,' *International Journal*, 1989–90: 35)

Environmental issues have always played a part in international relations. Mostly, they have been the subject of acrimonious disputes. Examples include disputes over international fishing quotas, over water allowances from international rivers, and over the resettlement of refugees from drought. However, never before have so many large and difficult issues appeared over such a short period of time. Ten years ago almost all environmental problems were dealt with (if at all) within national boundaries. Now, many of the most serious problems cannot be resolved in this way. Instead they require very broad and very long-term understandings among all the world's nations. Seriously, what is the chance of such cooperation occurring? What is the record so far?

The record is not encouraging. Other than the rapid signing of the Protocol on CFCs, the picture is generally one of no agreement at all, or lengthy negotiations that drag on for years with only partial resolution of the issues, as with the Law of the Sea and the Antarctica Treaty. It is true that some issues show promise of improvement – witness the controls on the dumping of toxic and radioactive waste at sea and an agreement (the Basel Convention) on the responsibilities of the exporters of toxic wastes. In general, though, progress is slow and difficult. The impediments to progress are many.

They include a lack of the specific information needed to formulate agreements and unwillingness on the part of governments to make any concessions that they fear will put them at a disadvantage in the world trading system. Finally, there is the political reality which recognizes that governments have other priorities, such as wars, ethnic strife, access to world markets, debt burdens, trade imbalances, inflation, and unemployment. These problems are more visible and easier for the public to follow when politicians neglect their promises. People are worried about environmental deterioration, but relatively few voters carefully track any one of the myriad problems. In many countries people neither vote nor have access to any environmental information beyond their daily problems of living.

Despite all these difficulties the environmental issues have become so intertwined with every aspect of a nation's economic and social life that they cannot simply be set aside until the time and resources can be found to deal with them. For example, it is the shortage of foreign exchange and the need to repay foreign debt that drives countries with tropical rain forests to cut down their hardwoods, even though it is understood that this will accelerate soil erosion. Furthermore, in countries like the Philippines and Ghana, there is not enough forest left to pay off the debt even if every hectare of the forest were clear-cut. Nevertheless, for want of other alternatives, Brazil, Côte d'Ivoire, the Philippines, Ghana, Indonesia, and other countries will continue to clear the forest and export their hardwoods. Thus, the reality of system closure makes it imperative that the fate of the forest be discussed at the same table as soil erosion, food security, and the management of unrepayable international debts.

It is just possible to believe that the community of nations is ready to think about bundling such problems together before it is too late. The reason for some optimism is that system closure brings an environmental awareness home to many very different countries at the same time. Nations certainly reacted more quickly than usual to the ozone-depletion problem, because the consequences were truly horrifying, quite as bad as the effect of aboveground nuclear testing, which was abandoned in the 1960s (*L'Express*, 6 March 1992). Other atmospheric problems could have consequences just as grave as ozone depletion, with entire regions becoming unproductive through drought, flooding, or acidification. Even if agricultural conditions do not deteriorate, the continued growth of population in low-income countries will become a global-scale problem, with more and more pressure to admit economic/environmental refugees to the rich countries. Where this is not possible legally, it will continue to happen illegally, as has been seen already in Europe, the United States, Hong Kong, and Australia.

The global commons under stress

The first topic dealt with in this book was global warming. It was discussed first because it is the largest issue in terms of its potential environmental impact, even though that impact is surrounded with controversy. No one denies that there is a CO_2 build-up in the atmosphere, but some deny that the build-up will lead to warming, while others concede that there is a warming effect but do not agree that warming will cause a rise in the ocean levels. At a seventy-two-nation conference on global warming in the Netherlands in November 1989 four of the major industrial producers refused to sign the proposal to stabilize CO_2 emissions by the year 2000 and reduce them by 20 per cent by the year 2005 (*Globe and Mail*, 7 November 1989: 5). The four refusals were from Japan, the United States, the former Soviet Union, and Britain. (A few weeks later, a new environment minister for Britain agreed to sign the proposal.) The United States wanted to wait for the publication of a United Nations study, and Japan stated that it was doing more than any other country to curb emissions already.

This disappointing result illustrates several important features of the complexity of international environmental issues. First, there is a great deal of uncertainty surrounding the scientific facts – much more uncertainty than in the average trade dispute or even the average fisheries dispute. Suddenly, we really need to know about things that until very recently were the concern of only small groups of specialists, if of anyone at all. Second, there is a lack of guiding principles for the resolution of the issues. Are these large pollution problems the responsibility of the large economies or of the inefficient economies? Japan has gone some way to making its industries cleaner, but has it done enough, or should the world economies impose a carbon tax on themselves which would hit all the large economies, whether relatively clean or not? Third, environmental issues are encouraging some very strange alliances. When was the last time Japan, the United States, the former Soviet Union, and Britain found themselves isolated on the same side of the table?

The second point is really fundamental, as it goes to the heart of the relevant negotiating mechanism for international environmental problem-solving. To support the Japanese argument (that they have done more to clean their house than other major industrial nations) the debate would have to be focused at the level of the output unit – and even then it would have to be selected from either the operating unit (the factory) or the corporate entity, as a company often includes several production facilities. A corporation could demonstrate that although it has carbon dioxide–producing factories, it also has carbon dioxide–absorbing forests. Indeed one company has already done exactly that (see Figure 11.1). To really get down to the required level of detail

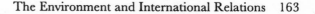

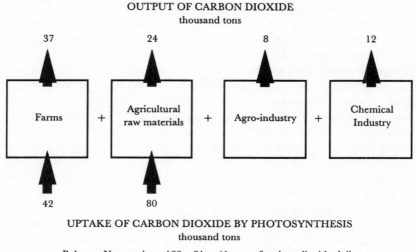

OUTPUT OF CARBON DIOXIDE
thousand tons

UPTAKE OF CARBON DIOXIDE BY PHOTOSYNTHESIS
thousand tons

Balance: Net uptake = 122 − 81 = 41 tons of carbon dioxide daily

Figure 11.1. Daily flux of carbon dioxide in the Ferruzzi Group of companies, 1988 (adapted from an advertisement placed in *Scientific American* [September 1989] by the Ferruzzi Group, an Italian conglomerate

you would need a production licensing system that was defined and policed by an international body. If the alternative approach were selected, and the big economies were the target (after all, the excess CO_2 is a by-product of the wealth they currently enjoy), then countries may be set targets, like the 'stabilization by year 2000, 20 per cent down by year 2005' proposed at the conference. There are many problems here (apart from Japan's objection), one being that this may tend to fix a nation's economic output at more or less the level it is now. Japan might settle for this, expecting to gain further production from greater efficiencies in processing materials and in using energy. However, the newly industrializing countries and the not-yet-industrializing countries would certainly not like it. Note the recent observation and warning: 'By 2020 China alone will produce one-fifth of the world's carbon-dioxide output. Add India, and the total rises to 30%. Watch for an alliance of third-world energy producers against the climate-change agreement next year' (*Economist*, 31 August 1991).

An alternative is to require a reduction from the most industrialized countries and to permit the expansion of developing countries (Flavin 1989: 35). The Delhi-based Centre for Science and Environment has even argued that the earth's absorptive capacity (sinks) for gases such as carbon dioxide and methane should be apportioned on a per capita basis; thus India, with 16 per cent of the world's population, should be permitted 16 per cent of the allowable emissions (IFDA 1991; Agarwal and Narain 1991). This proposal is not likely to be acceptable to any country of the North or to the less-populous, more-prosperous, countries of the South.

The problems do not end here. Two other knotty issues immediately intrude. National quotas are irrelevant, because so much production is in the hands of transnational companies. If the country of Japan had reached its given ceiling for CO_2 production and Thailand and the Philippines had not, then Japanese companies could simply expand their production in Thailand and the Philippines (as indeed they are already doing for economic reasons). The second, even knottier, issue is the development and transfer of clean technology. If Japan (whether defined as a state or as a set of companies) has developed a particular type of clean technology, would it not be in everyone's interests (including its own) to distribute that technology, free, to less efficient producers, or to potential producers who are too poor to do their own research and development, and too poor to import the clean technology, under licence, from the advanced industrial nations? This aspect of the problem extends the boundaries of the concept of aid. Even from this one example, the challenge to international relations is all too clear. Some European countries have begun to place carbon taxes on their own producers. This is a laudable step, but the fact remains that the CO_2 problem, like many environmental problems, is transboundary. Putting one's own house in order is a useful and necessary step, but it does not solve those problems which are operating on a global scale.

We have seen that, once the link between CFC production and stratospheric ozone depletion was established, the international industrial community moved quickly to agree on a solution, albeit a far too limited one and one that is being overtaken by events. The reasons for this display of relative alacrity were the acceptance of the scientific evidence, the public alarm caused by the idea of a 'hole' in the sky, and the fact that the people most threatened were the rich, especially those that had the money and the leisure time to lie on sunny beaches. In particular, the group most at risk were those fair-skinned people who had left their damp and draughty European homeland to populate sunnier places like Florida, California, and Australia. There is virtually no doubt that the threat is real. For example, an article published in *Retina* (1989) reported a correlation between an increase in the number of cases of solar eye-burn and record reductions in the ozone layer over New York in March 1986 (*Globe and Mail*, 17 January 1989). Even in this case, where the scientific evidence was not disputed, and where the threat directly pointed at the major producers of the problem, the resolution was far from complete. Ten years before the Montreal Protocol was signed, the United States Environmental Protection Agency had been among the first to ban CFC-using aerosol cans for frivolous and avoidable uses. Canada and some northern European countries did likewise. But frivolous uses still continue in other parts of Europe. As the *Economist* wryly noted, skiers, who are worried about the lack of snow in the Alps (1987–90), still spray their skis with CFC-using aerosols, even though CFCs, as greenhouse gases, are known to contribute to climate change and hence, possibly, to the lack of snow (*Economist*, 23 December 1989: 76).

On a more serious note, CFCs contribute to the material benefits of modernization through their use in refrigerators, solvents, and other non-frivolous applications. Refrigeration has played a major role in the improvement of the rich countries' diet, through both the long-distance transportation of food and the preservation of fresh food in shops and in the home. In the rich countries, under threat of the elimination of all CFCs, alternative chemicals are being developed. Probably alternatives can be found for all applications of CFCs, even though costs may go up and efficiency may go down. Again, however, there remains the problem of the terms of transfer of any new, CFC-free, technologies to poorer countries, which would benefit substantially from refrigeration of food stocks, but which probably lack capital and the scientific infrastructure to invent their own CFC-free products. What can be done? It seems inevitable that the aid agencies of the North will have to extend their responsibilities to the buying and the transfer of this sort of technology.

The acid-deposition problem involves several of the issues raised by the first two atmospheric concerns. The interesting new twist, from the perspective of international relations, is that, unlike the CO_2 and CFC residuals, the sulphur and nitrogen oxide particles (emitted during the combustion of fossil fuels and the smelting of sulphide ores) spend days (not years) in the atmosphere. So the depositions can be traced (roughly) from the destination back to the origin. In some ways this suggests that some of the obligatory internationalization of the previous issues, where everything is stirred into the same atmospheric soup, might be avoided, and 'acid treaties' may be worked out between sender and receiver. There are some possibilities of doing this, but – as noted in Chapter 5 – the winds are variable and there is still quite a lot of mixing. It seems likely, therefore, that the resolution of these problems will also lie in an internationally supervised agreement, similar to the agreements needed for CO_2 and CFC emissions. If the American/Canadian case is any indication, solutions will come very slowly. Canada has staunch American allies among the states of New England, which, like Canada, have been receiving doses of American acid precipitation for over twenty years. Yet, even with allies within the United States, and even with the readiness of

Americans to initiate legislation through local court rulings, progress has been painfully slow.

A new set of acid-deposition problems is emerging in those low-income countries with a significant industrial base located in areas that are highly susceptible to acidification. So far, the principal problem areas are found in Nigeria, Venezuela, India, and China. For such countries the familiar question of the terms of technology transfer reappears: where the richer countries have found effective methods for reducing acid emissions from power stations and smelters, under what conditions will such technology be transferred to other countries? For the gas that is wastefully flared from oilfields in Nigeria, Iran, and Venezuela the technology is already widely available, as the natural gas can be liquefied and shipped to the market for consumption. But the market 'does not justify' the $2 billion expenditure for Nigeria's first liquid natural gas plant although it has been under discussion for over twenty years. Meanwhile the acid deposition continues, to the detriment of Nigeria's already precarious agricultural sector. Surely, in such circumstances, we must look at an entirely new way of conducting global business.

In the realm of ocean management only one thing is fairly certain, and that is that the big problems have yet to surface. The ocean is the earth's greatest 'sink,' in Howard Odum's sense of a physical repository for what we no longer wish to be concerned with. From the shore facilities, like factories and cities, that evolved on the assumption of throwing all their wastes into the sea to the ships that regularly void their polluted holds in the ocean, all who are able to do so dump their waste in the ocean.

The oceans suffer from an additional disadvantage compared with the land. Every square metre of land (except Antarctica) is apportioned to some nation-state. Much of the ocean belongs to no one. Nations are jealous of the immediate portion of the continental shelf for strategic reasons and for fish; the 200-mile Exclusive Economic Zones staked out rights for more fish and for the drilling of oil and gas. The EEZs were agreed to in a hurry, because every coastal country thought it saw an advantage in establishing a claim to all the offshore resources it could grab. The government of the United States was very unhappy, but old colonial countries (with lots of little islands here and there) and the newly independent nations of the South saw their chance and seized it. (Some observers saw Britain's determination to recapture the Falkland Islands in 1982 as a response to the estimated oil potential of the shallow seas around the Islands.) What is important, from the perspective of this book, is that none of this 'sea-grab' had anything to do with the proper, sustainable management of the ocean. It is was simply a continuation of business as usual for old and new nation-states. In this situation we cannot even try to recast international relations on the basis of nation-states, although that is what the Law of the Sea has tried to do. For marine problems, even more than for land-based or atmospheric problems, we have to rethink our approach to the management of residuals on a global scale.

Regional variations in the impact of environmental deterioration will influence the way in which political alliances evolve. As we have seen, the Ozone Protection Protocol was agreed upon very quickly by the leading industrial countries once it appeared that their citizens would be the principal victims of continued neglect of the issue. International action on acidification and forest die-back is taking longer to develop because some of the causes of impact are still disputed and because some of the victims are also the major offenders. The impacts of marine pollution, groundwater depletion, and improper handling of wastes on land all entail localized disputes between a few parties in each case, rather than global representation. For example, the 1988 exposure of the international trade in toxic waste involved several pairs of countries; some transactions took place with official knowledge, and some without. The matter has been partially resolved by international agreement; however, the proposed improvements rely heavily on the goodwill of the exporting country and an understanding of the implied risks by the importing country.

The burning and break-up of the Iranian oil-tanker *Kharg V*, in January 1990, illustrates the complex international relations that can evolve from a relatively simple environmentally significant event. The incident involved Morocco (the likely victim), the Netherlands (the country of the salvage company), Spain (which sent technical help, but refused to have the damaged tanker towed closer to its shores), and France (which provided technical advice). Four days were wasted in salvage negotiations. Iran stayed out of the affair on the grounds that there was no problem and that this was 'an ordinary matter' (*Globe and Mail*, 2, 3, and 6 January 1990). A fortunate combination of weather conditions eventually broke up the oil slick before it could come ashore on Morocco's beaches. Eventually, of course, some of the oil will come ashore, but by then it will probably be indistinguishable from all the other oil globules floating in the world's major shipping routes. What was needed in the *Kharg V* affair was an international authority which could dispatch the salvage ship immediately and which could later extract full payment for the clean-up costs from the guilty party. Yet the only reaction so far to increased public concern about oil spills is that some of the major oil companies have withdrawn from the transportation sector of the business by contracting the work out to small (mostly single-tanker) companies. It is understandable if corporate pride in giant ships with names like *Amoco Cadiz* and *Exxon Valdez* is on the wane, but this shifting of liability is not a good development for the environment.

In the cases of toxic-waste exports and oil-tanker spills, the parties are few and can (usually) be identified fairly readily. Thus, there is a basis for systematic retribution, which should eventually translate into improved handling procedures. We have a much larger problem in the case of CO_2 build-up in the atmosphere and its possible impact on global warming and sea-level rise. First, the impacts are still being disputed, and such disputes provide an opportunity for prevarication. Second, it will probably affect every country in the world, although the impacts will vary greatly – and the way in which they will vary is one of the factors that is disputed. Third, the mitigation of the problem goes to the heart of the modern industrialization process – the provision of cheap energy from the burning of fossil fuels. The costs of converting to clean energy technology are almost beyond calculation, or, at best, the calculations have a large degree of error.

The atmosphere and the ocean, along with Antarctica, are readily recognized as global commons because so little of them has been allocated to nation-states. What is emerging now, however, is a realization that the biosphere as a whole should be treated as a global responsibility, because desertification, deforestation, and waste accumulation have now become large enough in their impact to threaten human occupancy of the planet just as directly as do climatic change and declining fish stocks.

From Stockholm to Rio

There is no doubt that attitudes to society's dependence on a healthy environment have changed considerably since the 1972 Stockholm conference. However, that conference was held twenty years ago and attitudes will have to change even more rapidly over the next ten years if we are to make use of the window of opportunity that an optimist might still think we have. What is certain is that any subsequent windows will become progressively smaller. Put in other words, any decision-maker who is ambitious to improve the global environment will never have a better opportunity than now, because it seems very likely that the human tenancy of the planet will become increasingly precarious. Although attitudes are changing, they are still lagging way behind events. We do not yet have a consensus on a global policy that will place us in a position to begin to mitigate the impact of our mistakes. Such a consensus may never emerge. We may just struggle on, arguing about the details of our too-late global clean-up campaign.

Many politicians still believe in growth at any cost. Their ideas are rooted in a time when the solution to the unemployment problem was seen as the creation of jobs through a vigorously expanding industrial economy. Thus, 'Smokestack America' provided proof that the American system worked.

Similarly, in the Eastern bloc smokestacks (and their pollution) were a powerful symbol of the drive to industrialization: 'Bitterfeld, in East Germany's industrial heartland 175 kilometres south of Berlin, has three smokestacks and nothing else on its civic coat of arms. The shield is an apt symbol ... for all around, more than 100 massive brick and concrete chimneys spew waste from state factories manufacturing steel, paint, film and dozens of industrial chemicals' ('East Germans Dwelling in Smokestack Forests See Poison Everywhere,' *Globe and Mail*, 19 January 1990: A1, A2).

The same approach was sold to the newly independent countries of Asia and Africa, in the 1960s, by economists from both East and West. Industry produced higher value-added goods than agriculture and therefore was to be encouraged. Agriculture itself was to be modernized by the intensive use of machinery and chemical inputs. The development agencies measured economic progress by the quantity of steel produced and by the kilograms of fertilizer applied per hectare of arable land.

It has slowly become apparent that a great many of the environmental side- effects of industrialization and industrialized agriculture, once dismissed as externalities, have a very tangible cost, not only to the enterprise itself, but also to the surrounding community and to the national economy. Water, air, and the ocean (as a garbage dump) had long been used as free goods, or only a nominal cost was paid for the water. Likewise forest lands were leased to timber companies, in exchange for the creation of a few jobs. Sometimes, especially in Canada and the United States, forestry activities were further subsidized by the public provision of roads and other infrastructure. In Brazil, one of the important factors behind the deforestation of Amazonia was a tax law which placed lower taxes on developed agricultural land than on undeveloped virgin forest. Other relevant factors included subsidies on settlement schemes, livestock ranches, and smelting projects (Mahar 1989: 46–50).

Since the Stockholm conference we have at least learned to count some of the costs of environmental neglect, even if we have not yet determined who is going to pay them. Formerly 'free goods' are now recognized as the environmental capital on which society rests. The notion of environmental capital was first brought to the popular attention by Stein and Johnson, in 1979, in their aptly titled book *Banking on the Biosphere*. Deforestation, desertification, marine pollution, and other destructive processes represent the depletion of this stock of natural capital. However, such processes are completely ignored by our present system of calculating the gross national product which measures only the value of goods and services sold during the accounting year. Thus, if 500 hectares of rain forest are cleared in Zaire, the only fact that is registered in the calculation of GNP is the commercial value of the timber that is sold.

Just as our national accounting system is still mired in the past, so are our institutions. The political counterpart of GNP is the nation-state itself. Once seen as the natural successor to the polyglot empires of the nineteenth century, it is now clearly an idea whose time is past. It is too small and inward-looking to begin to provide the kind of government we need to rehabilitate the planet. The transboundary and transgenerational nature of the current environmental problems has simply overwhelmed the capacity of the nation-state. As noted in the *Economist*: 'Unilateral action by, say, Sweden to contain emissions of nasty gasses that turn the world into a hot-house or punch holes in the ozone layer will be of little value; concerted action is required. Drugs, defence, terrorism all demand intervention beyond the boundaries of any one country. More co-operation is essential' ('Goodbye to the Nation State?' 23 June 1990: 11).

What is the likelihood of the seriousness of the environmental crisis forcing 'a new spirit of international cooperation' (MacNeill 1989–90)? Is the environment in such critical condition that it will act as a superordinate, or over-arching, issue which obliges national leaders to cooperate in their search for solutions? It has been observed that there is a growing number of interest groups distinct from national units, such as non-governmental organizations (NGOs), transnational corporations, and multinational organizations, to claim some part of an individual's loyalty (North–South Institute 1991). Are coalitions of such groups likely to define a broader purpose than narrow, short-term national interests, such that a cooperative path to sounder environmental practices might be charted? For environmental NGOs like Friends of the Earth and Greenpeace, and the United Nations Environment Programme, such a role is their *raison d'être*. Increasingly, other bodies are defining environmental policies, including most transnational corporations, national and international development agencies, and United Nations organizations not hitherto explicitly concerned with the environment, such as the United Nations Centre for Human Settlements (HABITAT) and the United Nations Development Programme. The work of the World Commission on Environment and Development strengthened many of these initiatives. New groups of nations have emerged to defend a particular environmental viewpoint, such as the Alliance of Small Island States, in response to the dangers associated with global warming.

Despite this proliferation of interests and activities, for the time being the major decisions will be taken by national governments at forums such as the Intergovernmental Panel of Climate Change (IPCC, created by WMO and UNEP) and the United Nations Conference on Environment and Development which took place in Rio de Janeiro in June 1992. At gatherings such as these the divisions between groups of national interests run deep, and as the crisis continues the divisions are likely to deepen. They will deepen as the cost of the crisis becomes more severe and as the differential impact of environmental change on the North and the South becomes more apparent. The attention of the North is focused on climate change, but for the South the urgent issue is poverty, which is believed to be rooted in the nature of international economic relations, especially trade, debt, and property rights. As Sir Crispin Tickell recently observed: 'The growing divergence of wealth between rich and poor countries would exacerbate the global crisis. A hundred years ago the difference between *per capita* income in Europe and India was 2:1, now it is nearly 70:1' (*Independent*, 27 August 1991: 1).

With differences this great it will be very difficult to find common ground. Even the most liberal of the countries of the North are not likely to be prepared to accept the proposition of New Delhi's Centre for Science and Environment that each individual's rights should be considered equal in the environmental debate, certainly not when an individual's rights are not equal within their national units anyway. What then can be used as a point of departure in the search for solutions?

12

Priorities for Analysis
and Mitigation

[At the Rio conference] ... according to certain sources, the emphasis will be
on atmospheric risks, or, more generally, on pollution, while most NGOs,
especially those from south of the Sahara, would hope that the priority
would be to deal with the ecological, economic and social problem of
poverty. (Jacques Bugnicourt, 'ONG: Tous les chemins mènent-ils à Rio?'
Ecodecision, 1991/1: 26–7)

The details of the many ways in which the expansion of the human domain
has affected the environment can be confusing. But the big picture is really
very simple, especially when we think of people as part of one of Howard
Odum's simple producer/consumer ecosystems. The big picture can be reduced to three propositions. First, improvements in material prosperity stimulate a rapid increase in population; then, once longevity is an established fact,
populations stabilize, and may even decline. The first stage in this transition
is now taking place among the poorest half of the world's people. Completion of this transition to a stable population is not inevitable. If material conditions do not improve, the transition may stall, thereby producing a
large-scale oscillation in the size of the human population, which may so
destabilize society that human die-back becomes general. We must admit the
possibility that the transition may not take place and we must understand
what the consequences of this failure may be.

The second essential ingredient for survival is a full understanding of our
use of somatic (or bodily) energy and our use of extra-somatic energy. The
way in which the North is currently availing itself of both forms of energy is
not sustainable. Heavy consumption of meat requires far more food inputs,
mainly grains, than are necessary to sustain human life. In order to provide
more grain for the world's population the rich need to modify their own

intake. More dramatic consequences follow from our dependence on burning fossil fuels. The residuals from this activity are polluting vegetation, soil, and water, and they are changing the composition of the atmosphere with potentially disastrous consequences. We should make the transition to sustainable agriculture and to renewable extra-somatic energy in the very near future. Third, we must review all our technologies for transforming materials into products in a way that assigns responsibility for the whole of the cycle. This means that someone, or some body, should accept responsibility for the proper disposal of all residuals from production. The concept of 'product life-cycle management' is already being introduced into legislation in Germany.

These three aspects of the problem – demography, energy, residuals – summarize the multitude of processes that we should reconsider in order to make the transition to sustainability. The fact that these three elements are inextricably linked should become ever more obvious as the consequences of global system closure become a reality. In this complex interplay of events there is a tendency to rely heavily on a technical analysis of the changing physical characteristics of the biosphere in the search for solutions. However, the major stumbling-block in this search is the political problem of poverty. It is poverty that accounts for the different environmental agendas of North and South. Until that problem is addressed there is little chance of broad international cooperation in dealing with the problems of the global environment, and without such cooperation there is little hope of a reversal of the trend towards environmental degradation.

Poverty

It was suggested in Chapter 1 that the postwar development effort had largely failed in the poorest countries of the South and the outlook was, at best, uncertain in many of the not-so-poor countries, such as Brazil and Mexico. The prescription of a little capital and a little technical help has been inadequate to transform traditional agrarian societies to modern, partly industrial, economies. In many of them the rate of population growth outstrips the rate of economic growth. We now believe that the North does not have a sustainable technology to transfer to the South, even if it had the political will to make such an effort. But prior to the question of the political will, in relation to the development and transfer of clean technology, is the abiding problem of poverty.

Logically, there are only two possible solutions to the poverty problem. Either the poor must be free to travel to the North to participate in its materially richer lifestyle, or a serious effort must be made to raise the standard of living in the South. The latter cannot be achieved by the multilateral and national aid agencies working at their present scale and within their present policy constraints. The South cannot be transformed simply by small injections of capital and technical aid. More than anything the South requires markets to which to export its resources. It is a double waste of money for the countries of the North to subsidize their own farmers and obsolescent industries and then fund their aid agencies to carry out a hopeless task. What might help more would be to shift their resources into research and development to create higher-value-added goods and services, freeing up the older market niches for exports from the South. The desperate need to develop environmentally friendly technology should provide a major incentive for expanded research and development. There is no reason to assume that this sectoral shift in the Northern economies will lead to a net loss in employment on a national, or even a regional, scale. This opening up of the North's markets will not be easy, as anybody who followed the Uruguay round of the General Agreement on Tariffs and Trade knows. However, it is a prerequisite for the eradication of poverty, providing drinking-water for all, and all the other ambitious objectives of the development effort. (I think the long-run alternative to opening up international markets is a doomed attempt to stem the tide of illegal migration.)

If the South has more markets to compete in, other elements of the aid program might make some headway. The new program should include an expanded commitment to the provision and maintenance of social and physical infrastructure, such as water, health, and education, which Jan Pronk has referred to as the 'global public sector' (Pronk 1990). Like public health in the nineteenth-century industrial cities, global public health should be accepted as being in everybody's interest and worth paying for. Despite the budgetary difficulties, this implies that additional resources need to be transferred from the North to the South. The additional resources can be justified only on condition that the South becomes committed to a reduction in the population growth rate. This can be done without recourse to Draconian measures, as has been demonstrated by the 'child-spacing approach' to family planning started in Malawi. Using this approach, health practitioners take as their objective the health of the mother and the children and propose that a greater lapse of time between births is one way to achieve this. The reduction in the number of births is then a by-product of the program, not its overt goal.

None of this will be easy. In the previous paragraph I have suggested the need to do two very unpopular things. The North is firmly against 'additionality' (i.e., providing additional resources) and the South is equally firmly against 'conditionality' (i.e., being told how to run its internal affairs). Nevertheless, both sides will have to yield if a solution to the poverty problem is to be found. Only when this has been assured can we turn to the technical side of the environmental crisis with some grounds for optimism.

Technology

Although the technical agenda may be approached in many different ways, the following four steps are essential:
- an environmental audit on all scales of activity, i.e., a materials balance assessment for each nation, each city, each company, and eventually, each household
- the setting of goals for emission reduction, moving towards zero discharge of the most problematic residuals
- the provision of financial and legal incentives to develop clean technology
- the free diffusion of clean technology

Some of the difficulties we may anticipate in implementing these steps have already been mentioned. Environmental audits and goals for emission reduction both suffer from the same difficulty of finding the best unit of account, as was first discussed in Chapter 3 in the context of carbon dioxide emissions. Along the road to emission reduction it is useful to set national goals in order to develop a coordinated global policy. In the long run, however, all producing units will have to conform to higher standards or go out of production. As was suggested in Chapter 3 this can be implemented effectively only if supervised internationally. Worldwide standards are a reasonable expectation only if the approved technology is freely available.

Financial and legal incentives to develop clean technology are discussed in the next section. If we assume for the moment that such technology can be developed, how can it most effectively be distributed? Existing means of distribution include transnational corporations and the development agencies. Additional use could be made of environmental NGOs and of 'twinned' cities from the North and South. So far the twinning of cities in the rich North and the poor South has been done altruistically, for the most part, to provide training for the South's city managers during brief visits to their partners in the North. The assumption is that the North has 'cities that work' that can serve as models for the South. This is a very questionable assumption, for at least two reasons. First, even if there are some successes in the North, they may be difficult to transfer to the cities of the South, for the reasons outlined in Chapter 9. The cities of the South are much poorer, they are growing much faster, and many are already much bigger. Second, the cities of the North have experienced some persistent failures, in that they have only just begun to contemplate the garbage crisis and most cities have remained indifferent to the long-term problems, such as homelessness and reduced life expectancy, of their own low-income and unemployed people. What might be more useful for citizens of the North and South would be for them to examine their problems together. When 'trainees' from the South come to the North they may be interested in a tour of the problems, not the showpieces. They may well be able to suggest to their Northern counterparts new approaches to handling the problems of street-people, new approaches to community participation, and new approaches to recycling waste materials.

Where might the money for this global public sector and global distribution of clean technology be found?

Incentives

There are at least four possible sources of financial resources for clean technology:

- taxes on pollution, such as a carbon tax
- the recovery, through the price mechanism, of the full cost of environmental goods, like water
- gains in efficiency from the reduction of waste and the reduced need for environmental rehabilitation, such as clean-ups after oil spills
- the 'peace dividend,' that is, the money no longer spent on armaments, as a result of *détente* between the former Soviet Union and the United States

A major source of financing should be from taxes on the production of all residuals, including carbon dioxide. A tax calculated in relation to the amount of carbon released would immediately create a financial incentive for a company to move to less-polluting forms of energy. The proceeds from these taxes could then be spent on developing and distributing improved technology, thus setting up a feedback loop in our production systems that should work progressively towards the elimination of unwanted residuals.

Other applications of the price mechanism, encouraged by legislation, could improve the environment at no net cost to society. For example, if the principle of full-cost recovery were legislated for environmental goods such as water, then users would have to pay to restore water to its original condition, i.e. (in most cases), so that is potable for human beings. Right now, in North America and Europe, some consumers are prepared to buy bottled water at many times the cost of tap water, because they do not trust the quality of the water in the tap. Other people put in cumbersome filtering systems, with little guarantee that the water coming through the filter is any better than the water in the tap.

If municipal waste water were better treated, then local beaches might become usable for recreation again, avoiding the need for lengthy trips just to find an outdoor place to swim in the summer, for those who have the means to travel. For households and for the public sector there are myriad ways in which higher environmental standards will result in reduced costs, not increased costs. (See, for example, *The Canadian Green Consumer's Guide*, by Pollution Probe, 1989.) The 'healthy city' concept is being promoted to help cities reduce the costs of health care (Ashton 1992; Toronto Board of Health 1988). A similar argument can be made for environmental rehabilitation in general. For the private sector the argument was made some time ago that there was *Profit from Pollution Prevention* (Campbell and Glenn 1982). But the word travels slowly, and there is still a general impression in the private sector that new equipment will represent a heavy cost, that prices must rise to cover this, that those companies forced to prevent pollution by overzealous governments will lose market share, and that plants will close. It is true, under existing legislation, that plants may close if they continue to pollute. But it does not follow that the continued existence of industrial firms depends on their freedom to pollute.

Other important entrenched attitudes of relevance to financing a global clean-up are improving. For example, advertising and the wasteful packaging and processing that goes with it are also under pressure. Now that the cost of municipal waste disposal is rising dramatically in Europe and North America, the fact that one-third of household waste is composed of containers and packaging is a matter of more than incidental concern (Uusitalo 1986: 77). When consumers have to pay significantly more for waste disposal they may begin to wonder how badly they need all the packaging they buy. On average, the packaging itself accounts for 10 per cent of the price of the goods; then the consumer-as-taxpayer has to pay to have the waste packaging taken away. Already some consumers accept that they do not have to have coffee filters and bathroom tissues bleached white, let alone have those white tissues later dyed pink or green. Judicious legislation of packaging will produce immediate savings for the consumer, the taxpayer, and the producer.

Finally, if the efficiency of pollution prevention does not convince the sceptics, then surely the evident costs of inaction and the eventual cost of clean-up should do so. The Exxon oil company put the direct costs of the *Exxon Valdez* oil spill in Alaska at more than two billion dollars. Yet technology exists at a fraction of that cost to greatly reduce the impact of an accident. If we want to look at the ultimate carelessness in industrial management the Bhopal case is sobering. The death toll has now reached nearly 4,000, and the Government of India has rejected the $470 million offer from Union Carbide; instead, it is reopening a claim for $2.5 billion in compensation (*Globe and Mail*, 23 January 1990). Costs such as these may seem small once the bill for global warming starts coming in.

For some years now, when people have begun to make estimates of the

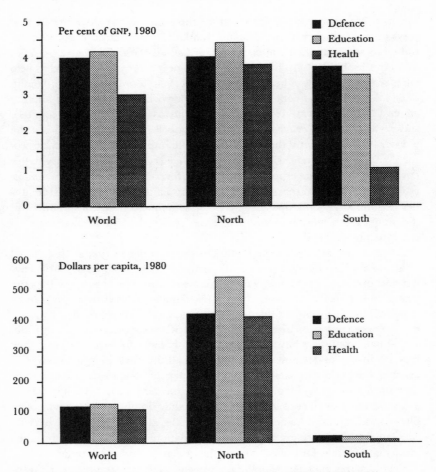

Figure 12.1. Military and social expenditures (from World Bank 1984: 150)

costs of environmental reform, they have made comparisons with the sums of money spent on military expenditure. As long ago as 1984, the World Bank made a comparison between military and social (health and education) expenditures (see Figure 12.1). It was useful to make such comparisons, just to put the number of billions of dollars in perspective. Yet matters went no further than the comparison, given that the pressure of the Cold War, the political weight of the military establishment, and the profitability of the arms trade seemed to preclude any serious discussion on the possibility of reducing armaments expenditures. Now, with the abandonment of communism in Eastern Europe and the former Soviet Union, a significant reduction in military expenditure looks distinctly possible.

Postscript

This book was in the final stages of production at the time of the United Nations Conference on Environment and Development, or Earth Summit, held in Rio de Janeiro in June 1992. As yet it is too soon to assess the achievements of the conference as most of the agreements were not legally binding, while the two treaties that were signed will not come into force until they have been ratified by at least thirty of the signatory nations. What was signed included the following:

- a Treaty on Climate Change which acknowledges the threat of global warming and possible sea-level rise and requires the signatories to submit reports on their emission levels; it is simply suggested that the North stabilize its emissions at the 1990 level by the year 2000
- a Treaty on Biodiversity which recognizes the need for nations to protect the biodiversity within their borders
- a set of 21 principles called the Rio Declaration which included a statement that nations should not damage the environment of other nations, but which reaffirms the sovereign rights of each nation to pursue policies of its own choosing
- an 800-page action plan known as Agenda 21, which lists many of the environmental problems mentioned in this book, from desertification to the international trade in toxic wastes
- a proposal to set up a Commission for Sustainable Development under the auspices of the United Nations
- a statement of Forest Principles which could serve as the basis for a later treaty

Individual countries from the North made pledges to support environmental programs in the South, but these were quite small compared with the estimated costs of fundamental environmental rehabilitation. No nation assumed a leadership position to fill the void left by the United States, which refused to sign the Treaty on Biodiversity and signed the Treaty on Climate Change only after it had been stripped of all operational significance. The European Community's Commissioner for the Environment did not attend the conference at all, on the grounds that nothing meaningful would be decided. The problems of rapid population growth in the South and overconsumption in the North were both buried in the small print.

By this reckoning it would not be difficult to dismiss the conference as a missed opportunity and a waste of money. It could easily be portrayed as a cynical charade designed to raise expectations and give the false impression that the world leaders were doing something about the environmental crisis.

It is also possible to see the conference in a more positive light as a first step along a cooperative path. About 170 nations were represented, including many heads of state. The president of the United States dined at the same table as Fidel Castro, although they did not converse. The fact that the North and the South have very different environmental priorities became abundantly clear and the confrontation that this difference provoked was probably inevitable. The fact that the countries of the South would not debate the population issue, or promise to preserve their forests, was to be expected. The fact that the United States would not sign the Biodiversity Treaty, which was full of ambiguous phrases about rights and patents, was not surprising either. The fact that the North's additional cash offers were for token amounts, and that any sizeable sums would go through the World Bank's Global Environmental Facility, was also predictable.

The most useful assumption, perhaps, is that the conference marked the beginning of an arduous process in which humanity commits itself to the rehabilitation of the planet. Nothing less than this is required. Indeed, it is no exaggeration to say that humanity is at a turning-point in its social evolution, a point which could be as significant as the moment when primates descended from the trees and began to dig around with sticks. The turning-point this time is the choice between continuing competition between nations and cooperation. As Robert Axelrod concluded in his book *The Evolution of Cooperation*: 'The core of the problem of how to achieve results from cooperation is that trial and error in learning is slow and painful ... Perhaps if we understand the process better, we can use our foresight to speed up the evolution of cooperation' (1990: 191).

Indeed, in the past few years some remarkable progress has been made in addressing the environmental crisis. The signing of the CFC Protocol, the meetings of the Intergovernmental Panel on Climate Change, the United Nations Commission on Environment and Development, and the Rio Conference itself would have been almost unthinkable twenty years ago. Perhaps there will even be a revival of interest in a comprehensive Law of the Sea. And, if the financial incentives are put in place, there is little reason to doubt that human ingenuity can develop clean technologies to power our production and transportation systems.

However, capital, technology, and material incentives can take us only so far, and that will not be far enough to escape the present crisis. System closure brings the survival of the species in question, as the poor are more numerous and more mobile than ever before in the history of the planet. Yet the nations of the world, divided as they are into North and South, face an institutional blockage. Our international institutions, such as the United Nations, are dependent on the nations themselves and thus they find it difficult to espouse a truly global perspective. Willy Brandt suggested that we need a Security Council of the Environment to do this. For such a council to take effective leadership, however, it would have to work towards harmony for humanity as a whole, not simply arbitrate between the separate interests of nations.

Glossary

The Glossary contains some technical terms used in the text which may be unfamiliar to the general reader, as well as some key environmental events.

acidification A process in which airborne pollutants such as sulphur oxides and nitrogen oxides react with water vapour to produce weak acidic compounds. When precipitated they reduce life in lakes and weaken the clay binding of minerals in soils. The soils become impoverished and the minerals may accumulate in the food chain. See **bio-accumulation** and **precipitation**.

albedo effect The effect of changes in the degree to which a land surface reflects sunlight. For example, snow has a high albedo; thus the extension of the area covered by snow, due to climate change, may have further impacts on the evolution of the climate.

algal blooms, algae Algae are primitive plants; some are aquatic. Pollutant-enriched water bodies may encourage algae to thrive, and they in turn will reduce the amount of oxygen available in the water to other aquatic life, such as fish. If sufficiently nourished by the accumulation of fertilizer wastes, like nitrogen and phosphorus, the algae may 'bloom' to cover extensive areas of surface water.

Amoco Cadiz A Liberian-registered oil tanker which foundered on the coast of Brittany in March 1978. The spillage of 228,000 tonnes of oil was nearly twice that of any other tanker spill up to that time.

anthropogenic climate change Global patterns of climate change constantly as a result of the interplay of a multitude of natural factors, such as variations in the earth's orbit around the sun. Anthropogenic climate changes are those caused by the influence of human beings, such as desertification resulting from overgrazing or an increase of carbon dioxide in the atmosphere caused by the burning of fossil fuels.

appropriate technology Some technology exported from advanced industrial countries is deemed to be inappropriate if it cannot be maintained in lower-income countries, or if it replaces some locally viable technology, or if it has adverse impacts on the environment.

aquifer, fossil aquifer an aquifer is an underground body of water, sometimes continuous, but more commonly residing in fissures in the rock. An aquifer is formed by the seepage of water through the ground until it reaches the local water-table. If there is no longer any seepage (because of climate change) to recharge the aquifer, then it is said to be a fossil aquifer.

Atlantic conveyor current A deep, salty current that regulates the exchange of heat within the global circulation of the oceans. It is believed that this particular deep current acts as a 'thermostat' which reacts to changes in the earth's climate.

atmosphere A thin layer of gases that surrounds the earth to a depth of 45 km, 99 per cent consisting of oxygen and nitrogen. The lower 10 km is known as the troposphere, the upper 35 km as the stratosphere.

available, or usable, energy Bodily or organic energy is known as somatic energy; organisms avail themselves of it by photosynthesis (in the case of plants) or by ingestion (in the case of mammals, fish, etc.). Fossil fuels, running water, and other planetary processes provide potential forms of extra-somatic (non-biological) energy for those creatures (such as human beings) that can harness it – for example, through combustion or by building dams or water-wheels.

Bhopal An industrial town in northern India that, in December 1984, was the scene of the world's worst industrial accident, in which over 2,000 people were killed outright by the escape of methyl isocyanate from a fertilizer factory. The victims' claims for compensation have still not been met.

bio-accumulation, bio-magnification Aluminum, heavy metals, and natural and synthetic compounds are being released into the environment in increasing quantities as a result of human activities. It is possible for these materials to build up at any place in the **food chain**. As lower members of the chain are consumed by higher members the materials tend to accumulate in heavier and heavier concentrations.

biogas Gas produced by the natural process of decomposition of vegetal matter. The most common biogas is methane, which is flammable. It is possible to build biogas digesters that make methane available in combustible form, which can then be used to produce electricity.

bio-geochemical cycles Chemicals such as oxygen, carbon, nitrogen, and phosphorus constantly cycle through the air, sea, and land components of the biosphere through their various **environmental pathways**. The concept of a bio-geochemical cycle attempts to relate the small-scale movements of chemicals through a farmer's field or a stream to shifts in their displacement on a global scale.

biomass Any vegetal matter. To estimate the vegetal productivity of a particular place the weight of vegetal matter in a sample area is measured.

biosphere 'That portion of the earth in which people and organisms can live, that is the biologically inhabitable soil, air and water' (E.P. Odum 1989: 28).

BOD Biological oxygen demand, which is an important measure of water quality. The more organisms, (including bacteria) that reside in the water, demanding

Glossary 185

oxygen, the less oxygen there is available for other organisms, such as fish. As BOD increases through increasing deposits of sewage, for example, established aquatic life, such as plants and fish, dies off.

boundaries The limits that define systems in general systems theory (GST).

Brandt Commission The International Commission on International Development Issues, chaired by Willy Brandt in 1980. See **North, South.**

Brundtland Commission and Report The World Commission on Environment and Development which met from 1983 to 1985, chaired by Gro Harlem Brundtland.

buffering, ocean and limestone The ability of the environment to reduce the impact of a chemical. For example, the ocean acts as a buffer for increased output of carbon dioxide, as it can absorb additional CO_2 by mixing at the air-sea interface. Limestone (calcium carbonate) acts as a buffer for acid deposition, as it is an alkali.

bush burning An agricultural practice of clearing the land for planting by burning off the vegetation, which is still common in low-income countries. It gives a one-time deposit of the nutrients that were stored in the trees. Traditionally this method was used as part of a system of bush-fallowing, which allowed the forest to return after a few years of agricultural use.

carbon tax Because carbon dioxide (CO_2) build-up is seen as the most potentially damaging human-induced environmental change, it has been proposed that all producers of carbon should pay a tax proportional to their output of carbon. This would encourage manufacturers to reduce their carbon emissions, and the payment of the tax would provide a fund for environmental rehabilitation.

CFCs Short form for chlorofluorocarbons, synthetic compounds used for aerosols, refrigerators, solvents, and foam packaging. In the stratosphere CFCs deplete the ozone layer which is shielding the earth from harmful ultraviolet radiation.

Chernobyl A nuclear power station in Ukraine that in April 1986 was the scene of the world's worst nuclear disaster. There were thirty-one immediate deaths when the reactor exploded, but this was followed by the threat of countless more deaths as the radioactive air mass spread out over Europe. For an analysis of the implications of the accident see Peter Gould's *Fire in the Rain* (1990).

clear-cutting The practice of cutting wide expanses of forests down to the ground, rather than selecting particular trees or stands of trees for removal. Clear-cutting is cheaper in the short term for the timber company, but it does much more damage to the soil than does selective cutting.

CO_2, CO_2 build-up, carbon dioxide The combustion of fossil fuels and trees releases additional carbon into the atmosphere, carbon that was formerly fixed in the ground or in the forest cover. It is generally believed that the build-up of carbon dioxide in the atmosphere will trap heat radiated from the earth's surface, leading to a gradual warming of the atmosphere.

continental drift In the 1920s Alfred Wegener proposed that the continental masses were not stable, but shifted slowly over the earth's surface as tectonic plates. Their movements explain the concentrated patterns of earthquakes and volcanic activity.

DDT Stands for Dichlorodiphenyltrichloroethane, an organochloride compound of chlorine, carbon, and hydrogen which was the first effective pesticide to be marketed worldwide in the 1940s. Among other uses, it proved to be a very effective pesticide against malaria-bearing mosquitoes. However, after a few years it became clear that pesticides like DDT threatened human health. Also they had only a short- term effectiveness against crop pests if they killed more of the pests' predators than the pests themselves, or if the pests developed a resistance to the treatment.

demographic transition The transition of the human population from an early stage of high death rates and high birth rates to a steady-state, replacement stage of low birth rates and low death rates.

developed, developing countries Developed countries are the early industrial powers of Western Europe and North America, later joined by Australia, New Zealand, and Japan. Developing countries are mostly former colonies of the European colonial powers which were expected to diversify their agrarian economies into modern industrial economies after decolonization. Some did; some did not.

diet transition As people become wealthier their diet moves away from traditional grains (such as millet and sorghum) to rice and wheat, and then from grains to meat.

directly productive activities (DPAs) Economic activities that produce a marketable product. Early orthodoxy in development economics in the 1950s held that international development agencies should leave DPAs to the private sector. After a period of interventionism in the 1960s and 1970s, this view of private-sector responsibility for DPAs came back in the guise of market forces.

DO Dissolved oxygen; the amount of oxygen available for respiration by aquatic organisms. As **BOD** increases, DO goes down.

draw-down. See **aquifer**. People, through drilling wells, gain access to **groundwater** in significant amounts. If they withdraw in excess of the natural recharge rate, the water-table will begin to fall; this is draw-down.

driving, or forcing, variables The variables, in terms of general systems theory (**GST**), that may change the nature of the system. For contemporary purposes, the driving variables behind the environmental crisis are the rapid growth of the human population and the increased access of the richer portion of that population to more and more of Nature's capital.

early chemical age An optimistic term of my own invention. Don Mackay first introduced me to the idea of the chemical age, that being the age when people began mastering naturally occurring chemicals and then creating chemicals of their own invention. We see the negative consequences of this development around us. I hope that we will soon learn to control the forces we have unleashed; then the era of early error might be characterized as the *early* chemical age.

energy, somatic and extra-somatic See **available, or usable, energy**.

energy transition As human societies become more complex they avail themselves of more energy, in both quantity and variety. Generally they move to energy sources of higher calorific value – for example, from wood to coal, then to oil. They access a higher calorie flow, but the environmental consequences of the transition become more complex.

entropy Disorder. According to the Second Law of Thermodynamics all systems pass inexorably towards entropy. In so far as we turn potential forms of energy (coal, oil) to waste heat, we accelerate the progression towards entropy. However, humans create complex systems that make more energy available to them. In a physical sense entropy is inevitable; in a social sense it is the constant challenge. The opposite of entropy is order, or negentropy.

environmental currency We are aware that dollars and cents do not measure the essential nature of humanity and the environment. We do not, however, have a simple, universal environmental currency as an alternative. Research into the development of an environmental currency has focused on the preservation of usable **energy**, the conservation of **biomass**, and the maximization of negentropy. See **entropy**.

environmental goods Includes clean air, water, and naturally productive soil; the goods that humans use, but do not usually pay for. Environmental goods used to be considered free goods in the language of economics. Now that we have overloaded natural systems, these formerly free goods are becoming scarce.

environmental pathway The route followed by any substance through environmental systems. For example, we can trace the pathway of **DDT** sprayed on a field, vaporizing into the atmosphere, sticking to vegetal matter, percolating through **groundwater** to a stream, being carried to the ocean, and then subsiding to the ocean depths.

eutrophication The natural process whereby water bodies absorb more and more oxygen-demanding material, such as plants and bacteria, and as the oxygen is depleted, aquatic life forms die out and the water body becomes dry land. This natural process is accelerated by human inputs of oxygen-demanding material, such as fertilizer run-off, and sewage. See **BOD**; **algal blooms**.

evolutionary paradigm Ilya Prigogine and his colleagues carried out several studies in the 1970s that showed that many natural systems did not degrade toward **entropy**, but at certain critical points (called bifurcations) formed new structures by undergoing irreversible change. It was this process of structure-forming that was responsible for the evolution of new systems, according to this paradigm.

externalities, economic Modern economics, like general systems theory (GST), defines elements as being either within, or external to, the system being studied. Thus, if there was no penalty for a factory that polluted the environment, then the pollution was an 'externality' to the economics of the factory.

Exxon Valdez An American oil tanker that ran aground in March 1989 shortly after leaving its home port of Valdez, Alaska. 'Only' 35,000 tonnes of oil were spilled, but the wind and current drove the oil onto a 300-mile stretch of wilderness coastline. The oil company paid out a record of more than two billion dollars in clean-up costs even before going before the courts to face compensation claims.

feedback, positive and negative Positive feedbacks encourage a system to grow or become more complex; negative feedbacks restrain a system, sometimes to the point of extinction.

food chain Higher life forms eat lower life forms in the biological pecking order. Krill are eaten by small crustaceans, which are eaten by fish, which are eaten by fish-eating birds and fish-eating humans. This is the food chain. Its relevance to the current environmental crisis lies in the **bio-accumulation** of contaminants, the vulnerability of higher orders to the demise of lower orders, and the change in overall food requirements demanded by humans in their tendency to eat more meat.

food gap Most countries import some foods and export others, to maintain their variety of diet and to provide foreign exchange. What has happened in some low-income countries is that they no longer provide the staple foodstuffs to feed their growing population. The difference between what the people need to stay alive and what their farmers produce (of the staple food products) is known as the food gap.

food security A country's ability to manage the **food gap**.

fossil fuels Fuels formed under earlier geological conditions, many of them in the Carboniferous Era, when much of the deposits of coal, oil, and natural gas exploited at present were laid down.

GDP Gross domestic product, or the value of goods and services produced in a country.

global warming Human activities are contributing to a build-up of **green-house gases** in the **atmosphere**. Most scientists think that this build-up will increase average surface temperatures of the earth by between 1° and 5°

Celsius over the next fifty years. This could lead to a worldwide rise in sea level and significant changes in worldwide climatic patterns.

GNP Gross national product, or the value of goods and services produced in a country, less the remittances paid abroad, plus the remittances received from abroad.

Grassy Meadows A village in northern Ontario where the accumulation of mercury in fish first led to a ban on fish consumption. See **heavy metals**.

green revolution In the 1960s international aid agencies introduced high-yielding varieties (**HYVs**) of rice, wheat, and maize to low-income countries. The initial results appeared as a technological breakthrough, especially in southeast Asia. However, these successes could not be replicated in Africa or Latin America for political reasons, and, even in Asia, some of the early successes faded in the face of resistant pests.

greenhouse effect Trace gases in the atmosphere reflect back the heat that is radiated up from the earth's surface, analogous to the effect of a greenhouse. This is what keeps the earth warm enough to be habitable. However, the anthropogenic increase in **greenhouse gases** now threatens to increase this heat-trapping effect and introduce widespread climate change, such as global warming and sea-level rise.

greenhouse gases Some are naturally occurring trace gases like carbon dioxide, methane, nitrous oxide, and ozone, but they are now greatly augmented by human activities. Artificial gases, like CFCs, also contribute to the **greenhouse effect**.

groundwater Fresh water that lies in the ground. Some of it is replenished by percolation from the surface. See **aquifer**.

GST General systems theory; a theory which represents all types of systems, natural, human, and theoretical. The main postulate is that the essential elements of a system may be defined by flows across boundaries.

habitat That part of the environment inhabited by a species or a group of species.

heat island The centres of modern cities contain massive concentrations of cement, steel, and other heat-absorbing materials. They also tend to include relatively little vegetation, and they are subject to waste heat emissions from buildings and vehicles. These factors tend to raise the temperature above that of the suburbs and surrounding countryside, especially in the summer months. This temperature elevation is known as the urban heat-island effect.

heavy metals Naturally occurring metals like cadmium, mercury, and lead which usually exist in low concentrations, in which state they are not harmful to humans or other species. In some circumstances they may become concentrated to levels that threaten health. For example, if a forest is **clear-cut**, then flooded by a reservoir, the tree stumps (which contain concentrated mercury) rot, releasing higher-than-usual concentrations of mercury, which could then accumulate through the **food chain**. See **bio-accumulation**.

hydrocarbons Compounds of hydrogen and carbon that occur in petroleum, natural gas, and coal. Sometimes used synonymously with **fossil fuels**.

hydrological cycle The cycle in which water continually passes over the land, to the sea, is evaporated into the atmosphere, and then precipitates back to earth. Some water rests outside this cycle for long periods, especially in fossil **aquifers**.

HYVs High-yielding varieties of crops, bred at experimental stations for distribution to smallholders. The HYVs of rice, wheat, and maize are key elements of the **green revolution**.

indicators Measurements that are taken to represent the status of a system. For example, mussels, which ingest and retain pollutants in the sea, are used as indicators of the degree to which the oceans are contaminated.

infant mortality rate The number of children per 1,000 live births who die in their first twelve months. In the poorest countries the rate is as high as 150; in richer countries it falls to 9 or 10.

infrastructure, physical and social Literally the framework of a system, usually in the context of human society. Thus, physical infrastructure includes transportation, communications, water supply, and electrical power. Social infrastructure refers to health and education services, and social security.

institution building Until the 1970s the development agencies concentrated their loans to developing countries in **infrastructure** and **directly productive activities**. Many of these project loans were ineffectual because the executing agencies (such as a Ministry of Public Works) in developing countries were inadequately staffed and too poorly equipped to respond. In the 1970s there was a shift to fund projects designed to strengthen the professional capacity of such institutions through training programs and reorganization.

interurban, intra-urban Interurban issues are those that concern relations between systems of cities, such as transportation links and trade. Intra-urban issues are those that reside within a particular city, such as urban land-use planning.

latitudes, higher and lower Latitude measures the distance north and south from the equator. Higher latitudes are far away from the equator (such as the poles); lower latitudes are close to the equator (such as the tropics).

linear, non-linear relationships Linear relationships describe two variables that are directly proportional to one another; non-linear relationships are those in which they are not. Many economic relationships are assumed to be linear; most biological relationships are non-linear.

Love Canal Abandoned canal in Niagara Falls, New York, used as a dump site by a chemical company; later it was filled in and sold to the local school board, which used it as a children's playground. In 1977 floodwaters exposed the toxic chemicals in the site, and the long-term hazards posed by the chemicals were linked to many illnesses that had been reported in the vicinity. Largely as a result of this one case the American public became concerned about toxic-waste dumps and Congress passed a new law that made the dumper of the wastes responsible for their proper disposal even if the company had subsequently sold the site.

materials balance assessment, or approach A mixed economics and engineering approach to the analysis of activities, such as factories and transportation systems, in which all the physical inflows and outflows associated with the production process are measured. This is a much more comprehensive form of analysis than traditional economic project analysis, which considers only those flows that have economic significance for the activity itself.

mean passage time The time taken for a particle to pass through a given segment of an **environmental pathway** – for example, the time it takes a water particle to pass from the inflow to the outflow of a lake.

metal uptake The absorption by plants and animals of a certain quantity of metals with which they come into contact. The rate at which absorption takes place is known as the rate of uptake.

metaprocesses Large-scale social and political processes that influence human life on all levels. For example, the political struggle which determines international trade agreements may affect the daily struggle for life of the marginal smallholder.

methane The main component of natural gas and an important contributor to the **greenhouse effect**. It occurs in underground fossil reserves and is also produced at the surface through agricultural activities such as livestock raising and paddy-rice cultivation.

Minamata, Japan A heavily industrialized region, whose inhabitants, in the 1950s, registered many new illnesses, some of which were crippling. Eventually the connection between the illnesses and pollution in the area (such as mercury contamination) was proved, and in the 1960s four landmark decisions were made by the courts, ordering the companies to pay compensation to the victims. Cases are still being heard.

mortality transition As the standard of living improves the mortality rate falls, especially the infant mortality rate. Gradually the highest death rates shift from the youngest members of the population to the oldest, while the major causes of death shift from respiratory and infectious diseases towards cardiac and carcinogenic diseases.

MSY Maximum sustainable yield is the maximum annual rate of exploitation of a natural resource that can be maintained without depleting the stock. The concept was first developed for ocean fisheries and subsequently used widely in forestry management.

mussel watch See **indicators**.

niche That part of a **habitat** occupied by a particular species. Also applied to markets; a country or a product might occupy a market niche.

NICs New industrializing countries; former developing countries that are making the transition from an agrarian society to an industrial one. Some of these are large in an absolute sense (Brazil, China); others are smaller, although industry accounts for a high percentage (30 or more) of total employment and total **GNP** (Taiwan, South Korea).

NIMBY syndrome Not in my backyard syndrome. Once people became aware of the dangers of toxic-landfill sites like **Love Canal**, there arose a widespread objection to any landfill site being developed in their particular neighbourhood, whether the wastes were harmless or not, or if toxic, the toxic substances were to be properly managed.

NO$_x$, nitrogen oxides NO$_x$ is used as a short form for nitric oxide (NO) and nitrogen dioxide (NO$_2$), which are produced by the combustion of **fossil fuels** and **biomass**. Both contribute to the **acidification** of the **biosphere**.

N$_2$O, nitrous oxide A by-product of **biomass** burning and the production of nitrogenous fertilizer; an important contributor to the **greenhouse effect**.

North, South Terms used to distinguish between rich countries and poor countries, popularized by the **Brandt Commission**. See also **developed, developing countries**.

nutrients, for plants All plant nutrients occur naturally, but unevenly. Thus, modern chemical agriculture has endeavoured to make up localized nutrient deficiencies by the application of fertilizer, especially to provide additional nitrogen, phosphorus, and potassium.

OPEC The Organization of Petroleum Exporting Countries, which was the first, and is so far the only, successful Third World commodity cartel. Its members are Algeria, Ecuador, Gabon, Indonesia, Iran, Iraq, Kuwait, Libya, Nigeria, Qatar, Saudi Arabia, the United Arab Emirates, and Venezuela. It raised the price for crude petroleum from $2 per barrel in 1972 to over $30 by 1980. In real terms this was a more than sixfold increase. After 1980 new supplies and energy conservation undercut OPEC's position in the market. In real terms oil prices are now back to the 1974 level.

optimization Obtaining the best possible result. In an economic context this might mean either the maximum output from a given set of inputs or the minimum input required for a given level of output.

ozone, O$_3$ A trace gas in the atmosphere that contributes to the **greenhouse effect** in the troposphere, but screens out harmful **ultraviolet radiation** in the stratosphere. See **atmosphere**.

PAHs Polycyclic aromatic hydrocarbons; an important contributor to urban air pollution derived from the incomplete combustion of fossil fuels.

PCBs Polychlorinated biphenyls; organochlorides used in the electrical and plastic industries, later found to be persistent and toxic.

pH Stands for positive hydrogen ions. A low pH value signifies **acidification.**

photosynthesis The process by which chlorophyll-bearing plants use sunlight to convert carbon dioxide (CO_2) and water to sugars.

potable water Water that can be drunk by human beings without adverse effects.

precipitation The condensation of water vapour in the atmosphere to form rain, snow, hail, fog, and dew.

primary energy The inputs used in the production of extra-somatic energy – **fossil fuels,** nuclear power, and hydroelectricity. This excludes energy in electrical form to avoid double-counting in the compilation of an energy budget. See **available, or usable, energy**.

product life-cycle engineering An approach to engineering which recognizes that the manufacture and use of goods produces unwanted **residuals** and that the safe disposal of these residuals should be an integral part of the design process.

R and D budget The budget spent in the public or private sector on the research and development of new products.

replacement cost, true price The market price of a good plus the cost of ensuring that the earth can continue to produce the good in question. Thus, agricultural products should carry the cost of cleansing the water and maintaining the soil productivity that made the production of the goods possible.

residuals, from economic activities Waste products – solids, polluted water, and polluted air. See **product life-cycle engineering**.

resilience The capacity of a system to return to proper functioning after a period of stress which may result in a temporary loss of output. This concept is juxtaposed with that of resistance, in which stress is withstood up to a certain degree, and then collapse follows.

Rio Conference The United Nations Conference on Environment and Development (UNCED), popularly known as the Earth Summit, which took place in Rio de Janeiro in June 1992.

savannah A tropical grassland zone lying between the tropical forest and the scrublands of the semidesert. The savannah is used for low-intensity cultivation and grazing. Generally this zone receives between 1,000 and 400 mm of rainfall per year, usually in one, or sometimes two, brief rainy seasons.

shoaling fish Fish that swim in large groups often close to the surface, and are thereby very susceptible to overfishing by large-scale trawlers; e.g., herring, mackerel, and anchovy.

sink A place in which **residuals**, such as waste heat, carbon dioxide (CO_2), or other unwanted substances, will collect.

SO_2, sulphur dioxide An important contributor to **acidification**, produced as a by-product of **fossil fuel** consumption and the smelting of sulphide ores, such as zinc, copper, and nickel.

solar radiation Energy reaching earth from the sun. Much of the **ultraviolet** and infrared ends of the spectrum are absorbed by trace gases, like **ozone**, in the stratosphere.

Stockholm Conference The 1972 United Nations Conference on the Human Environment which acted as a springboard for the modern environmental movement.

stratosphere, stratospheric ozone See **atmosphere** and **ozone**.

structural adjustment loan A type of loan developed in the 1980s by the World Bank for developing countries to encourage them to change their economic policies, principally by reducing public-sector involvement in the economy in favour of market forces.

systems ecology The application of general systems theory (**GST**) to ecological systems.

Third World The First World consists of the early industrialized market economies and the Second World consisted of the centrally planned (or communist) economies; the Third World is the rest – poor, mostly ex-colonial countries, sometimes referred to as **developing countries**, or the South. See **North, South**.

trace gases The gases that make up less than 1 per cent of the **atmosphere**, such as **carbon dioxide, ozone,** and **methane**.

transboundary, transgenerational pollution Pollution that crosses international boundaries; pollution that persists for more than one human generation. The major atmospheric pollutants and marine pollution fit both categories.

troposphere, tropospheric ozone See **atmosphere** and **ozone**.

ultraviolet radiation See **solar radiation**.

usufruct The right to use land without owning it; the most common form of land tenure in Africa, based on customary rights and lineage systems.

water-table See **aquifer**.

WCED, World Commission on Environment and Development; see **Brundtland Commission and Report**.

References

Agarwal, Anil, and Sunita Narain. 1991. *Global Warming in an Unequal World: A Case of Environmental Colonialism.* New Delhi: Centre for Science and Environment

Akbari, H., A. Rosenfeld, and H. Taha. 1989. Recent Developments in Heat Island Studies: Technical and Policy. In Garbesi, Akbari, and Martien (eds.), 14–31

Allen, Peter. 1980. *The Evolutionary Paradigm of Dissipative Structures*, AAAS Symposium Series 61. Boulder: Westview Press

Allen, Peter, and M. Sanglier. 1981. Urban Evolution, Self-organisation and Decision-making. *Environment and Planning, A* 13: 167–83

Anderson, Dennis. 1987. *The Economics of Afforestation: A Case Study of Africa.* World Bank Occasional Paper 1. New Series. Baltimore: Johns Hopkins

Anton, Danilo. 1990. *Urban Environments and Water in Latin America with Particular Reference to Groundwater.* IDRC Reports, October. Ottawa: International Development Research Centre

Arrhenius, Erik, and Thomas W. Waltz. 1990. *The Greenhouse Effect: Implications for Economic Development.* World Bank Discussion Papers 78. Washington, DC

Arrhenius, Svante. 1896. On the Influence of Carbonic Acid in the Air upon the Temperature of the Ground. *Philosophical Magazine*

Ashton, John (ed.). 1992. *Healthy Cities.* Milton Keynes: Open University Press

Axelrod, Robert. 1990. *The Evolution of Cooperation.* Harmondsworth: Penguin Books

Basta, Daniel J., and Blair T. Bower (eds.). 1982. *Analyzing Natural Systems: Analysis for Regional Residuals – Environmental Quality Management.* Washington, DC: Resources for the Future

Bingen, R. James. 1985. *Food Production and Rural Development in the Sahel: Lessons from Mali's Operation Riz-Segou.* Boulder: Westview Press

Bower, Blair T. 1977. *Regional Residuals Environmental Quality Management Modeling*, Research Paper R-7. Washington, DC: Resources for the Future

Bower, Blair T., and Rob Koudstaal. 1986. Managing Coastal Waters: Why, Who, What, How? In *Analyzing Biospheric Change: Final Report*, 38–61. Solna: IFIAS

Brandt Commission (Independent Commission on International Development Issues). 1980. *North–South: A Programme for Survival.* London: Pan Books

Briggs, David, and Peter Smithson. 1985. *Fundamentals of Physical Geography*.
London: Hutchinson

Broecker, Wallace, and George Denton. 1990. What Drives Glacial Cycles?
Scientific American, January: 49–56

Brown, Lester. 1988. *State of the World 1988*. A Worldwatch Institute Report on
Progress toward a Sustainable Society. New York: W.W. Norton

– 1989. *State of the World 1989*. A Worldwatch Institute Report on Progress
Toward a Sustainable Society. New York: W.W. Norton

Brundtland Commission (World Commission on Environment and Development).
1987. *Our Common Future*. Oxford: Oxford University Press

Bubenick, D.V. 1984. *Acid Rain Information Book*, 2nd ed. Park Ridge, NJ: Noyes

Bugnicourt, Jacques. 1991. ONG: Tous les chemins mènent–ils à Rio? *Ecodecision*
1: 26–31

Burton, Ian. 1983. The Vulnerability of Cities. In White and Burton (eds.),
Chapter 11

Campbell, Monica, and William Glenn. 1982. *Profit from Pollution Prevention*.
Toronto: Pollution Probe

Carson, Rachel. 1962. *Silent Spring*. Boston: Houghton Mifflin

CEEC (Centre Européen Echanges Commerciaux). 1988. A New Process for Sea
Water and Saline Water Desalination by Solar Energy. Unpublished document

City of Hannover. 1991. Ecology and Local Government Politics in the City of
Hannover. Landeshauptstadt Hannover. Unpublished document

City of Toronto. 1991. *The Changing Atmosphere: Strategies for Reducing CO_2 Emissions*,
vol. 1, *Policy Overview*; vol. 2, *Technical Volume*, Special Advisory Committee on
the Environment, Report No. 2, Toronto

Clark, R.B. 1989. *Marine Pollution*, 2nd ed. Oxford: Clarendon Press

Climate Institute. 1991. International Conference on Cities and Global Change,
Toronto, Canada, 12–14 June

Cogels, F.-X., and J.-G. Gac. 1983. Circulation et salinité des eaux du Lac de
Guiers: Problèmes de développement et modèle de gestion, and La chlorinité
des eaux du Lac de Guiers (Sénégal): Bilan quantitatif, qualitatif et perspec-
tives. In Institut des Sciences de l'Environnement, 25–59

Colby, Michael E. 1990. *Environmental Management in Development: The Evolution of
Paradigms*. World Bank Discussion Paper 80, Washington, DC

Colinvaud, Paul. 1982. *Why Big Fierce Animals Are Rare: An Ecologist's Perspective*.
Princeton: Princeton University Press

Commoner, Barry. 1971. *The Closing Circle*. New York: Knopf

Council on Environmental Quality and the Department of State. 1977. *The Global
2000 Report to the President: Entering the 21st Century*, vol. 1. Washington, DC: U.S.
Government Printing Office

Dekker, Lies, Blair T. Bower, and Rob Koudstaal. 1987. *Management of Toxic*

Materials in an International Setting, a Case Study of Cadmium in the North Sea. IFIAS Research Series 3. Rotterdam: A.A. Balkena

Dumont, René, and Marie-France Mottin. 1982. *Le Défi sénégalais.* ENDA Série Etudes et Recherches 74–82. Dakar: ENDA

Ekins, Paul, with Mayer Hillman and Robert Hutchinson. 1992. *Wealth beyond Measure: An Atlas of New Economics.* London: Gaia Books

Engelhard, Philippe, and Taoufik Ben Abdallah. 1986. *Enjeux de l'Après-barrage: Vallée du Sénégal.* Dakar: ENDA

Environment Canada. 1988. *The Changing Atmosphere: Implications for Global Security. Conference Statement.* Toronto, 27–30 July

Farman, Joseph, B. Gardiner, and J. Shanklin. 1985. Large Losses of Total Ozone in Antarctica Reveal Seasonal ClO_x/NO_x Interaction. *Nature,* May 16

Firor, John W. 1988. The Heating up of the World's Climate. In Thorkil Kristensen and Johan Paludan (eds.), Chapter 3, 52–67

Flavin, Christopher. 1989. *Slowing Global Warming: A Worldwide Strategy.* Worldwatch Paper 91. Washington, DC: Worldwatch Institute

Gac, J.-G., and F.-X. Cogels. 1986. An Assessment of the Impact on Lac de Guiers by Dam Construction on the Senegal River. *Water Quality Bulletin,* 11/2: 82–117

Garbesi, Karina, Hashem Akbari, and Phil Martien (eds.). 1989. *Controlling Summer Heat Islands.* Berkeley: Energy Analysis Program, Lawrence Berkeley Laboratory

Garcia, Rolando. 1981. *Drought and Man – The 1972 Case History.* Volume 1 of *Nature Pleads Not Guilty.* Oxford: Pergamon Press

Gasherebuka, T. 1985. Comportements energetiques des ménages à Dakar: Le cas de la Gueule Tapée. Thesis for the Diplôme des Etudes Approfondies en Sciences de l'Environnement, Université de Dakar, Dakar

Glantz, Michael. 1987. Impacts of the 1982–83 Climate Anomalies in the West African Sahel. In Glantz, Katz, and Krenz (eds.), Chapter 10

Glantz, Michael, Richard Katz, and Maria Krenz (eds.). 1987. *The Societal Impacts Associated with the 1982–83 Worldwide Climate Anomalies.* Boulder: National Center for Atmospheric Research, in association with WMO and UNEP

Gordon, David (ed.). 1990. *Green Cities: Ecologically Sound Approaches to Urban Space.* Montreal: Black Rose Books

Goubert, Jean-Pierre. 1989. *The Conquest of Water: The Advent of Health in the Industrial Age.* Oxford: Polity Press and Basil Blackwell

Goudie, Andrew. 1983. *Environmental Change,* 2nd ed. Oxford: Clarendon Press
– 1990. *The Human Impact on the Natural Environment,* 3rd ed. Oxford: Basil Blackwell

Gould, Peter. 1990. *Fire in the Rain: The Democratic Consequences of Chernobyl.* Cambridge: Polity Press

Government of Canada. 1990. *Canada's Green Plan for a Healthy Environment.*
Ottawa: Ministry of Supply and Services

Graedel, Thomas, and Paul Crutzen. 1989. The Changing Atmosphere. In
Managing the Earth, special Issue of *Scientific American*, September, 58–68

Grenon, Michel, and Michel Batisse (eds.). 1989. *Futures for the Mediterranean Basin:
The Blue Plan.* Oxford: Oxford University Press

Hamel, Pierre, Luc-Normand Tellier, Rodney White, and Joseph Whitney. 1986.
Forces et faiblesses des méthodes d'évaluation des impacts environnementaux. Quebec:
Bureau d'Audiences Publiques sur l'Environnement

Head, Ivan. 1991. *On a Hinge of History: The Mutual Vulnerability of South and North.*
Toronto: University of Toronto Press

Hills, Peter, and Joseph Whitney (eds.). 1988. *Environmental Quality Issues in Asian
Cities.* Hong Kong: University of Hong Kong with the University of Toronto
and IFIAS (Project Ecoville)

Hirschman, Albert O. 1984. *Getting Along Collectively: Grassroots Experiences in Latin
America.* New York: Pergamon Press

Holling, C.S. (ed.). 1978. *Adaptive Environmental Assessment and Management.* New
York: Wiley

Homer-Dixon, Thomas I. 1990. *Environmental Change and Violent Conflict, Emerging
Issues.* Occasional Paper Series of the American Academy of Arts and Sciences.
Cambridge, MA

Houghton, J.T., G.J. Jenkins, and J.J. Ephrauns (eds.). 1990. *Climate Change: The
IPCC Scientific Assessment.* Cambridge: Cambridge University Press for WMO and
UNEP

IFDA (International Federation for Development Alternatives). 1991. A Case of
Environmental Colonialism: Indian Citizens Challenge UN-US Study on Third
World's Role in Global Warming. *IFDA Dossier* 81 (April/June): 79–80

IIED/WRI. 1987. *World Resources 1987.* New York: Basic Books. See, especially, Air
Pollution and Acid Rain in the Third World: A Case Study of China

IMF (International Monetary Fund). 1989. *World Economic Outlook.* Washington, DC

Institut des Sciences de l'Environnement. 1983. *Le Lac de Guiers: Problématique de
l'environnement et de développement.* Conference proceedings of the Institut des
Sciences de l'Environnement, Université de Dakar, Dakar

IRRI (International Rice Research Institute). 1990. Rice Researchers Launch
Major Study on Global Warming. *IRRI Reporter*, December

Jäger, J., and H.L. Ferguson (eds.). 1991. *Climate Change: Science, Impacts and Policy:
Proceedings of the Second World Climatic Conference.* Cambridge: Cambridge
University Press for WMO and UNEP

Kates, Robert, and Ian Burton (eds.). 1986. *Geography, Resources and the Environment*,
vol. 1, *Selected Writing of Gilbert F. White*, vol. 2, *Themes from the Work of Gilbert F.
White.* Chicago: University of Chicago Press

Keeling, Charles D. 1987. Measurements of the Concentration of Carbon

Dioxide at Mauna Loa Observatory, Hawaii, 1958–86. Final Report of the Carbon Dioxide Information and Analysis Center, Martin-Marietta Energy Systems Inc. Oak Ridge, Tennessee

Kellogg, William, and Robert Schware. 1981. *Climate Change and Society: Consequences of Increasing Atmospheric Carbon Dioxide*. Boulder: Westview Press

Koffi, Attahi. 1989. Côte d'Ivoire: An Evaluation of Urban Management Reforms. In Stren and White (eds.), Chapter 5, 112–46

Kornprobst, J.M. (ed.). 1983. *Chimie Marine pour le Développement*. Joint publication of the Faculté des Sciences, Université de Dakar, and ENDA, Dakar

Koudstaal, Rob. 1987. *Water Quality Management Plan, North Sea: Framework for Analysis*. IFIAS Research Series 2. Rotterdam: A.A. Balkena

Kristensen, Thorkil, and Johan Paludan (eds.). 1988. *The Earth's Fragile Systems*, IFIAS Research Series 4. Boulder: Westview Press

Lagadec, Patrick. 1981. *Le risque technologique majeur: Politique, risque et processus de développement*. Paris: Pergamon Press. English translation published as *Major Technological Risk: An Assessment of Industrial Disasters*. Oxford: Pergamon Press

Laikin, Richard, Michael Jones, and Joseph Whitney. 1985. *A Simulation Model of Metropolitan Toronto's Solid Waste Management System*. Project Ecoville, Working Paper 19, Institute for Environmental Studies, University of Toronto

Lal, R. 1984. Assessment of Productivity of Tropical Soils and the Effects of Erosion. In Rijsberman and Wolman (eds.)

Lamson-Scribner, Frank, and John Huang. 1977. *Municipal Water Supply Project Analysis: Case Studies*, vols. 1 and 2. Washington, DC: Economic Development Institute of the World Bank

Lappé, Frances Moore. 1976. *Diet for a Small Planet*, rev. ed. New York: Ballantine Books

Lawrence, Peter (ed.). 1986. *World Recession and the Food Crisis in Africa*. London and Boulder: James Curry and Westview Press

Lipton, M. 1977. *Why Poor People Stay Poor: Urban Bias in World Development*. Cambridge: Harvard University Press

Lohani, Bindu N. 1982. *Urban Solid Wastes: Recovery and Recycling*. ENDA Third World Document. Dakar

Lovelock, James. 1988. *The Ages of Gaia: A Biography of Our Living Earth*. Oxford: Oxford University Press

McDougall, E. Ann (ed.). 1990. *Sustainable Agriculture in Africa*. Trenton: Africa World Press

Mackay, Donald. 1991. *Multimedia Environmental Models: The Fugacity Approach*. Chelsea, Maine: Lewis

MacNeill, Jim. 1989. Strategies for Sustainable Economic Development. *Scientific American*, September: 155–65

– 1989–90. The Greening of International Relations. *International Journal*, 451 (Winter): 1–35

MacNeill, Jim, Pieter Winsemius, and Taizo Yakushiji. 1991. *Beyond Interdependence: The Meshing of the World's Economy and the Earth's Ecology.* Oxford: Oxford University Press

Mahar, Dennis. 1989. *Government Policies and Deforestation in Brazil's Amazon Region.* Washington, DC: World Bank

Mangin, Jean-Marc. 1989. Rural Water Supply in Southern Ethiopia. Unpublished paper. Toronto: University of Toronto, Institute for Environmental Studies

Meade, Melinda, John Florin, and Wilbert Gesler. 1988. *Medical Geography.* New York: Guildford Press

Meadows, Donella H., Dennis L. Meadows, Jørgen Randers, and William W. Behrens. 1972. *The Limits to Growth.* New York: Signet Books/Potomac Associates

Metropolitan Toronto Government. 1991. *Strategic Plan, May 1991.* Toronto

Molina, M.J., and F.S. Rowland. 1974. Stratospheric Sink for Chlorofluoromethanes: Chlorine Atom–Catalysed Destruction of Ozone. *Nature,* 249/5460: 810–12

Morris, D.M. 1979. *Measuring the Condition of the World's Poor: The Physical Quality of Life Index.* Oxford: Pergamon Press

Mortimer, Michael. 1989. *Adapting to Drought: Farmers, Famines and Desertification in West Africa.* Cambridge: Cambridge University Press

Munn, R.E. 1986. Global Environmental Prospects. In Kates and Burton (eds.), 326–38

Myers, Norman (ed.). 1985. *The Gaia Atlas of Planet Management.* London: Pan Books

Ngom, T. 1989. Appropriate Standards for Infrastructure in Dakar, Senegal. In Stren and White (eds.), Chapter 7, 177–203

Nicolis, G., and Ilya Prigogine. 1977. *Self-organization in Non-equilibrium Systems: From Dissipative Structures to Order through Fluctuations.* New York: Wiley

North–South Institute. 1991. Globalization and the Nation State. In *Review '90, Outlook 91,* 12–14. Ottawa: North–South Institute

O'Brien, R.C. (ed.). 1979. *The Political Economy of Under-development: Dependence in Senegal.* Beverly Hills: Sage Publications

Odum, Eugene P. 1989. *Ecology and Our Endangered Life-support Systems.* Sunderland, MA: Sinauer Associates

Odum, Howard T. 1983. *Systems Ecology: An Introduction.* New York: Wiley

OECD. 1985a. *State of the Environment, 1985.* Paris

– 1985b. *OECD Environmental Data, 1985.* Paris

– 1991a. *State of the Environment.* Paris

– 1991b. *Environmental Indicators: A Preliminary Set.* Paris

Ogalla, Laban. 1987. Impacts of the 1982–83 ENSO Events on Eastern and Southern Africa. In Glantz, Katz, and Krenz (eds.), Chapter 9

Okpala, Donatus. 1984. Urban Planning and the Control of Physical Growth in Nigeria: A Critique of Public Impact and Private Roles. *Habitat International*, 8/2: 73–94

Onibokun, Adepoju. 1989. Urban Growth and Urban Management in Nigeria. In Stren and White (eds.), Chapter 4, 68–111

Ontario Ministry of Energy. 1990. *Global Warming: Towards a Strategy for Ontario.* Toronto: Queen's Park

Pandey, G., and B. Bowander. 1987. Decision-making in Crisis: The Case of Bhopal Disaster. Unpublished paper. Hyderabad: Staff College of India

Passet, René. 1979. *L'Economique et le vivant.* Paris: Payot

Peltier, W.R. 1990. Global Sea-level Rise and Global Warming. Special lecture series on Global Change, Erindale College, University of Toronto

Perez-Trejo, Francisco, and Rodney White. 1991. A Simulation Model of the Response to an Industrial Emergency in a Third World City. *Third World Planning Review*, 13/3: 261–75

Petit-Maire, Nicole. 1984. Le Sahara, de la steppe au désert. *La Recherche*, 160: 1372–82

Petit-Maire, Nicole, and J. Riser (eds.). 1983. *Sahara ou Sahel? Quaternaire Récent du Bassin de Taoudenni (Mali).* Luminy-Marseille: Laboratoire du Quaternaire du Centre National de la Recherche Scientifique

Please, Stanley. 1984. *The Hobbled Giant: Essays on the World Bank.* Boulder: Westview Press

Pollution Probe. 1989. *The Canadian Green Consumer Guide: How You Can Help.* Toronto

Postel, Sandra. 1989. *Water for Agriculture: Facing the Limits.* Worldwatch Paper, 93. Washington, DC: Worldwatch Institute

Prigogine, Ilya. 1980. *From Being to Becoming: Time and Complexity in the Physical Sciences.* San Francisco: W.H. Freeman

Prigogine, Ilya, and Isabelle Stengers. 1984. *Order out of Chaos: Man's New Dialogue with Nature.* New York: Bantam Books

Pronk, Jan. 1990. We Need a Global Mixed Economy and a Global Public Sector. *IFDA Dossier*, 78 (July–September): 1–2, 44

République du Sénégal. 1982. *Substitution du butane au charbon de bois.* Rapport d'Etude par Trans Erg (Paris), Ministère du Développement Industriel et de l'Artisanat, Dakar

– 1983a. *Doublement de la conduite Thiès-Dakar: Etude de factabilité et avant projets sommaires.* Rapport de RRI (Rhein-Ruhr), Ministère de l'Hydraulique, Dakar

– 1983b. Loi No. 83–05 du 28 janvier portant sur le Code de l'Environnement.

Journal Officiel de la République du Sénégal, 23 April: 324–32

– 1984a. Décret fixant le régime des prix des certains produits et services, no. 84–404. Direction du Commerce Intérieur et des Prix, Dakar

– 1984b. *Schéma national d'amenagement du territoire: Version préliminaire.* Ministère de l'Intérieur, Dakar

– 1985. Seminaire national sur une politique concertée de protection de l'environnement avec le secteur industriel, Dakar, 18–19 janvier. Ministère de la Protection de la Nature, Dakar

– 1986. Conférence atelier sur l'importance des technologies propres pour un dévéloppement économique durable, Dakar, 12–25 février. Ministère de la Protection de la Nature, Dakar

Richmond, Amos. 1988. Greening of the Desert. In Thorkil Kristensen and Johan Paludan (eds.), Chapter 4, 71–95

Rifkin, Jeremy. 1989. *Entropy: Into the Greenhouse World*, rev. ed. New York: Bantam Books

Rijsberman, Frank R., and M. Gordon Wolman (eds.). 1984. *Quantification of the Effect of Erosion on Soil Productivity in an International Context.* Delft: Delft Hydraulics Laboratory

Rijsberman, Frank R., and M. Gordon Wolman. 1985. Effect of Erosion on Soil Productivity: An International Comparison. *Journal of Soil and Water Conservation*, 40/4: 350–4

Roan, Sharon L. 1989. *Ozone Crisis: The 15 Year Evolution of a Sudden Global Emergency.* New York: Wiley

Rodhe, Henning, and Rafael Herrera (eds.). 1988. *Acidification in Tropical Countries: SCOPE 36.* Chichester: Wiley for SCOPE

Salas, R.M. 1986. *The State of World Population 1986.* New York: UNFPA

Sanders, David. 1985. *The Struggle for Health: Medicine and the Politics of Underdevelopment.* London and Basingstoke: Macmillan Education

Schneider, Stephen. 1989. The Changing Climate. *Scientific American*, 261/3 (September): 70–8

– 1990. *Global Warming: Are We Entering the Greenhouse Century?* New York: Random House

Shea, Cynthia P. 1988. *Protecting Life on Earth: Steps to Save the Ozone Layer.* Worldwatch Paper 87. Washington, DC: Worldwatch Institute

Smil, Vacliv, Paul Nachman, and Thomas Long II. 1983. *Energy Analysis of Agriculture: An Application to U.S. Corn Production.* Boulder: Westview Press

Somerville, Carolyn M. 1986. *Drought and Aid in the Sahel: A Decade of Development Cooperation.* Boulder: Westview Press

Stein, R., and B. Johnson. 1979. *Banking on the Biosphere.* Lexington: D.C. Heath

Stren, Richard. 1986. *The Ruralization of African Cities: Learning to Live with Poverty.*

Project Ecoville Working Paper Series, 34. Institute for Environmental Studies, University of Toronto

Stren, Richard, and Rodney White (eds.). 1989. *African Cities in Crisis: Managing Rapid Urban Growth*. Boulder: Westview Press and IFIAS

Stren, Richard, Rodney White, and Joseph Whitney (eds.). 1992. *Sustainable Cities: Urbanization and the Environment in International Perspective*. Boulder: Westview Press

Tibesar, Arthur, and Rodney White. 1990. An Analysis of Household Energy Use in Dakar, Senegal. *Journal of Developing Areas*, 25: 33–48

Tickell, Sir Crispin. 1990. Human Effects of Climate Change. Lecture to the Royal Geographical Society, London, 26 March

Toronto Board of Health. 1988. *Healthy Toronto 2000: A Strategy for a Healthier City*. Toronto: City of Toronto Board of Health

Turk, Jonathan, and Amos Turk. 1988. *Environmental Science*, 4th ed. Philadelphia: Saunders College Publishing

UNDP. 1990. *Human Development Report 1990*. New York: Oxford University Press

– 1991. *Human Development Report 1991*. New York: Oxford University Press

UNEP. 1986. *The State of the Environment: Environment and Health*. Nairobi

– 1987a. *Hazardous Chemicals*. UNEP Environmental Brief 4. Nairobi

– 1987b. *Cleaning up the Seas*. UNEP Environmental Brief 5. Nairobi

– 1988. *Safeguarding the World's Water*. UNEP Environmental Brief 6. Nairobi

– 1989. A Total Phase-out of Ozone-depleting Chlorofluorocarbons (CFCs), *UNEP North American News*, 4/3 (June): 1

UNEP/GEMS. 1987a. *The Greenhouse Gases*. UNEP/GEMS Environment Library 1. Nairobi: UNEP

– 1987b. *The Ozone Layer*. UNEP/GEMS Environment Library 2. Nairobi: UNEP

UNEP/NCAR. 1990. CO_2 Backlash – Editorial. *Network Newsletter* (Boulder), Winter: 1

Uusitalo, Liisa. 1986. *Environmental Impacts of Consumption Patterns*. Aldershot: Gower Publishing

Viaud, Paul. 1984. *Energie et biomasse au Sahel*. Dakar: Ecole Nationale Supérieure Universitaire de Technologie

von Bertalanffy, L. 1968. *General Systems Theory: Foundations, Development, Application*. New York: George Braziller

Wane, Oumar. 1983. Utilisation urbaine de l'eau du Lac de Guiers et planification écologique intégrée de la ville. In Institut des Sciences de l'Environnement, 63–77

– 1985. La croissance urbaine au Sénégal: Urbanisation et extension de Dakar. *Mondes en Développement*, 13/52: 553–81

Wekwete, Kadmiel. 1992. Human Settlements and Sustainable Development in Africa. In Stren, White, and Whitney (eds.), Chapter 5, 104–40

White, Gilbert F. 1973. *Domestic Water Supply: Right or Good? Human Rights in Health.* Ciba Foundation Symposium 23, London, 4–6 July. Amsterdam: Associated Scientific Publishers. Reprinted in Kates and Burton (eds.), vol. 1, 357–76

White, James C. (ed.). 1989. *Global Climate Change Linkages: Acid Rain, Air Quality and Stratospheric Ozone.* New York: Elsevier

White, Rodney. 1989–90. Environmental Management and National Sovereignty: Some Issues from Senegal. *International Journal,* 45/1: 106–38

– 1990. Agricultural Policy Options in the Face of Uncertainty: The Case of Senegal. In E. Ann McDougall (ed.), Chapter 5, 151–63

White, Rodney, and Ian Burton. 1983. *Approaches to the Study of the Environmental Implications of Contemporary Urbanization.* MAB Technical Notes No.14. Paris: UNESCO

White, Rodney, and Joseph Whitney. 1992. Cities and the Environment: An Overview. In Stren, White, and Whitney (eds.), Chapter 2

Whitney, Joseph. 1981. Urban Energy, Food and Water Use in Arid Regions and Their Impact on Hinterlands: A Conceptual Framework. Khartoum: Institute for Environmental Studies

Wilson, Alan. 1981. *Geography and Environment: Systems Analytical Methods.* Chichester: Wiley

Wolman, M. Gordon, and Abel Wolman. 1986. Water Supply: Persistent Myths and Recurring Issues. In Kates and Burton (eds.), vol. 2, 1–18

World Bank. 1984. *World Development Report 1984.* See, especially, Part 2, Population Change and Development. Washington, DC

– 1978 to 1992. *World Development Report.* (An annual publication.) Washington, DC

– 1989. *Striking a Balance: The Environmental Challenge of Development.* Washington, DC

– 1990. *The World Bank and the Environment: First Annual Report, Fiscal 1990.* Washington, DC

World Resources Institute. 1990. *World Resources 1990–91.* New York: Oxford University Press

Worrest, Robert C., Katie D. Smythe, and Alexander M. Tait. 1989. Linkages between Climate Change and Stratospheric Ozone Depletion. In James C. White (ed.), 67–78

Xoomsai, Tawanchai. 1988. Bangkok: Environmental Quality in a Primate City. In Hills and Whitney (eds.), Chapter 1

Index

absorptive capacity (of the biosphere), 23

acidification and acid precipitation, 15, 18, 20, 37, Chapter 5 passim, 58; bilateral treaties regarding, 165–6; emissions by country, 74–6; regional impacts of, 72–8

additionality. *See* aid

Africa: cities and property tax, 134; land management, 108–9; river basin schemes, 116; toxic-waste imports, 157–8. *See also* Ethiopia, Ghana, Morocco, Nigeria, Senegal

Agarwal, Anil, and Sunita Narain, 163–4

Agenda 21 (Rio Conference), 179

agriculture: incentives for smallholder production, 108–9, 113, 137, 143; irrigation, 118–22; modernization and social change, 106–8; revolution in Europe, 104

aid: additionality of, 174; agencies, 11, 106, 124–5, 143; conditionality of, 18, 174; technology transfer, 154, 165. *See also* technology transfer, World Bank

AIDS, 16, 20, 31, 61, 124; and ozone depletion, 61

Akbari, H., A. Rosenfeld, and H. Taha, 142

algal blooms, 85, 89–90

Allen, Peter, 24–5

Alliance of Small Island States, 170

American Meteorological Society, 18

Analysing Biospheric Change (ABC) project, xii

Anderson, Dennis, 111

Antarctic: global warming, 49; ozone depletion, 60

anthropogenic climate change, 39, 41–50

Anton, Danilo, 123

Arctic: global warming, 49–50; ozone depletion, 60; smog and acidification, 69

Argentina: fishery, 81; ozone depletion, 60

Arrhenius, Svante, 42

Ashton, John, 177

'Atlantic Conveyor' (ocean current), 41

Axelrod, Robert, 180

Bangkok, 133

Banking on the Biosphere, 169

Basel Convention on International Trade in Hazardous Wastes, 160

Basta, Daniel, 144

Bhopal accident, 23, 140–1, 177

Bingen, James, 109, 120

bio-accumulation, 22, 27, 67, 84, 89

biodiversity, 99, 126; treaty on (Rio Conference), 179

bio-geochemical cycles, 30; and the ocean, 82–4

biological oxygen demand (BOD), 28

biomass, 85, 113; biomass fuels, 33

Bower, Blair, 27, 92, 144